BROOKINGS-WHARTON

papers on URBAN AFFAIRS

2009

*Gary Burtless and
Janet Rothenberg Pack
Editors*

BROOKINGS INSTITUTION PRESS
Washington, D.C.

ISSN 1528-7084
ISBN 978-0-8157-0300-6

BROOKINGS-WHARTON

papers on URBAN AFFAIRS

2009

Robert A. Margo *Boston University and NBER*
Christopher Mayer *Columbia Business School, NBER,*
  and Visiting Scholar, Federal Reserve Bank of New York
Tomoya Mori *Kyoto University*
Eleonora Patacchini *University of Rome "La Sapienza"*
Tomasz Piskorski *Columbia University*
John M. Quigley *University of California–Berkeley*
Tony E. Smith *University of Pennsylvania*
Christopher Timmins *Duke University*
Joseph Tracy *Federal Reserve Bank of New York*
Bruce A. Weinberg *Ohio State University, IZA, and NBER*
Shouyue Yu *Duke University*
Yves Zenou *Stockholm University and IFN*

Conference Nathaniel Baum-Snow *Brown University*
Participants Alan Berube *Brookings Institution*
Xavier de Souza Briggs *Massachusetts Institute of Technology*
William Collins *Vanderbilt University*
William Dickens *University of Maryland*
Anthony Downs *Brookings Institution*
Joseph Gyourko *University of Pennsylvania*
Amy Liu *Brookings Institution*
Edwin S. Mills *Northwestern University*
Carol O'Cleireacain *Brookings Institution*
Katherine O'Regan *New York University*
Howard Pack *University of Pennsylvania*
Alice Rivlin *Brookings Institution*
Martha Ross *Brookings Institution*
Alberto Saiz *University of Pennsylvania*
Raven E. Saks *Federal Reserve Board*
Amy E. Schwartz *New York University*
Michael Stoll *University of California–Los Angeles*
Richard Voith *Econsult Corporation*
Susan Wachter *University of Pennsylvania*
Cliff Winston *Brookings Institution*
Hal Wolman *George Washington University*
Grace Wong *University of Pennsylvania*

Preface

Brookings-Wharton Papers on Urban Affairs has for ten years been devoted to publishing forward-looking research on urban policy issues in a form accessible to a diverse audience. This is the tenth and final volume in the series. It contains a symposium on international urban issues and three other papers on the inventiveness of cities, on discrimination in subprime mortgages, and on job decentralization and suburbanization.

It is appropriate at this point to acknowledge the people and institutions that have helped make the ten years of conferences and volumes so rewarding. The many authors and discussants over the past decade deserve special thanks for intellectual contributions to the conferences as well as their efforts to draft arguments in a clear and accessible style for the volumes. We are also grateful to all the other conference participants for making the annual meetings lively and enlightening.

Since its launch in 1999, the collaboration between the Wharton School and the Brookings Institution has drawn on resources and personnel in both academia and the policymaking community. We hoped to create a series of volumes that would be of interest and use to a wide audience, including policymakers and their staffs, practitioners in the private sector, journalists, students, and others.

The conferences at which the papers were initially presented as well as the resulting volumes owe much to the efforts of key people at both Brookings and Wharton. Brookings presidents Michael H. Armacost and Strobe Talbott supported this project. Bruce Katz, director of the Metropolitan Policy Program, has been a loyal and generous supporter of the project, and his research program provided major financial support.

At Wharton, Peter Linneman and Joseph Gyourko, former and current director, respectively, of the Samuel Zell and Robert Lurie Real Estate Center, have supported the project intellectually and financially from its inception. We have also received financial support the past five years from the Urban Research

Institute at the University of Pennsylvania, which is codirected by professors Eugenie Birch and Susan Wachter. For two years, the Wharton Dean's Office also provided support for the conference and volume.

Several people at Brookings made vital contributions to the conferences, where drafts of papers were first presented, and to the resulting volumes. Budgetary assistance and oversight have been provided by Jamaine Fletcher (Metropolitan Policy Program) and Linda Gianessi (Economics Studies) of Brookings. Over the decade, Saundra Honeysett, Jeanine Forsythe, Teresa Brown, and Kathleen Kruczlinicki at Brookings organized conference logistics and managed the paper flow. Lael S. Harris ably performed these duties for the current volume. Many Brookings research assistants provided splendid assistance in helping the coeditors fact-check the submissions and prepare summaries of the major articles. This year we thank Sean Hardgrove, Rosanna Smart, and Pavel Svaton for providing this crucial help. Janet Walker and Anthony Nathe of the Brookings Institution Press have managed the production of the conference volumes creatively and efficiently.

The conferences were organized and the volumes edited by Janet Rothenberg Pack of the Business and Public Policy Department at Wharton in collaboration with William G. Gale from 1999 to 2004 and Gary Burtless from 2005 to 2009. Gale, now the director of Economic Studies at Brookings, held the Arjay and Frances Fearing Miller Chair in Economics while he was coeditor of the volumes; Burtless holds the John C. and Nancy D. Whitehead Chair in Economics.

Thank you all!

Editors' Summary

Brookings-Wharton Papers on Urban Affairs presents new research on urban economics to a broad audience of interested policy analysts and researchers. The papers and comments contained in this volume, the tenth in the series, were presented at a conference on November 13–14, 2008, at the Brookings Institution. The papers examine a range of issues that are relevant to urban economics, including the effects of job location in an urban area on residential choice patterns, racial bias in mortgage lending, and the effects of urban characteristics on the development of new patents. The volume also contains three papers on urban developments outside of the United States. The topics treated include urban sprawl in Europe, rural-to-urban migration patterns in Brazil, and locational patterns of establishments across Japanese cities.

After World War II, a growing percentage of Americans moved to the nation's suburbs, and a shrinking percentage chose to live in central cities. This shift in residential patterns occurred at the same time as a shift in the location of jobs. Compared with job locations in the early postwar period, a smaller share of U.S. employment is now concentrated in central cities and a bigger share is located in the suburbs. For regional planners and urban economists, this raises an important question: Have residents of metropolitan areas flocked to the suburbs because that is where the jobs are? Or have employers followed urban migrants out into the suburbs?

In their paper "Job Decentralization and Residential Location," Leah Platt Boustan and Robert A. Margo offer a partial answer to this question using information on the residential choices of state government employees who hold jobs inside and outside of state capitals. The location of state capitals was chosen many decades ago, and no state has chosen to relocate its capital since the early twentieth century. State government employment in capital cities tends to be concentrated near the historical heart of cities, usually in or near the central business district. The persistence of state employment patterns in state capitals gives analysts evidence that can be helpful in determining the effect of the geographical distribution of employment on employees' residential choices.

There are two kinds of contrast that are useful in determining the impact of job location on residential choice. First, state government employees who work in capital cities can be compared with employees who work for other kinds of establishments in the same metropolitan areas. Since state government employees in those cities are much more likely to work in the central city, the difference between their residential choices and those of employees of other kinds of establishments sheds light on the impact of job location on the decision of workers to live inside or outside of the central cities. Second, state government employees who work outside of capital cities are considerably less likely to work in the central city of a metropolitan area. The distribution of their employment inside and outside of central cities is similar to that of employees of other kinds of establishments that are located in the same metropolitan areas. Boustan and Margo combine information for these two sets of contrasts to determine how the geographical concentration of state government employment in capital cities affects the choice of employees to live inside or outside of the central city.

The authors use individual-level information from the 1980 decennial census to assess the impact of job location on residential choice. They find that state government employees in capital cities are about 13 percent more likely than state employees in other locations to work in the central city. At the same time, the state employees who work in capital cities are 3 to 4 percentage points more likely to reside in the central city. From this the authors infer that the increased concentration of employment in the central city has a nontrivial effect on the residential choices of state employees. They estimate that the addition of 100 new employment positions in the central city would add 25 new working residents to the population of the central city. The authors attempt to verify their findings by performing some sensitivity tests. For example, they compare the residential choices of postal letter carriers, whose employment is widely dispersed across metropolitan areas, with the choices of other postal employees, whose employment tends to be concentrated in central cities. The residential choices of these two kinds of employees strengthen the case for believing that working in the central city tends to raise the chances that a worker will also choose to live in the central city. By implication, the movement of employment back from the suburbs to the central city could play a noticeable role in bringing working residents back into central cities.

ECONOMISTS AND OTHER RESEARCHERS have assembled considerable evidence of racial bias in mortgage lending. Much of the early evidence focused on differential denial of mortgage credit to minority borrowers. More recent research also uncovered evidence of higher interest charges to some minority borrowers. A great deal of this evidence was accumulated before the explosion of subprime lending, which occurred during the past decade. In a paper in this volume, "Subprime Mortgage Pricing: The Impact of Race, Ethnicity, and Gender on the Cost of Borrowing," Andrew Haughwout, Christopher Mayer, and Joseph Tracy assemble a new dataset to examine lending bias from a novel perspective. Their data are derived from a merge of records in the LoanPerformance and the Home Mortgage Disclosure Act databases. Using information on individual loans that is common to the two files, the researchers create a merged file that contains more comprehensive information about the loans than has been available to previous researchers.

The focus of their analysis is a single type of loan commonly referred to as a 2/28 mortgage. This is a thirty-year adjustable rate mortgage (ARM) in which borrowers are charged a specified interest rate for the first two years of the loan. The interest rate is then reset at two-year intervals, usually according to a formula that sets the mortgage rate as a specified increment over a particular short-term interest rate, such as the London Interbank Offered Rate (LIBOR). At the peak of the subprime lending boom, the 2/28 mortgage was one of the most popular forms of subprime mortgage. The authors' sample consists of all subprime borrowers who obtained 2/28 mortgages originating in a single month, August 2005. Although the merged file contains fairly complete information about borrower characteristics, the characteristics of their neighborhoods, and the terms of their loans, it is missing some information about the points and fees that borrowers paid when the loan was taken out. If lenders charged discriminatory upfront fees, this form of discrimination will not be detected in the analysis.

As the authors note, there are three possible ways that lenders can discriminate against credit applicants from disadvantaged groups. They can decline to make loans, steer disadvantaged borrowers into more costly types of loans, or impose higher charges on disadvantaged borrowers who are offered a particular kind of loan. By focusing solely on borrowers who obtained a particular kind of mortgage, the authors cannot shed light on the first two forms of discrimination. However, their study provides a rich and unique investigation into the third kind of discrimination.

Among 2/28 subprime borrowers, the authors find little systematic evidence of discrimination against historically disadvantaged groups. If anything, some minority groups obtained slightly more favorable terms on their loans than non-minority borrowers did. For example, both African American and Hispanic borrowers were offered slightly lower initial rates than other borrowers received, though the difference was small—0.025 percentage points. The interest rate resets were also slightly more advantageous for African American and Hispanic borrowers. In contrast, Asian borrowers may have paid slightly higher initial and reset interest rates than other borrowers. In all cases, however, the differences were economically small. Loan terms were the same for male and female borrowers.

Controlling for the creditworthiness of borrowers, the authors also find that loan terms were more favorable in neighborhoods with a higher percentage of African American, Hispanic, and Asian residents and in neighborhoods with above-average unemployment. This surprising finding may have a simple explanation. Because subprime borrowers are more plentiful in minority and high-unemployment neighborhoods, subprime lenders may have been more likely to compete for business in those areas. In neighborhoods with few potential customers, it may not be worthwhile for subprime lenders to establish a business presence. The greater competition for business in minority and high-unemployment neighborhoods may have pushed lenders to offer somewhat better loan terms in those areas. Less surprising, the authors find that loan terms were more advantageous for borrowers in metropolitan areas that had experienced faster appreciation of housing prices in the recent past. This result makes sense if lenders thought that faster past price appreciation signaled a smaller risk that subprime borrowers would default on their loans. In summary, while there may be substantial discrimination in the home mortgage market, the authors' results suggest that it does not take the form of discrimination in the terms offered to subprime borrowers who obtain 2/28 mortgages.

A MAJOR FINDING IN THE regional economics literature is the inventive productivity of cities, where inventive productivity is measured by the number of patents generated. Many urban economists attribute this productivity to agglomeration economies. In an earlier study, Gerald Carlino, Satyajit Chatterjee, and Robert Hunt (2007) found employment density and local research and development (R&D) inputs, in particular human capital, to be major factors explaining this phenomenon. In "What Explains the Quantity and Quality of Local Inventive Activity?" Carlino and Hunt extend this earlier research. One contribution of the paper is the development of a broader measure of inventive productivity. The authors consider not only the number of patents, as in the earlier literature, but also the relative importance of local inventions, defined by the number of citations a patent receives in patents obtained by later inventors. Equally important, they also include several additional variables to explain local inventive productivity. These include the nature of R&D performed in different fields, the source of funding for local R&D, the differential effects of funding for basic versus applied research, and the impact of congressional earmarks for R&D performed by colleges and universities.

The authors estimate the importance of the determinants of the variation in the two inventive productivity variables across 280 metropolitan areas. Their explanatory variables include the R&D variables mentioned above and several measures of agglomeration potential: the log of metropolitan area (MA) size and its density, both in terms of jobs and the log of the inverse of average establishment size; the share of the adult population with a college degree; and measures of local government, academic, and private R&D inputs.

The pattern of results, with a few important exceptions, does not differ when the dependent variable changes from patents per capita to citation-weighted patents per capita. An educated workforce is the decisive explanatory factor in both cases. The authors find that higher employment density in the metropolitan area increases the per capita output of patents. In contrast, larger average establishment size in a region has a negative effect on patent intensity. A possible implication is that cities with a more competitive market structure generate greater productivity with respect to inventiveness. When the authors focus on citation-weighted patents rather than patents, they uncover a couple of differences in their results. Total employment in a region has a positive impact on citation-weighted patents, indicating increasing returns to scale among cities with a population of about 1.8 million or less. When the dependent variable is unweighted patents, the minimum efficient size of a productive city is found to be smaller.

When the authors compare the relative effectiveness of different sources of R&D funding, they find federal government funding to be the least productive source of funds. The authors also try to distinguish between the effectiveness of different types of federal funding, estimating the separate effects of basic and applied research funding. Both kinds of federal funds seem to decrease patenting intensity, relative to university-funded R&D, though only the coefficient on applied funding is statistically significant. The result is insufficiently robust to conclude that federally funded basic R&D is less productive than university R&D, or more productive than federally funded applied R&D, but it weakens the case for believing that applied R&D is more closely related to final products, and thus to patenting.

The authors conclude with a discussion of a number of policy implications of their findings. Their main recommendation focuses on policies that encourage the accumulation of local human capital. This recommendation is based on the authors' finding that the intensity of local human capital has overwhelming importance in explaining the rate of local inventive activity. They discuss several other important possible policy implications but stress the importance of establishing the microfoundations of spillover effects before their introduction. More generally, the authors are cautious about making policy recommendations that are based upon their examination of the impact of different sources of R&D funding and suggest directions for future research.

URBAN SPRAWL HAS BEEN a major topic of study in the United States. The phrase *urban sprawl* and most of its variants—*urban decentralization, suburbanization*, and *low density development*—usually have a negative connotation. Because U.S. urban planners are typically critical of sprawl, they offer numerous policy prescriptions to contain it. These ideas include urban growth boundaries, zoning changes to increase density, and protection of agricultural land on the urban fringe. The urban economists Jan Brueckner and Ann Largeyb offer a more descriptive phrase, *excessive decentralization*, which they define as decentralization that fails to take into account market failures, that is, negative externalities (Brueckner and Largeyb 2008).

In contrast to the voluminous U.S. literature on urban sprawl, there have been comparatively few studies of the subject in Europe. There are a number reasons for this. First, many observers have the erroneous impression that European cities remain fairly compact. According to this view, suburbanization has not played a major role in changing the basic European urban form. Another problem in analyzing European urban sprawl is the lack of comparability in the definitions of and data organization for urban areas. In their paper, "Urban Sprawl in Europe," Eleonora Patacchini and Yves Zenou make use of a new dataset, the Urban Audit. One of the limitations of these data is that the authors cannot define the "core" of a metropolitan region in the same way as can be done in the United States. This leads the authors to measure sprawl as the variation over time of the total land area or the population density of a given city. The authors argue that "there is no effective and standard definition of the concept of a city in Europe." They use the notion or terminology of sprawl to investigate sprawl in Europe, but they clearly recognize that their analysis is by no means comparable to similar studies in the United States.

The authors hypothesize that decentralization or sprawl is the result of increased automobile ownership, improvements in income, changing employment patterns, and higher crime rates in the cities. In the United States, higher proportions of minorities are sometimes associated with high crime rates and in turn are often assumed to encourage suburbanization or urban sprawl. By contrast, in Europe ethnic minorities are concentrated in the suburbs, and thus it is believed that they retard suburbanization from the city centers, that is, retard urban sprawl.

The authors begin their empirical analysis with straightforward regressions in which the dependent variable is the growth in urban population density. The authors find that urban density tends to fall the higher the proportion is of higher-income households, defined either by income or employment. Density also tends to decline where there is faster growth in the number of registered cars. In cities where there is a higher percentage of non-European residents, urban density tends to remain high. (Recall that non-European residents tend to live in European suburbs rather than in the urban core.) When the growth in the crime rate is included in the model, the authors find the same negative correlation, but it is not statistically significant.

Given the differences between the U.S. and European definitions of cities and in data coverage, the authors properly caution against interpreting their results as a clear basis for comparing urban sprawl in the United States and in Europe. Their findings suggest, however, that Europeans and Americans respond to many of the same factors that determine urban density patterns. These common factors include rising income and increased automobile ownership. Some of the important differences between Europe and the United States are connected to differences in the location of poor residents and high crime. In Europe the poor and high crime tend to be concentrated in the suburbs, while in the United States they are concentrated in the cities.

FOR CITIZENS IN DEVELOPING COUNTRIES, a well-trodden path to economic betterment is the road to a big, fast-growing city. Rural-to-urban migration has swollen the size of cities and contributed to the deterioration of urban amenities in many metropolitan areas of the developing world. The economic logic of this migration from the point of view of the rural poor is straightforward. Wages in large metropolitan areas are higher than in the countryside and in small towns and cities. Somik V. Lall, Christopher Timmins, and Shouyue Yu investigate another possible impetus for this kind of migration, namely, differences in the availability of important public services in different regions of a country. In their paper "Connecting Lagging and Leading Regions: The Role of Labor Mobility," the authors try to assess the relative contribution of regional differences in wages, on the one hand, and the availability of public services, on the other, in stimulating regional migration in Brazil. Their evidence is derived from the 1991 and 2000 censuses, and the authors' statistical analysis focuses on migration between county-level political jurisdictions in Brazil.

Many analyses of migration behavior have examined the impact of regional wage differences in encouraging migration. Analysts have only rarely examined the influence of regional differences in the availability of public services. Lall, Timmins, and Yu focus on three basic types of public services: local infrastructure, availability of health care, and the cost of transportation. They analyze the impact of access to three kinds of local infrastructure: piped water, sewage systems, and the electric grid. As a measure of access to modern health care, the authors determine the availability of hospital care in different Brazilian regions. Access to the transportation system is measured using the cost of transportation to the state capital and to Brazil's largest city, São Paulo. The statistical model that the authors use to determine migration decisions includes measures of regional public services and regional wages. Since the estimation is performed at the individual level, it is possible for the authors to measure variations in the importance of different public amenities for potential migrants who have different baseline characteristics, including educational attainment.

The authors find that differences in the availability of public services as well as regional wage differences play a significant role in Brazilians' migration decisions. Their analysis suggests that migrants with very low levels of schooling are attracted to regions where transportation to the state capital is inexpensive and to regions where a higher percentage of residents have access to a sewage system and a hospital. Potential migrants with more schooling are attracted to destinations where residents have access to hospitals and to electric lights. These findings suggest a policy approach that developing countries might adopt to reduce overcrowding in the nations' largest cities. This kind of overcrowding is a common side effect of the wide wage differential between the biggest urban areas and the less densely populated areas in the same developing country. The authors' findings imply that migration to the biggest urban areas would slow if public services were introduced or expanded in the lagging regions of the countries. The authors also note that potential migrants would be much better prepared for work, either in their home region or in a megacity, if they had better access to schooling when they were young. This provides another powerful argument for strengthening public services in lagging regions of the country, in this case, access to good public schools.

THE LAST PAPER, "A Reconsideration of the NAS Rule from an Industrial Agglomeration Perspective," by Tomoya Mori and Tony E. Smith is an expanded version and technical treatment of an old literature on urban hierarchies and a newer literature on urban agglomeration. In previous work, the authors developed the Number-Average Size (NAS) Rule, defined as the negative log-linear relation between the average population size of cities, with an industry present, and the number of these cities (Mori, Nishikimi, and Smith 2008).

In this paper the authors try to determine which cities host a "significant" agglomeration of an industry and are thus subject to the NAS Rule. They call these cities "cluster-based (cb-choice) cities" for each industry and proceed with their analysis using this new boundary criterion. In sum, they use an existing statistical technique to distinguish cities that share part or all of a significant spatial cluster for an industry, confirm industry concentration in cb-choice cities, examine changes in the number of and concentration in cb-choice cities over time, and verify that the NAS Rule, Hierarchy Principle, and Rank Size Rule hold up under this new partitioning procedure.

Using manufacturing industry and population data for Japan in 1980 and 2000 and constructing cluster schemes for each of the industries, the authors analyze 139 industries. The mean percentages of establishments included in clusters are 95.7 percent in 1981 and 94.1 percent in 2001. The authors can thus define a cb-choice city for a given industry if and only if "it shares at least one positive employment municipality with some cluster" in the universe of cluster cities. The average number of cb-choice cities is 116.3 cities in 1981 and 101.7 in 2001.

These cb-choice cities for a given industry do appear to have larger concentrations of industry, as exhibited by the frequency distribution of the ratios of mean employment (number of establishments) among all cb-choice cities for that industry to the means of employment (number of establishments) among all other cities. For all industries, and in both time periods, all ratios are greater than one.

Although there is remarkable similarity in the frequency distributions of these concentration ratios over time, it is also the case that industrial location decisions are subject to significant churning over the twenty-year period. Small and less diversified cities tend to stay that way, while large and more diversified cities also tend to stay large and diversified. The dramatic adjustments of industrial location take place within the intermediate levels of industrial diversity.

The NAS Rule holds just as well in 2000–01 as in 1980–81, despite the churning. Plotting and regressing the log of the average size of cb-choice cities on the log of the number of cb-choice cities for the 139 manufacturing industries, the fit is indistinguishable from perfect linearity (with $R^2 = 0.996$) in both periods. In addition, the slopes of the two regression lines are almost equivalent (–0.734 and –0.716 in 1981 and 2001, respectively). This implies that while "the numbers and average sizes of cb-choice cities for individual industries have changed, they have done so in a manner that leaves their elasticity of substitution invariant." The NAS Rule thus seems to hold over time and under this new definition of cb-choice city boundaries.

The Hierarchy Principle, as loosely based on that originally proposed by Christaller, also holds true with remarkable stability over time. In their version of the Hierarchy Principle, Mori and Smith find that "industries in cities with a given level of industrial diversity (that is, a given number of cb-choice industries) will also be found in all cities with larger industrial diversities." They reject the null hypothesis that this result is due to stochastic random processes in both time periods.

The stability of the NAS Rule, Hierarchy Principle, and Rank Size Rule underscore their close relationship. When taken together, the NAS Rule and Hierarchy Principle imply (under strict theoretical standards) that cities could only hope to attract a given industry for which those cities qualified as cb-choice cities for that industry, and for which all more industrially diverse cities were already cb-choice cities for that industry. This indicates that cities are more likely to attract industries that would create local clustering of that industry, and that would be consistent with the existing locational hierarchy for that industry. Smaller cities would do better to attract lower-ranked industries while larger, more diverse cities could attract higher-ranked industries. The authors plan to examine such policy implications in later work.

References

Brueckner, Jan K., and Ann G. Largeyb. 2008. "Social Interaction and Urban Sprawl." *Journal of Urban Economics* 64 (1): 18–34.

Carlino, Gerald, Satyajit Chatterjee, and Robert M. Hunt. 2007. "Urban Density and the Rate of Invention." *Journal of Urban Economics* 61 (3): 389–419.

Mori, Tomoya, Koji Nishikimi, and Tony E. Smith. 2008. "The Number-Average Size Rule: A New Empirical Relationship between Industrial Location and City Size." *Journal of Regional Science* 48 (1): 165–211.

LEAH PLATT BOUSTAN
University of California–Los Angeles
National Bureau of Economic Research

ROBERT A. MARGO
Boston University
National Bureau of Economic Research

Job Decentralization and Residential Location

This paper addresses an old and central question in urban economics: how does the spatial distribution of employment opportunities influence residential location? Over the past fifty years, both employment and population left central cities for the suburban ring. Between 1960 and 2000, the share of metropolitan Americans who lived in the suburban ring increased from 48 to 68 percent. Over the same period, the share of metropolitan residents who worked outside the city rose from 41 percent to 58 percent. The decentralization of employment and population has led economists to ask whether workers followed jobs out to the suburbs or jobs followed workers. Answering this question is complicated by the fundamental simultaneity of the location decisions of workers and firms.

We adopt a novel approach to disentangling the causal relationship between the location of employment and population. Our main focus is on a single industry—namely, state government—whose primary location is predetermined with respect to current residential patterns. State government is concentrated in capital cities. The choice of capital city was established long before the process of suburbanization began. In many cases, core state buildings, such as the state capitol and the state supreme court, were built in the historic central business district (CBD) well over a century ago and have never been moved. As a result, state workers in capital cities are disproportionately likely to work downtown compared with other workers in the area (75.6 per-

We would like to thank Gary Burtless and Janet Rothenberg Pack for their editorial guidance and Edward Glaeser, Janice Madden, and the other participants of the Brookings-Wharton Papers on Urban Affairs conference for their helpful insights. This paper also benefited from the valuable suggestions of Steven Ross, Todd Sinai, Joel Waldfogel, Bruce Weinberg, and seminar participants at California State University–Fullerton, the University of California–Los Angeles, and the Wharton School. We acknowledge financial support from the Richard S. Ziman Center for Real Estate at UCLA.

1

cent versus 55.4 percent). However, state employees are also present in every major metropolitan area. State workers in noncapital cities are not much more likely than other workers in the area to work in the central city (57.9 percent versus 52.0 percent).[1]

If job location is an important determinant of residential location, we expect state workers in capital cities to be more likely to live in the central city relative to either state workers in other metropolitan areas or private sector workers in the capital . This set of comparisons naturally suggests a difference-in-differences estimation strategy. The first difference contrasts state workers in capital and noncapital cities to control for socioeconomic characteristics and differences in the taste for urban living that may be unique to state employees. The second difference contrasts state and nonstate workers within metropolitan areas to control for any relevant structural differences between capital and noncapital cities or their residents.

Our main empirical investigation is based on individual census records from the 1980 Integrated Public Use Microdata Series, or IPUMS (Ruggles and others 2008).[2] We find that state employees in capital cities are 12 to 14 percentage points more likely than state workers elsewhere to work downtown, relative to others in their metropolitan area, and 3 to 4 points more likely to live downtown. We find no observable differences in age, gender, education level or wage rates that could account for this residential pattern. Furthermore, this residential gap is robust to controlling for the industrial distribution of state workers in capital and noncapital cities. These figures imply that adding 1,000 jobs to the typical central city would increase the number of working residents in the central city by approximately 250 people.

Similar to state capitals, other government or government-related employment is characterized by historically determined locations that are very difficult to alter. We extend our basic analysis by considering employment in defense-related industry and at the United States Postal Service. Shortly after the Second World War, Congress specified that defense contractors should locate outside of existing city centers as a countermeasure against conventional or nuclear

1. A rich, related literature in economics, geography, and sociology has focused on potential inefficiencies in capital cities due to rent-seeking behavior. See, for example, Rosen and Resnick (1980); Carroll and Meyer (1983); Ades and Glaeser (1995). However, to the best of our knowledge, this paper is the first to point out the physical centralization of state government activity in capital cities and to assess the implications for residential location.

2. We focus on 1980 for pragmatic reasons. The census did not record employment locations before 1960; metropolitan area of residence is not reported in the 1960 IPUMS; and in 1970, the IPUMS sample reports either metropolitan area of residence or household location (central city versus suburbs), but not both. In 1990 and 2000, IPUMS does not distinguish between working in the CBD or in any other part of the central city.

attack (O'Mara 2006). We use census data to identify workers who are likely to have been affected by this policy and demonstrate that they were significantly more likely to both work and live outside of central cities in 1980.

In prior work, we used the location of postal employment to study the role of spatial mismatch in black employment outcomes (Boustan and Margo 2009). Central to our earlier analysis is the fact that postal processing and distribution plants were located in or near central business districts before the postwar era of employment decentralization and are politically difficult to relocate. As a result, postal clerks are likely to work in central cities, while mail carriers are distributed throughout metropolitan areas. In comparing occupations within the postal service, we find that noncarriers are more likely to work and live downtown. Our estimates using defense and postal workers are very similar in magnitude to our state capital results.

State Capitals as a Natural Experiment for Central City Employment

Our goal is to estimate the impact of employment location on residential location. An ideal experiment for this purpose would randomly allocate the location of a given industry to either the center or the periphery of metropolitan areas and observe where workers in that industry might choose to live. This experiment has two important features:

—Industry location would vary across metropolitan areas. In some areas, the industry would be located in the center, while in others it would be located in the suburbs.

—This variation would be exogenous by design to current residential patterns.

In reality, workers may locate close to firms to minimize commuting costs, and firms may locate close to residential areas, offering compensation to workers in the form of a shorter commute. Thus, any observed relationship between worker and firm locations could be driven by either worker or firm decisions. By manipulating industry location, this experiment would focus on worker decisions alone, avoiding concerns about reverse causality.[3] Furthermore, varying industry location across metropolitan areas would help to address selection bias.

3. Of course, one could also imagine a thought experiment in which households are randomly allocated to central versus periphery locations. We focus on how people respond to (quasi-) randomly assigned job locations rather than the reverse because, relatively speaking, it is easier to find real-world analogs to the random assignment of job location rather than to the random assignment of residential location. As a result, we estimate only one of the causal parameters of interest—how residential choice responds to employment location, not the reverse.

Industries that tend to locate in the central city—such as finance, insurance, and real estate—may be those that benefit most from agglomeration economies. These industries may also employ educated workers who have a preference for suburban living. In this case, selection bias would understate the true relationship between job location and residential location.

Employment in state government provides a real world analog to the experiment described above. Every state has a capital city where core state business is carried out. The location of virtually every state capital, even for former territories, has not changed since the nineteenth century. The one exception, Oklahoma City, was declared the capital of Oklahoma in 1910. In other words, the founding of state capitals long predates—and is therefore plausibly exogenous to—the decentralization of the population to the suburbs, which overwhelmingly occurred in the twentieth century.

Much of the government activity in state capitals takes place in buildings that were constructed in the nineteenth century and remain in the historic central business district. Examples of such buildings are obvious: the state capitol, where state legislatures hold sessions; official state libraries and archives, which are adjuncts to the legislature; and state supreme judicial courts. However, in noncapital cities, there is no inherent reason—and indeed no empirical pattern—for state government workers to be employed in central cities. For example, Bureaus of Motor Vehicles, where individuals acquire or renew their licenses, are often located well outside of central business districts, close to major highways to facilitate access by automobile.

State government satisfies our two experimental criteria: it is an industry whose main location varies across metropolitan areas for historical reasons unrelated to current residential patterns. However, state capitals were established many years ago and may have evolved differently from other cities over time. As a result, unique aspects of capital cities and their residents may confound our analysis. For instance, workers in capital cities are better educated than the typical American worker. To address potential differences between capital and non-capital cities, we compare state workers to the remainder of the workforce (both private and other public sector workers) in their metropolitan area.

Using within-metropolitan area variation has two main advantages. First, every metropolitan area is configured differently. Because of topography or local politics, central cities vary enormously in size relative to the area as a whole. For a given (square mile) size of the metropolitan area, these differences alone will generate a positive but spurious correlation between the share of any two activities occurring in the city (here, working and residence).

Secondly, comparing workers within metropolitan areas absorbs other omitted local characteristics that may be correlated with the share of activity occurring downtown. For example, a central city might be crime-ridden, encouraging firms and workers to relocate to the suburban ring. We could also imagine characteristics that repel firms from the central city but attract residents. A center city with a high local tax rate may create adverse business conditions, but the collected revenue may be used to fund local government services that attract residents.

Our empirical strategy thus compares the employment and residential locations of state workers in capital and noncapital cities to other, nonstate workers in the same set of metropolitan areas. The key identifying assumption is that state workers in both city types are otherwise identical but for their "assignment" to the state capital. However, as table 1 demonstrates, state workers in capital cities are engaged in different tasks from those of their counterparts in noncapital cities. In the capital, state employees are more likely to participate in government administration and less likely to work in a state-run hospital or university. These differences encourage us to test whether observable characteristics of the state workforce vary between capital and noncapital cities. We estimate:

$$(1) \quad \mathbf{X}_{ijk} = \alpha + \beta_1(\text{state worker} \times \text{capital city})_{ijk} + \alpha_2(\text{state worker})_{ijk} + \beta_3(\text{capital city})_{ijk} + \epsilon_{ijk},$$

where i indexes individuals; j, metropolitan areas; and k, class of worker (state worker or not). $\mathbf{X}$ is a vector of individual characteristics, including race, gender, age, and educational attainment. Our interest is in the coefficient β_1 on the interaction between being a state worker and living in a capital city. The indicator for being a state worker allows state employees to have systematically different characteristics than nonstate workers in all cities. In later specifications, we replace the main effect of living in a capital city with metropolitan area fixed effects, which absorb both the effect of capital city status and other local attributes.

Our sample contains more than 700,000 full-time workers in 127 metropolitan areas, 25 of which are state capitals.[4] Appendix table 1 presents summary statistics for this sample. A list of the capitals that can be identified in the data

4. We focus on individuals between the ages of 18 and 64 who were not in school, living in group quarters, in the armed forces, or in the farm sector. Sample individuals must live in a metropolitan area large enough for place of residence to be revealed in the public use data and must be in the subsample asked to report employment location (around half of all respondents indicated by the MIGSAMP variable).

Table 1. Top Industries for State Workers in Capital Cities and Noncapital Cities, 1980[a]
Percent

Industry[b]	Capital	Noncapital
Colleges and universities	18.67	22.83
General government	15.44	5.18
Hospitals	10.62	17.92
Administration of human resource programs	9.62	7.76
Justice and public order	8.03	8.77
Elementary and secondary schools	7.97	10.96
Administration of economic programs	7.24	4.19
Public finance and taxation	3.68	1.14
Administration of environmental programs	1.55	1.04

Source: 1980 IPUMS 5 percent sample.
a. Sample: Individuals aged 18–64 who are employed full-time for the full year and are not in school, living in group quarters, in the armed forces, or in the farm sector. Restricted to the subsample asked to report their location of employment and to metropolitan areas large enough for place of residence (central city versus suburb) to be revealed.
b. Industries reflect 1990 census categories using the 1990 IPUMS IND variable.

is presented in appendix table 2. The smallest metropolitan area anchored by a capital city in our sample is Trenton, New Jersey, and the largest is Minneapolis-St. Paul, Minnesota. The median capital area is larger in size than the median noncapital area, contributing 3,900 in contrast to 2,800 observations to the sample. Noncapital cities overtake state capitals at the 75th percentile of the size distribution, a pattern that is driven by the nation's ten largest cities (for example, New York City and Los Angeles).

The top panel of table 2 compares the personal attributes of state workers in capital and noncapital cities relative to other workers in their respective metropolitan areas. The main effects of being a state worker and living in the capital city are large and significant. State workers are older and more educated than the rest of the workforce, and they are also more likely to be female and black. Workers in capital cities are also better educated and more likely to be female, but they tend to be younger than workers in other areas. However, state workers in capital cities do *not* differ from state workers elsewhere along any of these dimensions, with the exception of race. State workers in capital cities are less likely to be black. The other point estimates are orders of magnitude smaller than the main effects and are not statistically significant. If anything, the racial differences will work against our main findings because African Americans are more likely to live in central cities.

The bottom panel of table 2 compares the labor market characteristics of state workers in capital and noncapital cities. While state workers earn 3 percent less than nonstate workers outside of capital cities, this gap is not present in capital cities. We speculate that this discrepancy may reflect the different

Table 2. Are State Workers in Capital Cities Different from State Workers Elsewhere?[a]

Variable	= 1 if some college	= 1 if college graduate	= 1 if female	= 1 if black	Age
= 1 if capital	0.011	0.019	0.016	−0.011	−0.912
	(0.004)	(0.011)	(0.005)	(0.012)	(0.154)
= 1 if state worker	−0.022	0.200	0.135	0.082	1.549
	(0.004)	(0.014)	(0.008)	(0.010)	(0.181)
Capital × state worker	−0.001	0.002	−0.003	−0.048	0.033
	(0.007)	(0.019)	(0.013)	(0.014)	(0.344)

	= 1 if married	ln(wage)	ln(wage) industry FE	Hours per week	Hours per week industry FE
= 1 if capital	−0.001	−0.032	−0.022	0.178	0.147
	(0.008)	(0.016)	(0.014)	(0.078)	(0.071)
= 1 if state worker	−0.032	−0.032	−0.035	−0.698	−0.326
	(0.006)	(0.012)	(0.012)	(0.012)	(0.111)
Capital × state worker	−0.002	0.033	0.007	−0.505	−0.240
	(0.012)	(0.019)	(0.016)	(0.193)	(0.187)

Source: 1980 IPUMS 5 percent sample. N = 707,506.
FE = fixed effects.
a. Regressions include state fixed effects. Standard errors are reported in parentheses and are clustered at the metropolitan area level. Sample restrictions are listed in the notes to table 1.

industrial distributions of state workers by city type. Indeed, adding dummy variables for three-digit Standard Industrial Classification (SIC) industry codes erases the wage differences between state workers in capital and noncapital cities. A similar pattern holds for hours of work per week. We show below that our main results are robust to including a full set of industry dummies.

The similarity of state workers in capital and noncapital cities, at least along observable dimensions, supports our use of a difference-in-differences estimator. However, our strategy requires the additional assumption that the presence of state government in the central business district has no effect on the job locations of private sector and other public sector workers (our control group). We will underestimate the parameter of interest if private firms in state capitals are more likely than firms elsewhere to locate downtown—perhaps because there are employment spillovers in providing services to centralized state employees. Alternatively, we will overestimate the parameter of interest if private firms in state capitals are less likely to locate downtown—for example, if state agencies outbid private firms for the fixed supply of land in the central city.

Table 3. State Workers in Capitals Are More Likely to Work and Live in Central Cities[a]

Dependent variable	Base (1)	Add industry dummies (2)	Weight equally (3)	Include college towns (4)
Panel A				
= 1 if work in city	0.137	0.119	0.124	0.143
	(0.029)	(0.027)	(0.031)	(0.028)
= 1 if work in CBD	0.082	0.051	0.087	0.070
	(0.023)	(0.023)	(0.023)	(0.022)
Panel B				
= 1 if live in city	0.034	0.027	0.031	0.039
	(0.016)	(0.015)	(0.018)	(0.015)

Source: 1980 IPUMS 5 percent sample. N = 707,506.
CBD = central business district.
a. Sample restrictions are listed in the notes to table 1. Standard errors are reported in parentheses and are clustered at the metropolitan area level. All regressions include metropolitan area fixed effects and individual-level controls, including a fourth-order polynomial in age and dummies for being female, black, and for each year of completed schooling. The second column adds a vector of dummy variables for each industry using the 1990 industry categories. The rows report coefficients on the interaction between capital city and state worker.

Empirical Results

We begin by demonstrating that state workers in capital cities are more likely to work downtown, a pattern that corresponds to the historical placement of government buildings. Table 3 examines the work and residential locations of state workers in capital and noncapital cities relative to other workers in their metropolitan area. The regressions underlying this table follow the form of equation 1 but replace the dependent variable with an indicator for either working or living downtown. Panel A shows that state workers in state capitals are 12 to 14 percentage points more likely than state workers elsewhere to work in the central city and 5 to 9 points more likely to work in the central business district.[5] These effects are large relative to the sample mean, increasing the probability of working in the central city by 25 percent and doubling the probability of working in the central business district.

If workers based their residential location decisions on their job location we would expect that state workers in capital cities are also more likely to live downtown. We test this proposition in panel B. We find that state workers in capital cities are indeed 3 to 4 percentage points—or 10 percent—more likely to live downtown. The results are again robust to adding dummy variables for three-digit SIC industry codes or weighting each metropolitan area equally. In the

5. It is interesting to note that, with the exception of state workers, employment in capital cities was no more decentralized than anywhere else by 1980. If we replace the metropolitan area fixed effects with state fixed effects, we can identify the main effect of living in a capital city. The resulting coefficient is –0.003 (standard error = 0.027).

final column (column 4), we add eight university towns to the treatment group, including Ann Arbor, Michigan; Fayetteville, Arkansas; and Lexington, Kentucky. The logic of our research design—namely, that many state buildings were constructed in the nineteenth century and are very difficult to move—may also apply to state universities. This specification yields very similar results.

Our focus on capital cities is motivated by an interest in the relationship between place of work and place of residence. The estimating equation that we have in mind is the following:

$$(2) \quad = 1 \text{ if live in city}_{ijk} = \alpha + \beta(= 1 \text{ if work in city})_{ijk} + \Phi X_{ijk} + j + k + \epsilon_{ijk}.$$

The results in table 3 suggest that a state worker's placement in the capital city is a viable instrumental variable for working in the central city.

Table 4 begins by estimating equation 2 by ordinary least squares (OLS). Working in the city increases the probability of living in the city by 26 percentage points, while working in the CBD only increases the probability of living in the city by 13 points. This pattern appears to be inconsistent with virtually all economic models of urban areas, which have at their core a trade-off between commuting costs and land prices. Such models imply that the attraction of living in the city should be strongest for those who work closest to the center.[6] The contrary evidence found in the OLS regression suggests the presence of a selection bias. Workers with a college degree are 70 percent more likely that those without to be employed in the central business district. Educated workers may prefer to live in the suburbs, despite—rather than because of—their distance from work.

The second column of table 4 uses the interaction between being a state worker and living in the state capital as an instrumental variable for working in the center city. By comparing state workers in capital and noncapital cities, we aim to minimize the presence of such selection bias. The relationship between working and living in the central city is little changed by this procedure, but the effect of working in the CBD on residential location triples in size. It now appears that working in the CBD increases the probability of living in the city by approximately 36 points, a larger effect than that of simply working in the city. Adding industry dummies further increases the estimated effect of working in the CBD.

Although our estimates are expressed as probabilities that a single individual lives in the central city, the empirical magnitudes can be usefully interpreted

---

6. This argument might not be strictly true if we think about urban transportation systems and interstate highways, many of which are geared to funnel commuters into the CBD.

Table 4. The Relationship between Place of Work and Place of Residence[a]

Variable	OLS (1)	IV (2)	IV Add industry dummies (3)
= 1 if work in city	0.263	0.246	0.239
	(0.025)	(0.135)	(0.139)
= 1 if work in CBD	0.130	0.356	0.548
	(0.012)	(0.223)	(0.380)

Source: 1980 IPUMS 5 percent sample. N = 707,506.

CBD = central business district; IV = instrumental variables; OLS = ordinary least squares.

a. Sample restrictions are listed in the notes to table 1. Dependent variable: = 1 if live in city. Standard errors are reported in parentheses and are clustered at the metropolitan area level. All regressions include metropolitan area fixed effects and individual-level controls, including a fourth-order polynomial in age and dummies for being female, black, and for each year of completed schooling. The instrument for working in the central city is an indicator equal to 1 for state workers in capital cities. The third column adds a vector of dummy variables for each industry using the 1990 industry categories.

as the predicted number of working residents living in the central city for 1,000 new centrally located jobs. Adding 1,000 jobs to the CBD would attract 356 working residents to the central city, while adding 1,000 jobs to the rest of the city would attract 227 working residents; together, these results imply that adding 1,000 jobs to the city as a whole would attract 246 new residents.[7] If one's goal is to attract residents to central cities and the policy at hand involves relocating 1,000 jobs, adding these jobs to the historical CBD appears to be more effective at the margin. Note, however, that the opposite conclusion would be drawn from the OLS specification, illustrating the value of our use of state capitals as a natural experiment.

We estimate the number of residents that stay in the central city for each job that remains. If we assume that the same relationship holds for jobs that *leave* the city (and residents who follow), we can use the parameter to assess the role of employment decentralization in the historical process of suburbanization. While our estimation is based on the 1980 cross section, we apply the resulting parameter to the time series variation in the location of employment. From 1960 to 2000, the share of workers who worked in the city fell from 59.3 to 42.3 percent (17 percentage points). The instrumental variable estimate implies that the share of workers who lived in the city would correspondingly fall by 4.2 points (= 17 × 0.246; second column of table 4). The central city share of the metropolitan population fell by 18.8 points over the same period. Combining the figures, we can infer that employment decentralization explains around 22 percent (= 4.2/18.8) of the observed suburbanization of population from 1960 to 2000. While we view this magnitude as plausible it should obvi-

7. Fifteen percent of city jobs are located in the CBD. Therefore, we calculate the effect of adding 1,000 jobs to the rest of the central city as X in the expression $0.15(356) + 0.85X = 246$.

ously be viewed with caution because we are using the results from a single case study to extrapolate to the broader economy over a (needless to say, lengthy) forty-year period of substantial social and economic change.[8]

This caveat aside, our results suggest that employment decentralization per se appears to have been a quantitatively important—but by no means sole— cause of population suburbanization. The bulk of suburban growth occurred after World War II, an era marked by rising real incomes, the diffusion of the private automobile, and new state and federal road building projects. Margo (1992) argues that rising real incomes can account for 40 percent of the movement to the suburbs from 1950 to 1980. According to Baum-Snow (2007), each interstate highway built through a central city reduced urban population by 16 percent. Households were also attracted to the suburbs by their racial and income homogeneity. Boustan (2010) finds that reversing the black migration from the rural South would have slowed the loss of urban white population by 17 percent.

Our results contribute to a long literature in urban economics on the empirical relationship between employment and residential locations. The canonical monocentric model of an urban area begins with the assumption that all production, and therefore all employment, occurs in a central location, such as the central business district (Alonso 1964; Mills 1972). In this framework, suburbanization cannot be driven by changes in employment location by construction. White (1999) summarized a set of more complex models that make the locations of both workers and firms endogenous but noted that the difficulty of the problem has limited their usefulness for quantitative analysis. As a result, the relationship between the spatial distribution of employment and population has become an inherently empirical issue.

In the 1980s and 1990s, a substantial empirical literature applied thenfashionable simultaneous equations methods to estimate the impact of job decentralization on population suburbanization and vice versa (see, for example, Steinnes 1982; Grubb 1982; Palumbo and Hutton 1987; Palumbo, Saks, and Wasylenko 1990; Greenwood and Stock 1990; Thurston and Yezer 1994; Boarnet 1994). A standard approach was to posit an econometric model linking, for example, the share of workers living (or working) in the central city to the share working (or living) in the central city and then to use lagged values of the endogenous variables as instrumental variables (for example, the share of workers working in the central city in 1970 as an instrument for the share

---

8. One concern about external validity is that the state government may provide more stable employment arrangements than the typical firm in the private sector. As a result, workers in state government may be more likely than others to base their residential location decisions on their place of employment.

working in the central city in 1980). All of these studies found that employment followed population to the suburbs, and a substantial minority also presented evidence that households followed jobs (Steinnes and Boarnet are exceptions).

We believe that this earlier empirical literature suffers from two conceptual problems. First, if location decisions are forward looking, it is entirely possible that households will move to the suburbs in expectation that firms will soon do so (and vice versa). The absence, in other words, of a relationship between today's suburbanization of population and yesterday's decentralization of employment does not necessarily rule out the possibility that people follow jobs. More fundamentally, the direction of the relationship hinted at in this literature is not sufficient to establish causality. In particular, if the error term in the regression is serially correlated at the metropolitan area level—which is almost certainly the case—then the use of lagged values of the endogenous variables as instruments will be invalid. Our approach to measuring the impact of employment on residential location avoids these econometric problems and thus (in our view) produces a more reliable estimate of the causal parameter of interest. In thinking about our results, it should be kept in mind that we are estimating a "reduced form" linking two economic outcomes—where people live and where they work. As such, we have not attributed employment decentralization or population suburbanization to more fundamental causes.[9]

Robustness Checks

In this section we explore the robustness of our main finding in three ways. First, we examine differences in the size of the treatment effect of work location on residential location by education, migrant status, and marital staus. In the second and third checks, we develop alternative instrumental variables based on employment in two additional industries for which work location is predetermined or (arguably) exogenous.

Results by Education and Migration Status

Our analysis establishes an empirical relationship between an individual's place of work and place of residence. One model that may give rise to this finding is that workers take into account their (given) work location when selecting

9. Or to put it another way, we are not estimating a structural model linking household and firm location decisions to preferences and technology. For an example of such a structural estimation, see Kopecky and Suen (2009).

their place of residence. However, we cannot directly rule out an alternative model: individuals choose their residential location for other reasons—for example, because of amenities or proximity to family—and then select a job that maximizes wages net of commuting costs conditional on their place of residence. In this case, we would find that state workers in capital cities are more likely to both live and work downtown simply because individuals who are *already* living downtown find work in nearby state buildings. However, we could not accurately describe these workers as having "followed" their jobs to the central city.[10]

Although we can never fully dispel the possibility that residential location precedes job choice, we argue that it is less likely to be operative among certain subgroups of the population—in particular, college graduates and recent migrants. College graduates function in a national labor market, and therefore their employment outcomes are not restricted to a narrow geographic band around where they happen to live (Wozniak 2006). Similarly, recent migrants to a metropolitan area have demonstrated their willingness to participate in a labor market that is much broader (in the geographic sense) than their immediate residential area. If we find a stronger relationship between the place of work and place of residence among these mobile workers, we feel confident in interpreting the relationship as the effect of work location on residential location. On the other hand, we expect the residential locations of married women to be less sensitive to their place of employment because of the need to make joint location decisions with a spouse (Madden 1981). If we continue to find a strong relationship between place of employment and place of residence for this subgroup, we will be concerned that our findings are driven by job searches conducted close to home.

Table 5 replicates our main analysis while allowing for interactions with migration activity, educational attainment, marital status, and gender. Recent migrants and college graduates are more responsive to place of employment than is the rest of the workforce. Having been "assigned" to a job in the central city increases the likelihood that a college graduate or recent migrant lives in the central city by 33 and 37 points, respectively, compared with a base effect

10. An even more complicated alternative is that workers simultaneously determine whether to work in the public or private sector, whether to live in the central city or the suburbs, and the metropolitan area in which to live. In this case, workers who prefer both urban living and the steadiness of state employment may choose to settle in Albany rather than in Buffalo in the state of New York. If this model holds, our difference-in-differences estimator may simply be identifying a group of workers with a strong taste for city life. However, if this were true, we might also expect to see observable differences between state government workers in state capitals as opposed to other workers, and as we demonstrated previously, we generally do not.

Table 5. Heterogeneous Effects of Work Location on Residential Location[a]

Demographic variable	OLS = 1 if work in city (1)	OLS = 1 if live in city (2)	IV = 1 if live in city (3)
A. Migrants			
Main effect	0.138	0.027	0.202
	(0.029)	(0.016)	(0.097)
Interact with recent migrant[b]	–0.008	0.025	0.167
	(0.022)	(0.018)	(0.102)
B. College graduates			
Main effect	0.156	0.025	0.172
	(0.028)	(0.016)	(0.086)
Interact with college graduate	–0.045	0.015	0.153
	(0.025)	(0.025)	(0.147)
C. Ever married women[c]			
Main effect	0.128	0.037	0.285
	(0.028)	(0.017)	(0.106)
Interact with married woman	0.023	–0.017	–0.123
	(0.018)	(0.010)	(0.058)

Source: 1980 IPUMS 5 percent sample. N = 707,506.

IV = instrumental variables; OLS = ordinary least squares.

a. Sample restrictions are listed in the notes to table 1. Standard errors are reported in parentheses and are clustered at the metropolitan area level. All regressions include metropolitan area fixed effects and individual-level controls, including a fourth-order polynomial in age and dummies for being female, black, and for each year of completed schooling. In columns 1 and 2 we report coefficients for the main effects of being a state worker in the capital city along with the interaction with the demographic variable in question. Column 3 reports the parallel IV regression in which the main effect of being a state worker in the capital city is used to instrument for working in the central city. The rows report coefficients on being a state worker in a capital city (or working in the central city) and the interaction with the relevant demographic variable.

b. "Recent migrants" include all individuals who moved between counties, states, or countries in the previous five years.

c. "Ever married women" includes women who are currently married, divorced, or widowed. We did not find a significant difference between the responsiveness of single men and women or married men to place of employment. Hence, we compare married women to all other categories in this specification.

of 20 percentage points (see column 3). In contrast, the residential location of married women is less responsive to place of own employment than the rest of the workforce. Taken together, these patterns are more consistent with a model in which workers choose where to live given a known work location rather than a model in which workers search for jobs close to home.

Alternate Case Study: The "Cold War" Instrument

Thus far, we have drawn sharp conclusions about the relationship between job and residential location on the basis of a single case study. It is highly desirable, therefore, to see if the basic findings carry over to other case studies. In this section and the next, we conduct similar exercises for two additional industries whose primary location was either initially determined by or has been kept in place by government rulings.

In the expansion of national defense industries during the cold war, the federal government encouraged firms with defense contracts to locate outside of central cities, which were thought to be prime targets for nuclear attack (O'Mara 2006). Manufacturing plants in defense-related industries are, as a result, more likely to be in the suburbs and—by the logic of our analysis—we might expect their workers to be more likely to live in the suburbs.

The census does not clearly identify workers in defense-related industries. We opt for a narrow definition of *defense-related workers*, focusing on those in the "guided missiles, space vehicles, and parts" manufacturing industry. We exclude industries such as aircraft manufacturing that may conduct substantial business with the federal government but that also have a sizeable civilian component. Although more than 95 percent of workers in the guided missiles industry report working in the private sector, there can be little doubt that these firms had federal contracts.

Table 6 examines the work and residential locations of workers in the guided missiles industry. Each column corresponds to a different choice of control group. In the first column, the comparison group contains around twenty heavy manufacturing industries from farm machinery to household appliances. In the second column, the comparison group is restricted to transportation manufacturing industries (except guided missiles). The third column leaves out ship building, which often takes place at harbors adjacent to the central city and therefore is disproportionately centralized.

Workers in a defense-related industry are 8 to 10 percentage points more likely to work in the suburban ring than are workers in comparable manufacturing industries in the same metropolitan area. Defense workers are also 2 points more likely to *live* in the suburban ring. These results imply that working in the suburbs increases the probability of living in the suburbs by 22 to 24 percent, a very similar magnitude to the results obtained with the state capital instrumental variable.

Workers in a defense-related industry are much more likely than workers in the various comparison groups to hold a college degree; for example, in the subgroup represented in the regression shown in column 3 (transport equipment, without ship building), 40 percent of defense workers were college graduates versus 14 percent for the comparison group. The fourth column restricts the analysis to workers in this particular subgroup without a college degree. This restriction has no effect on the substantive findings; indeed, the treatment effect of suburban employment on suburban residence for the non-college sample is even larger than in the unrestricted sample.

Table 6. Are Workers in a Defense-Related Industry More Likely to Work and Live in the Suburbs?[a]

	All workers			Without college degree
Dependent variable	*Electrical machinery, computer, and transport equipment* *(1)*	*Transport equipment, without guided missiles* *(2)*	*Transport equipment, without ship building* *(3)*	*Transport equipment, without ship building* *(4)*
OLS				
= 1 if work in suburb	0.102	0.098	0.081	0.085
	(0.030)	(0.032)	(0.029)	(0.030)
= 1 if live in suburb	0.023	0.024	0.019	0.035
	(0.014)	(0.016)	(0.016)	(0.016)
IV				
= 1 if live in suburb	0.223	0.249	0.239	0.418
	(0.141)	(0.162)	(0.208)	(0.235)
N	82,166	32,288	29,520	22,518

Source: 1980 IPUMS 5 percent sample.

IV = instrumental variables; OLS = ordinary least squares.

a. Sample restrictions are listed in the notes to table 1. Further restrictions are reported in column headings. "Defense-related industry" is narrowly defined here as the manufacturing of "guided missiles, spacecraft, and related parts" according to the 1990 industry categories. Standard errors are reported in parentheses and are clustered at the metropolitan area level. All regressions include metropolitan area fixed effects and individual-level controls, including a fourth-order polynomial in age and dummies for being female, black, and for each year of completed schooling. The first and second rows report coefficients on an indicator for working in a defense-related industry. In the third row, working in a defense-related industry is used as an instrument for working in the central city.

Alternate Case Study: The Postal Employment Instrument

Because of the difficulty of finding an exact control group for workers in defense-related industry, we turn to a within-industry comparison of two types of postal workers—mail carriers and postal clerks—whose job locations differ for historical reasons. The qualifications for entering the postal service are roughly uniform across these occupations. Job seekers take a civil service exam and available positions are filled by one of the three top-scoring candidates (the so-called Rule of Three), with a preference given to veterans.[11]

The location of mail carrying follows population patterns. As businesses and households moved out to the suburban ring, mail carriers followed suit. In contrast, noncarriers tend to work in the central city. The centralization of mail processing dates from the early twentieth century, when the bulk of intercity mail was transported by rail. At the time, central post offices were built near the main downtown rail terminal. Even as trucking and air travel eclipsed rail transport, postal facilities have remained downtown and face a number of regulatory and political impediments to relocation.

11. Mail carriers and postal clerks differ along a few observable dimensions. Mail carriers are less likely to be female (8 versus 25 percent) or black (10 versus 25 percent). They are also slightly

Table 7. Are Postal Clerks More Likely to Work and Live in the Central City?[a]

Dependent variable	= 1 if non–mail carrier
OLS	
= 1 if work in central city	0.152
	(0.015)
= 1 if live in central city	0.036
	(0.009)
IV	
= 1 if live in central city	0.238
	(0.065)

Source: 1980 IPUMS 5 percent sample.

IV = instrumental variables; OLS = ordinary least squares.

a. Sample restrictions are listed in the notes to table 1. In addition, these regressions are restricted to individuals employed by the U.S. Postal Service. $N = 8,669$. Standard errors are reported in parentheses and are clustered at the metropolitan area level. All regressions include metropolitan area fixed effects and individual-level controls, including a fourth-order polynomial in age and dummies for being female, black, and for each year of completed schooling. The first and second rows report coefficients on an indicator for working in an occupation other than mail carrier. In the third row, working as a non–mail carrier is used as an instrument for working in the central city.

Boustan and Margo (2009) exploit this contrast between the typical job location of mail carriers and other postal employees to investigate the effect of employment decentralization on the economic activity of urban black residents. Following a similar strategy here, we compare the work and residential location of mail carriers to other postal employees. Table 7 demonstrates that other postal employees are 15 percentage points more likely than mail carriers to work in the central city. Correspondingly, these noncarriers are also 3.6 points more likely to live in the central city, which implies that working downtown increases the probability of living downtown by 24 points. The numerical stability of this parameter across the three case studies—state workers, postal workers, and employees in defense-related industry—is remarkable.

Concluding Remarks

Urban economists have long been interested in the relationship between the spatial distributions of employment and population. This paper examines whether working in the central city increases the likelihood of living in the central city, using state workers in capital cities as a natural experiment. Many government buildings in state capitals were constructed in the nineteenth century and have not been (and we believe never will be) moved to an outlying

---

less likely to have some college education (31 versus 35 percent). While we control for these and other attributes, we cannot account for any differences in the taste for urban living in these two populations.

location. As a result, state workers in state capitals are more likely to work in the central city than are state workers in other metropolitan areas.

We use the interaction between being a state worker and living in the state capital as an instrumental variable for working in the central city. We find that residential location strongly responds to employment location. According to our estimates, moving 1,000 jobs into the central city would encourage 246 working residents to reside in the city. Patterns of very similar magnitude obtain in other industries whose job location is determined by government policy—including defense-related industry or the postal service. Applying our core parameter of interest, we argue that about one-fifth of the suburbanization of population between 1960 and 2000 can be attributed to employment decentralization.

By using a natural experiment to explore a long-standing issue in urban economics, our paper also makes a methodological contribution. While natural experiments have been widely employed in labor economics and public finance, they have been less prevalent in urban economics, perhaps because of a belief that locations are rarely determined by exogenous forces. Although this belief may be true in general, we feel that there are more such experiments in urban economics than generally recognized and that careful examination of the historical record will yield other examples.

Although the primary purpose of this paper is to advance understanding of a central issue in urban economics, our results are also relevant to urban policy in two ways. First, and perhaps most important, our paper provides a useful rule of thumb as to the quantitative effect on a central city's population if jobs are added or subtracted from the urban core, perhaps in response to other local policies—for example, because of changes in the level of business taxes (Bollinger and Ihlanfeldt 2003). Urban politicians have obvious political interests at stake if their constituencies rise or fall in size; urban planners may be concerned with population loss as a harbinger of building decay and neighborhood decline. Some fraction of the incomes of central city residents will be spent on locally produced goods and services, including owner-occupied housing, thereby generating tax dollars for local government expenditures. Our rule of thumb is that for every X jobs added or subtracted to the center city's base, the center's working population will increase by $0.25*X$, or (roughly) one resident for every four jobs.

Secondly, our results have implications for the recent debate over consumption-led urban revival. In particular, Glaeser, Kolko, and Saiz (2001), Glaeser and Gottlieb (2006), and others have suggested that there may be economies of scale in consumption associated with dense populations. Thus, for example, rising incomes might lead consumers to demand certain consumption goods—art museums or symphony orchestras, among others—that might be more efficiently produced in central cities. Investing in the infrastructure associated with the production of such goods, according to the logic of this argument, might lead to a resurgence of downtown areas. However, our results suggest that the current level of employment decentralization will limit any return of residents to urban cores, at least in the short run. That is, unless cities remain productive in the sense of job creation, providing employment opportunities in the urban core, the draw of a shorter suburban commute will prevent an entirely consumption-led urban revival.

Appendix

Table A-1. Summary Statistics, by Metropolitan Area, 1980[a]

	Mean	*Standard deviation*
Share work in center city	0.556	0.163
Share work in CBD	0.083	0.045
Share live in center city	0.309	0.238
Share state worker, all metro areas	0.047	0.039
Share state worker, capital areas	0.093	0.056

Source: 1980 IPUMS 5 percent sample.
CBD = central business district.
a. Means are measured at the metropolitan area level (N = 127). The last row presents statistics for the metropolitan areas anchored by a capital city (N = 25).

Table A-2. Capital Cities Identified in the Sample

State	*Capital city*
AR	Little Rock
AZ	Phoenix
CA	Sacramento
CO	Denver
CT	Hartford
GA	Atlanta
HI	Honolulu
IA	Des Moines
IN	Indianapolis
LA	Baton Rouge
MA	Boston
MI	Lansing
MN	Minneapolis-St. Paul
NC	Raleigh-Durham
NJ	Trenton
NY	Albany-Schenectady-Troy
OH	Columbus
OK	Oklahoma City
PA	Harrisburg
RI	Providence
SC	Columbia
TN	Nashville
UT	Salt Lake City
VA	Richmond
WI	Madison
	College towns
AR	Fayetteville
AZ	Tucson
KY	Lexington
MI	Ann Arbor
NM	Albuquerque
NJ	New Brunswick
OR	Eugene
TN	Knoxville

Comments

Edward Glaeser: For forty years, economists have argued about whether jobs follow people or whether people follow jobs. Across metropolitan areas, this debate concerns the relative importance of amenities or productivity differences across space. Within metropolitan areas, this debate focuses on the causes of suburbanization. Does the fact that people and jobs have decentralized reflect the allure of suburban living or the advantages of suburban productivity?

Leah Platt Boustan and Robert Margo enter this debate with a straightforward paper about state capitals. They argue, quite plausibly, that the location of capitals is essentially exogenous. State governments chose their locales in the nineteenth century (except for Oklahoma City), and they have not moved since. The changing vicissitudes of urban fortunes have not caused the Texas state government to move to a Houston suburb or the California state government to locate near Hollywood. The capital's golden domes and office buildings are essentially fixed and therefore provide a means for identifying the impact of job location on housing location.

Boustan and Margo's strategy is essentially a simple difference-in-differences estimator. They compare state employees in metropolitan areas that are state capitals with employees in areas that are not. They find that in capital cities, state government employees are 8 percent more likely to labor in the central business district and 13 percent more likely to work in the capital itself. They then use this variation to estimate the impact of working in a city on the propensity to live in a city.

The ordinary least squares relationship between these two variables is that workers are 26 percent more likely to live in a city if they work in a city. If the workers labor in a central business district or CBD, they are 13 percent more likely to live in a city. Using the interaction between being a state employee and being in a state capital as an instrument, they find that working in a city increases the propensity to live in the city by 25 percent, which is astonishingly close to the ordinary least squares estimate. Somewhat less plausibly, they find that the effect of working in a central business district almost triples, so that working in the CBD increases the propensity to live in a central city by 36

21

percent. With industry level controls, that coefficient rises to 55 percent, but it is measured with a fair degree of error. The greater precision of the city-on-city estimates, and their stability across regressions, lead me to be more confident about these estimates.

Boustan and Margo then look at demographic subgroups and find effects that are significantly stronger for unmarried women, relative to married women, which makes sense since married women may be more tied to their spouse's place of work. There are also big point estimates of the interactions with being a migrant or college graduate, but these estimates are statistically insignificant. There is some evidence that effects are similar for postal workers.

What problems plague these estimates? State capitals are, of course, different from noncapital cities. Generally governments have spent resources to make their home cities more pleasant. The capital building itself may be, like Bulfinch's Boston dome, a pleasant piece of architecture. Other memorials and parks may be disproportionately present in the capital. In some cases, such as Columbus, Ohio, or Madison, Wisconsin, the state's flagship university is also located in the capital. Surely, these amenities may also be pulling people into the central city.

However, if this pull impacts all workers equally, Boustan and Margo's point estimates will be unbiased. If workers are all the same, then the amenities will draw everyone to the center of the capital and have no disproportionate impact on state government employees. Their difference-in-differences approach will handle the problem, if state workers and other employees have similar tastes.

The problem arises if state workers have a different taste for these amenities. If state workers like the fruits of government spending more than private employees do, which is not entirely implausible, then the capital's amenities will draw them disproportionately into the urban core. In this case, the effect that Boustan and Margo identify as coming from workplace location is the impact of amenities. One imperfect means of addressing this concern would be to control for area-level amenities and interact them with being a state employee.

A second problem, related to personal heterogeneity, is that working as a state employee in a state capital may disproportionately attract people who like living in big cities. The location of the workplace may be exogenous, but the workers are not. Those workers who like living in the state capital will be particularly likely to apply for jobs that are located in that area. In that case, the perceived workplace location effect will actually reflect the tastes for living in the urban center. Unless we had some experiment where workers were randomly assigned to state government jobs, I know of no means of addressing this problem.

While these estimates are imperfect, they still have value. After all, it is not as if there are great alternative means of estimating the impact of workplace location on housing location. Despite my concerns, I am perfectly willing to accept that their figure of .25 is a reasonable estimate of the impact of workplace location on job location. What does this value mean for the larger question of the causes of suburbanization?

A .25 figure means that for every job that leaves the city, one-fourth of a worker also leaves the city. That figure should be multiplied up by the total number of people in the worker's household to understand the impact of job decentralization on population decentralization. In two-person families, a one job exodus means an exodus of one-half of a family. But does this mean that one-half of the suburbanization of population can be attributed to an exodus of employers?

Consider the following simple model, where S_{City}^{Job} is the share of the total jobs in a metropolitan area that are in a city and S_{City}^{Homes} is the share of homes that are in the city. Assume that $S_{City}^{Job} = \alpha S_{City}^{Homes} + Z_{Jobs}$ and $S_{City}^{Homes} = \beta S_{City}^{Jobs} + Z_{Homes}$, where α and β are parameters and Z_{Jobs} reflects exogenous forces determining the location of jobs and Z_{Homes} reflects exogenous forces determining the location of homes. Solving these equations reveals

$$S_{City}^{Job} = \frac{1}{1-\alpha\beta}(\alpha Z_{Homes} + Z_{Jobs})$$

and

$$S_{City}^{Homes} = \frac{1}{1-\alpha\beta}(\beta Z_{Jobs} + Z_{Homes}).$$

Boustan and Margo essentially treat state capitals as variation in Z_{Jobs}, which can identify the value of β.

To understand the causes of a change in job and housing centralization, I assume that these exogenous variables have changed over time, which implies the change equations

$$\Delta S_{City}^{Job} = \frac{1}{1-\alpha\beta}(\alpha\Delta Z_{Homes} + \Delta Z_{Jobs})$$

and

$$\Delta S_{City}^{Homes} = \frac{1}{1-\alpha\beta}(\beta\Delta Z_{Jobs} + \Delta Z_{Homes}).$$

The share of job decentralization that is caused by housing decentralization is

$$\frac{\alpha\Delta Z_{Homes}}{\alpha\Delta Z_{Homes} + \Delta Z_{Job}};$$

the share of housing decentralization that is caused by job decentralization is

$$\frac{\beta\Delta Z_{Jobs}}{\beta\Delta Z_{Jobs} + \Delta Z_{Homes}}.$$

To identify the relative importance of the two types of changes, we have two equations, and we know the values of three variables ΔS_{City}^{Job}, ΔS_{City}^{Homes}, and β, but we need to solve for three unknowns α, ΔZ_{Homes}, and ΔZ_{Jobs}. This is not enough information. For example, suppose we know that ΔS_{City}^{Job} was $-.4$ and ΔS_{City}^{Homes} was $-.6$ and β equals .5. If α equals zero, then ΔZ_{Jobs} equals $-.4$ and ΔZ_{Homes} equals $-.4$. The share of housing decentralization that is caused by job decentralization in that case would equal one-third; the share of job decentralization that is caused by housing decentralization would equal zero. Conversely, if α equals .5, then $\Delta Z_{Jobs} = -.1$ and $\Delta Z_{Homes} = -.4$. The share of housing decentralization that is caused by job decentralization in that case would equal one-fifth; the share of job decentralization that is caused by housing decentralization would equal two-thirds. The exercise yields wildly different answers depending on the value of α, and that value is unknown.

This little algebraic exercise is not meant to disparage the important contribution of Boustan and Margo to understanding the roots of urban change. They have provided a new estimate of a potentially important coefficient. However, we are still far from having the full range of parameter estimates needed to get a handle on the roots of suburbanization. Yes, people do follow their jobs, but jobs also surely follow people. Both coefficients are needed to estimate the complete relationship. This is a pressing topic for future research.

Janice F. Madden: Leah Platt Boustan and Robert Margo have developed a creative approach for measuring the extent of residential suburbanization that is caused by job suburbanization. They have an imaginative new way of answering the question: do jobs follow people or do people follow jobs? Although numerous studies have tried to answer this question with a variety of econometric techniques designed to sort out cause from effect, they have all ultimately been plagued by the problem that people may suburbanize in anticipation of job suburbanization or jobs may suburbanize in anticipation of residential suburbanization. Therefore, simply tracing the order or timing of observed job and residential moves does not show that the move that came first was the cause and the move that came next was the effect.

Boustan and Margo try to solve this problem by comparing the residential locations of employees whose jobs are in the central city and cannot move with the residential locations of employees whose jobs may locate anywhere within the metropolitan statistical area (MSA). Specifically, they analyze the residential locations of state workers in MSAs where the state capital is located relative to nonstate workers in state capital MSAs and also relative to state workers in non–state capital MSAs. They find that, on average, state capital employees are 25 percent more likely to reside in the central city than are non–state capital employees in the same MSA and than are state employees located in non–state capital MSAs. They conclude that an employer that locates in the central city, rather than in the suburbs, will cause an additional one-quarter of its employees to reside in the central city (relative to the residential distribution of employees were the same employer to locate in a suburb).

The basic idea is straightforward but clever. Simply, state employees working at the state capital have a predetermined central city work location. Unlike other employers, the locations of state capitals have not adjusted to the locations of potential employees, and there are no expectations that such adjustments will occur. Therefore, the differences between the rates of suburbanization for state employees in the state capital MSAs and the rates for state employees in other MSAs and for nonstate employees in the state capital MSAs measure the residential suburbanization effects of employers changing locations to follow employees. The approach (the key identifying assumption) requires that there are no differences, relevant to residential location preferences, in the selection of employees into state jobs versus nonstate jobs in the state capital MSAs and into non–state capital MSAs versus state capital MSAs among state workers. Therefore, for the greater incidence of central city residential locations of state workers in state capital MSAs to be attributable to their central city workplace locations, it is necessary that state workers in the state capitals not be different from nonstate workers in state capitals and from state workers in non–state capitals with respect to characteristics, other than workplace location, that affect their residential location choices.

Boustan and Margo have not clearly demonstrated that these groups of workers are the same with respect to their residential location preferences, given their workplace. They provide evidence on the similarity of state workers in the state capital MSAs to other workers in the state capital MSAs and to state workers in non–state capital MSAs. I do not find that evidence sufficient, however, to dismiss completely the possibility that these workers could systematically differ in their residential preferences. Boustan and Margo focus on whether state workers in state capital MSAs are significantly different *both* from state workers in non–state capital MSAs and nonstate workers in the state capital MSAs. This approach does not consider many plausible ways that residential preferences could differ between these groups of workers.

First, there are potential interactions between the characteristics of workers that are more important than the characteristic alone in affecting residential location decisions. For example, the effects of gender are likely to differ by marital and parental status (and vice versa). Boustan and Margo show that state workers outside state capital MSAs are substantially more likely to be female than are other workers in the same MSA, but in the state capital MSA, state workers are slightly less likely to be female. State workers are less likely to be married, both in the state capital and elsewhere. But the characteristics that matter in decisions on residential location and commuting are not marriage alone or gender alone, but the combination of marriage, gender, and parental status.

Second, if state workers have *more* of a characteristic than other workers while workers in non–state capitals have *less* than workers in state capitals, these offsetting differences in a particular characteristic (which yields no statistically significant interaction effect for being a state worker and residing in a state capital in Boustan and Margo's table 2) may still yield systematically different residential location outcomes depending on the connections between the characteristic and residential location preferences or between the characteristic and the potentially differential characteristics of state capital and non–state capital MSAs. For example, consider a situation in which state workers were older than nonstate workers but workers in the state capital MSA were younger than workers in other MSAs. In this case, the interaction effect of being a state worker in a state capital is zero (similar to the situation indicated by the last column in the top panel of Boustan and Margo's table 2). If state capital MSAs have central cities that are less attractive to younger workers (because they do not have an entertainment focus) than are central cities in non–state capital MSAs, then state (that is, older) workers would be more centralized in state capitals, but the difference would not arise from the differential employment locations of state workers in state capitals but from the interactions of differences in characteristics (age) between state workers and nonstate workers (or preferences) and in the (central city) characteristics of state capital and non–state capital MSAs (or choice sets).

Table 8. Characteristics of State Capital and Non–State Capital MSAs, 1980
Percent, except where noted

MSA	Population (1000s)	MSA population		MSA employment in durable manufacturing	Poverty rates
		In central city	*African American*		
Boston	2,763	25	5	12	9
Minneapolis	2,114	31	2	16	7
Atlanta	2,030	25	19	9	12
Denver	1,619	32	3	10	8
Phoenix	1,509	52	3	14	11
Indianapolis	1,167	60	10	18	9
Columbus	1,093	52	12	13	11
Sacramento	1,014	28	4	4	11
Salt Lake City	936	18	1	11	8
Nashville	851	54	16	11	12
Oklahoma City	834	49	9	10	11
Providence	817	30	4	25	10
Albany	795	15	3	10	10
Honolulu	763	48	2	8	10
Hartford	726	26	8	19	8
Richmond	632	36	19	6	11
Raleigh	531	34	19	10	12
Baton Rouge	494	48	20	4	15
Lansing	472	30	6	17	10
Harrisburg	447	12	5	11	8
Columbia	410	27	20	7	13
Little Rock	394	40	21	10	12
Des Moines	338	63	4	7	8
Madison	324	54	1	6	10
Trenton	308	30	13	12	9
Means					
State capitals	935	37	9	11	10
Remaining MSAs	1,109	29	10	20	12

Source: 1980 IPUMS 5 percent sample.
MSA = metropolitan statistical area.

I am particularly concerned about the interactions between worker characteristics and the differences between state capital and non–state capital MSAs.
The state capital MSAs are different from other MSAs in important ways that
are likely to affect how a central city job location affects residential decisions
of workers. If residential choices are affected by the interactions between
worker characteristics (preferences) and MSA characteristics (choice sets),
then state capital MSAs can be used to measure the effects of central city work
locations that can be generalized to other MSAs only if state capital MSAs are
otherwise similar to non–state capital MSAs. Table 8 lists the state capital MSAs

included in the study and some of their characteristics. The two bottom rows of the table show the averages of these characteristics for the included state capitals and also for the remaining MSAs included in the group of the largest 125 in the nation in 1980. The non–state capital MSAs average 20 percent more population (1.109 million versus 935,000), 10 percent lower representation of African Americans (10 percent versus 9 percent), and 20 percent higher poverty rates (12 percent versus 10 percent). Manufacturing accounts for almost twice as much (20 percent versus 11 percent) of private sector employment in non–state capital MSAs. The choice sets are different in state capital MSAs and non–state capital MSAs.

As Boustan and Margo indicate, the nine largest MSAs in the nation are not state capitals, so the state capital results may not reflect the employment location effects for large MSAs. Because many studies have connected suburbanization of residences to flight from central city poverty or African Americans, and because state capitals have fewer African American and poor residents, the state capital results may overstate the employment location effects for MSAs with more African Americans and more poor. Because MSAs with more manufacturing have slower growth and higher central city poverty and because state capital cities have less manufacturing, the state capital results may not reflect the employment location effects for MSAs with more manufacturing.

State capital cities also include a larger share of the MSA residents (37 percent versus 29 percent) than do non–state capital cities. This difference, if it is the result of the state capital being in the central city and state workers being more likely to locate in the central city, is not a problem. If, however, there are more people living in the central cities in state capitals because of other unmeasured characteristics that are not the result of the presence of the state capital (such as less regional political fragmentation), then the state capital is not a good instrument for the effects of central city workplace locations in more suburbanized MSAs.

Boustan and Margo show that state workers in state capitals are substantially less likely to be African American than are state workers outside the state capital and a bit less than are other workers in the state capital. Because African Americans are more likely to reside in cities than whites are, they state that this racial difference in state capitals "work(s) against (their) main findings." If the instrumental variable is working so that the race composition of the MSA does not matter and if the main finding is that the decentralization of jobs causes the decentralization of population, then the statement is correct. If, however, the main finding is that for every four jobs created in the center, there will be one new worker resident in the central city, then the estimate is too small; more worker residents in the central city would be expected. If there are interactions between the choice set (MSA characteristics such as fewer African Americans in state capital MSAs) and preferences (worker characteristics such as race) that are not accounted for in the analysis, then the effect may work "with the main findings" resulting in an overstatement of the effects of central city employment locations on central city residential locations.

Finally, consider the analyses if the causation is reversed so that workers search for jobs from their residences rather than select residences on the basis of their job locations. State jobs in the central city of state capitals may be of particular appeal to some workers residing nearby who are less likely to commute longer distances. Consider two categories of workers that may be overrepresented among state workers in state capitals, relative to state workers elsewhere and to non–state workers in state capitals. Boustan and Margo show part-time workers to be more prevalent in non–state capital MSAs and among state workers, especially those in state capital MSAs. Part-time workers typically make shorter commutes because their time at work does not justify longer commuting. Virtually all commuting research also finds that mothers take jobs closer to home. Mothers of children under the age of 18 make shorter commutes because the value of their nonmarket time is high and also because the value of proximity is high, for example, when children have unanticipated needs for their parents. Because state workers in state capital MSAs are more likely to work part-time (consistent with the results on hours per week reported in Boustan and Margo's table 2) and may be more likely to be mothers of young children (not considered), then state jobs in the state capital would be correlated with central city residence because they attract nearby part-timers and mothers more than do state jobs in non–state capitals or nonstate jobs in state capitals.

Boustan and Margo's additional results for postal workers and defense plant workers, which give similar estimates of the effects of central city employment locations on residential locations, provide impressive tests of robustness of their findings for state workers in state capital MSAs. But these two analyses pose the same set of questions as the analysis of central city residential locations for state workers in state capitals. For the postal workers, in particular, the reverse causality discussed above seems particularly likely.

References

Ades, Alberto F., and Edward L. Glaeser. 1995. "Trade and Circuses: Explaining Urban Giants." *Quarterly Journal of Economics* 110: 195–227.

Alonso, William. 1964. *Location and Land Use*. Harvard University Press.

Baum-Snow, Nathaniel. 2007. "Did Highways Cause Suburbanization?" *Quarterly Journal of Economics* 122: 775–805.

Boarnet, Marion G. 1994. "The Monocentric Model and Employment Location." *Journal of Urban Economics* 36: 79–97.

Bollinger, Christopher R., and Keith R. Ihlanfeldt. 2003. "The Intraurban Spatial Distribution of Employment: Which Government Interventions Make a Difference?" *Journal of Urban Economics* 53: 396–412.

Boustan, Leah P. 2010 (forthcoming). "Was Postwar Suburbanization 'White Flight'? Evidence from the Black Migration." *Quarterly Journal of Economics* 125.

Boustan, Leah P., and Robert A. Margo. 2009. "Race, Segregation, and Postal Employment: New Evidence on Spatial Mismatch." *Journal of Urban Economics* 65: 1–10.

Carroll, Glenn R., and John W. Meyer. 1983. "Capital Cities in the American Urban System: The Impact of State Expansion." *American Journal of Sociology* 88 (3): 565–78.

Glaeser, Edward L., and Joshua D. Gottlieb. 2006. "Urban Resurgence and the Consumer City." *Urban Studies* 43 (8): 1275–299.

Glaeser, Edward L., Jed Kolko, and Albert Saiz. 2001. "Consumer City." *Journal of Economic Geography* 1 (1): 27–50.

Greenwood, Michael J., and Richard Stock. 1990. "Patterns of Change in the Intrametropolitan Location of Population, Jobs, and Housing, 1950–1980." *Journal of Urban Economics* 28: 243–76.

Grubb, W. Norton. 1982. "The Flight to the Suburbs of Population and Employment, 1960–1970." *Journal of Urban Economics* 11: 348–67.

Kopecky, Karen, and Richard M. H. Suen. 2009. "A Quantitative Analysis of Suburbanization and the Diffusion of the Automobile." Working Paper. University of Western Ontario, Department of Economics.

Madden, Janice. 1981. "Why Women Work Closer to Home." *Urban Studies* 18: 181–94.

Margo, Robert A. 1992. "Explaining the Postwar Suburbanization of Population in the United States: The Role of Income." *Journal of Urban Economics* 31: 301–10.

Mills, Edwin. 1972. *Studies in the Structure of the Urban Economy*. Johns Hopkins University Press.

O'Mara, Margaret Pugh. 2006. "Uncovering the City in the Suburb: Cold War Politics, Scientific Elites, and High-Tech Spaces." In *The New Suburban History*, edited by K. Kruse and T. Sugrue, pp. 57–79. University of Chicago Press.

Palumbo, George, and Patricia Hutton. 1987. "On the Causality of Interurban Location." *Journal of Urban Economics* 22: 1–13.

Palumbo, George, Seymour Saks, and Michael Wasylenko. 1990. "Population Decentralization within Metropolitan Areas: 1970–1980." *Journal of Urban Economics* 27: 151–67.

Rosen, Kenneth T., and Mitchel Resnick. 1980. "The Size Distribution of Cities: An Examination of the Pareto Law and Primacy." *Journal of Urban Economics* 8: 165–86.

Ruggles, Stephen, Matthew Sobek, Trent Alexander, Catherine A. Fitch, Ronald Goeken, Patricia Kelly Hall, Miriam King, and Chad Ronnander. 2008. *Integrated Public Use Microdata Series: Version 4.0* [machine-readable database]. Minneapolis: Minnesota Population Center.

Steinnes, D. 1982. "Do People Follow Jobs or do Jobs Follow People? A Causality Issue in Urban Economics." *Urban Studies* 19: 187–92.

Thurston, Lawrence, and Anthony M. J. Yezer. 1994. "Causality in the Suburbanization of Population and Employment." *Journal of Urban Economics* 35: 105–18.

White, Michelle J. 1999. "Urban Areas with Decentralized Employment: Theory and Empirical Work." In *Handbook of Regional and Urban Economics*, edited by E. S. Mills and P. Cheshire. Oxford, United Kingdom: Elsevier.

Wozniak, Abigail. 2006. "Why Are College Graduates More Responsive to Distant Labor Market Opportunities?" Working Paper. University of Notre Dame, Department of Economics.

ANDREW HAUGHWOUT
Federal Reserve Bank of New York

CHRISTOPHER MAYER
Columbia Business School
National Bureau of Economic Research
Federal Reserve Bank of New York

JOSEPH TRACY
Federal Reserve Bank of New York

Subprime Mortgage Pricing: The Impact of Race, Ethnicity, and Gender on the Cost of Borrowing

The subprime lending boom increased the ability of many Americans to get credit to purchase a house. Yet concerns persist that not all borrowers have been treated equally. Previous research suggests that subprime loans were particularly concentrated in neighborhoods with a high concentration of black and Hispanic residents (Mayer and Pence 2007). Some commentators have been concerned that minority borrowers were steered into subprime loans in some cases when they might have qualified for cheaper conforming loans or that minority borrowers were given subprime loans that had fees or rates that were too high.

Previous research on housing markets suggests that such concerns might be warranted. Beginning in the early 1990s, data collected from lenders through the Home Mortgage Disclosure Act (HMDA) indicate that black or Hispanic applicants were more likely to be rejected for a mortgage relative to a white applicant, even when controlling for credit scores or other observable individual risk factors (Munnell and others 1996). Subsequent research showed that minority borrowers might also have been more likely to default on loans, but these findings were less clear in that they did not control for basic ex-ante risk factors (Ladd 1998). Even controlling for the likelihood of default, Canner,

The authors wish to acknowledge especially valuable comments and discussions with Robert Avery, Glenn Canner, and Karen Pence. Ebiere Okah and Rembrandt Koning provided extremely careful and excellent research assistance as well as many suggestions. The Paul Milstein Center for Real Estate at Columbia Business School provided funding to help support this analysis. The views expressed are those of the authors and do not necessarily reflect the views of the Federal Reserve Bank of New York or the Federal Reserve System.

Gabriel, and Wooley (1991) argued that minorities still face reduced access to conventional lending markets.

Recent studies of consumer loans have amplified concerns that minorities still face disparate treatment when applying for credit. For example, Charles, Hurst, and Stephens (2008) showed that blacks pay appreciably higher rates than other borrowers when financing a new car. Some portion of the higher payments comes from a higher proportion of blacks who use more expensive finance companies, but even among borrowers with comparable risk profiles using finance companies, blacks still pay higher rates. Similarly, Ravina (2008) found that black borrowers on Prosper.com, a successful online lending market, pay rates that are more than 1 percent higher than comparably risky white borrowers. Ravina attributed the higher rates for blacks to the fact that black lenders, who do not charge higher rates to black borrowers, are relatively under-represented on Prosper.com relative to black borrowers.

Despite the size of the mortgage market, as well as previous evidence on racial and ethnic differences in access to lending for housing, there are no recent studies that we have found on mortgage rates for minority borrowers. Below, we examine mortgage rates charged to a group of subprime mortgage borrowers using an innovative new dataset created by merging information on the race, ethnicity, and gender of mortgage borrowers (as reported under HMDA) with mortgage pricing and risk variables reported by LoanPerformance (LP). Through extensive work, we have been able to match approximately 70 percent of loans in LP to a unique mortgage in HMDA. The merged dataset allows us to examine racial, ethnic, and gender differences in mortgage lending, controlling for both the risk profile of the mortgage and the characteristics of the neighborhood where the property is located.

As the subprime market took off between 2000 and 2006, a variety of new products became available for financing housing. The available contracts were differentiated along many dimensions, including term, amortization schedule, and the allocation of future interest rate risk between borrower and lender. Because each of these features has effects on the value, timing, and probability of repayments, the precise way that they are combined into products will affect their value to borrowers and lenders. Thus, if we are to understand the pricing of loans, it is important that we examine a specific part of the market at a particular time, so that loan features and credit conditions are common for all the contracts we observe.

We focus on so-called 2/28 mortgages originated in August 2005. The 2/28 is a hybrid adjustable rate mortgage (ARM) in which borrowers are charged an initial mortgage rate for two years, followed by biannual rate resets based on a margin over a short-term rate. The 2/28 was a very popular form of subprime borrowing, and it accounted for approximately 80 percent of subprime variable rate loans and over 53 percent of all subprime loans outstanding at the end of 2007 (Sherlund 2008). We choose August 2005 for our analysis because LP coverage of the subprime market was very high in that year, and August was the peak month for originations of subprime loans. As we will see below, our initial dataset includes more than 80,000 subprime 2/28 loans originated in that month. In spite of its wide appeal and importance in the overall subprime universe, however, the 2/28 contract is only one part of a very large market—about 4.4 million first-lien mortgages were originated in 2005—and our results may be specific to the part of the market that we analyze.

There are at least three dimensions along which mortgage lenders may treat similar groups of borrowers differently. First, as discussed in much of the literature reviewed above, they may simply refuse to offer credit at all. Second, they may steer accepted applicants into less attractive or more costly products, like subprime loans. Finally, even at a particular time, they may price a given product differently for different borrowers.

Our approach precludes analysis of important questions related to selection of the borrower into the 2/28 product. Our data do not allow us to determine whether some borrowers were steered into subprime mortgages, or into 2/28s in particular, on the basis of their demographic characteristics. Instead, within the 2/28 product category, we examine determinants of both the initial interest rate as well as the margin used to adjust the rate after two years. As well, we add one more important caveat: we are unable to directly observe the points and fees paid when the borrower initially took out the mortgage, so it is possible that we are missing data that might show disparate treatment in loan origination costs.

In contrast to previous findings, our results show that if anything, minority borrowers get slightly favorable terms, although the size of these effects are quite small. Black and Hispanic borrowers pay very slightly lower initial mortgage rates than other borrowers pay—about 2.5 basis points (0.025 percent) compared with a mean initial mortgage rate of 7.3 percent. Black and Hispanic borrowers also have slightly lower margins (about 1.7 to 5 basis points, or 0.0017 to 0.005 percent) compared with a mean margin of 5.9 percent. Asian borrowers pay slightly higher initial rates and reset margins (about 3 basis points). We find no appreciable differences in lending terms by the gender of the borrower. These results control for the mortgage risk characteristics and neighborhood composition. While many of these differences are statistically significant, they are economically insignificant.

A second important finding is that 2/28 mortgages were cheaper in zip codes with a higher percentage of Asian, black, and Hispanic residents, as well as in counties with higher unemployment rates, once we control for the individual risk characteristics of the borrower. Taken in conjunction with the results in Mayer and Pence (2007) that showed that high minority neighborhoods and locations with higher unemployment rates have a higher concentration of subprime loans, this is consistent with a small but positive credit supply shock in these neighborhoods. The fact that subprime loans were cheaper in high minority neighborhoods and counties with higher unemployment, possibly because of economies of scale, might help explain why these neighborhoods had higher concentration of subprime loans.[1] Of course, these results cannot provide insight into whether some of the subprime borrowers would have qualified for a lower-cost conventional loan, as some have alleged.

Finally, our results also show that subprime loans were less expensive in metropolitan areas with greater past rates of house price appreciation. This finding is consistent with the idea that lenders may have expected higher rates of future house price appreciation in these neighborhoods and thus were willing to accept lower mortgage rates.[2] Such a finding can help explain why subprime mortgages were also more prevalent in markets with high house price appreciation (Mayer and Pence 2007), although the question of whether this was due to excessive expectations of borrowers or lenders or both can not be answered with our data.

The next section of the paper examines the data and describes the merging process for HMDA and LP data. Next we summarize the data and consider regressions of the cost of borrowing. The paper concludes with a brief policy discussion and a path for future research.

Data

Much of the innovative analysis in this paper is driven by our data. We merge together two datasets to examine the role of race, ethnicity, and gender in borrowing costs. The LoanPerformance database contains information on home location, mortgage amount, lending terms, mortgage risk factors, and monthly payments for the bulk of securitized loans. The Home Mortgage Disclosure

---

1. Previous research also found that FHA loans, the government-insured predecessor to subprime lending, also were much more highly concentrated in minority neighborhoods.
2. Piskorski and Tchistyi (2008) developed a model showing that lenders optimally lend more in markets with faster rates of house price appreciation.

Act requires lenders to report data on borrower demographics, income, geographic location, lender name, and in some cases, the mortgage yield for almost all loan applications in the United States. Therefore most LP mortgages should be contained in the HMDA database. We identify matching loans using the common data fields across the databases. Our analysis is limited to subprime mortgages to focus on the portion of the market with the riskiest loans. We also focus on mortgages originated in 2005, when LP appears to have the strongest coverage of the subprime market (Mayer and Pence 2007).

LoanPerformance

First American LoanPerformance, a subsidiary of First American CoreLogic Inc. provides information on securitized mortgages in subprime pools. The data do not include mortgages held in portfolio; securitized mortgages in prime, jumbo, or alt-A pools; or loans guaranteed by government agencies such as the Federal Housing Administration (FHA) and the Department of Veterans Affairs or by government-sponsored enterprises such as Fannie Mae, Freddie Mac, or Ginnie Mae. The data also exclude loans handled by servicers that do not report to LoanPerformance.

We classify loans as subprime if they were packaged into a deal classified as subprime in LoanPerformance. The guidelines for what type of mortgage can be sold into a subprime pool vary across securitizers. In general, borrowers in subprime pools tend to have low credit scores and high loan-to-value ratios. On occasion, securitizers include a handful of near-prime or prime loans in these pools.

The LP data contain extensive information on the characteristics of the loan, such as the mortgage type, the interest rate, the loan purpose (whether it was for purchase or refinance), and whether the loan has a prepayment penalty. However, data on upfront points and fees are not included. LP has less detailed information about the borrower, reporting the FICO credit score, the borrower's reported debt-to-income ratio, and the extent to which that income is documented. There is relatively little information about the property beyond the sale or appraised price, the type of property, and its state and zip code.

We use the following LP data fields: "zip code," "origination date," "first payment date," "lien," "occupancy" (owner-occupied or not), "purpose" (purchase or refinance), "loan amount," and "originator name." As well, we use the rating of the deal that the loan was packaged in. The five-digit zip code and loan amount are retained as reported. The origination date is used as reported. However, a variable is created reporting whether the origination date is imputed or not. LP often imputes the origination date by assuming origination two months before the first payment date. Therefore we classify any loan with an origination date exactly two months before first payment date as having an imputed origination date. Lien is classified as first lien or subordinate. We restrict our analysis to first-lien mortgages.

HMDA

Under the Home Mortgage Disclosure Act, most originators must report basic attributes of the mortgage applications that they receive in metropolitan statistical areas (MSAs) to the Federal Financial Institutions Examination Council. These data are considered the most comprehensive source of mortgage data and cover an estimated 80 percent of all home loans nationwide (Avery, Brevoort, and Canner 2007) and a higher share of loans originated in metropolitan statistical areas. Depository institutions that are in the home lending business, have a home or branch office in an MSA, and have assets over a certain threshold ($35 million in 2006) are required to report to HMDA. Mortgage and consumer finance companies that extend 100 or more home purchase or refinancing loans a year are also required to report for any MSA in which they receive five or more applications. We use the following HMDA data fields: "census tract," "action date," "loan amount," "occupancy," "loan purpose," "originator," "high cost annual percentage rate" (APR), and "lien."

Merging and the Combined Sample

We use HMDA and LP loans originated in 2005. Only loan applications that are marked as originated, as used for home purchase and refinance, and as one-to four-family properties are considered. Any HMDA loans marked as sold to Fannie Mae, Ginnie Mae, Freddie Mac, and Farmer Mac are not included since LP only reports loans that were privately securitized. Only loans originated on working days, that is, not weekends and not on holidays (as defined by the Office of Personal Management) are included. Finally, loans with missing information on purchase and refinance, occupancy, lien, or five-digit zip code are dropped.

We clean the originator name in LP to match originators in HMDA, which are likely accurate given that the HMDA data are reported by the originators themselves. We match the most common originator names in LP, which make up approximately 95 percent of loans with nonmissing originator names, to the corresponding HMDA originator name by hand. However, the originator name is missing in LP about 60 percent of the time. In addition, we classify the originator name as missing in LP if the originator name cannot be hand matched into an originator name that is in the HMDA data.

Finally, we combine census tracts in HMDA into zip codes to match the geographic data in LP. We cross walk each census tract, as defined in the 2000 U.S. census, to 2006 zip codes using the proportion of a census tract that is fully contained in the zip code.

The appendix describes our merging process in more detail. The data used for our analysis below represent the set of unique, one-for-one merges between LP and HMDA.

Interest Rates and Spreads in LP and HMDA

The presence of interest rate information in LoanPerformance and an APR spread over Treasury rates data in HMDA provides an additional check on our merge and on the key variables in our analysis. HMDA reports the difference between the APR on each loan and the rate on comparable maturity Treasuries for all loans in which this spread is at least 300 basis points (3 percent).[3] This APR, which is calculated by the institution reporting the HMDA data, is based on the full cost of the loan, including both interest costs and such up-front charges as points and fees, amortized over the full loan term.[4] Future rate adjustments for all of the loans we analyze are tied to the six-month LIBOR, plus the margin, and in every case this expected future rate will exceed the initial rate assuming no change in the six-month LIBOR rate since origination. Thus, if we have correctly merged the same loan across the two data files, the initial interest rate provided in LP should *never* exceed the APR that is reported in the HMDA data.

For each loan in our data, we calculated the spread between the initial interest rate as reported in LP and the comparable maturity Treasury (the same used to calculate the APR spread). Comparing this LP spread with the HMDA spread provides us with a data consistency check on our merge between the two data files. Table 1 reports the various combinations of spreads calculated from LP in relation to those obtained from the HMDA data. Start with mortgages in the southwest corner of the table. For these mortgages the HMDA APR spread is censored indicating that it was less than 3 percent. However, the LP spread—defined as the difference between the initial rate and the comparable Treasury—exceeded 3 percent. These mortgages fail this consistency check. Move now to the southeast corner. In this cell, both HMDA and LP indicate

---

3. See Avery, Brevoort, and Canner (2006, p. A126). The HMDA measure of spread is censored for loans with APRs that are less than 3 percent above the Treasury rate.

4. For details on calculating an APR, see (www.efunda.com/formulae/finance/apr_calculator.cfm).

Table 1. Spreads in LP and HMDA, 2/28 ARMs[a]

LP	HMDA Spread < 3	HMDA Spread > 3
Spread < 3	5,349	41,204
Spread > 3	**2,571**	**479**[b] 29,191[c]
Total		78,794
Sample size		75,744

Source: Authors' calculations.
ARM: adjustable rate mortgage; LP: LoanPerformance; HMDA: Home Mortgage Disclosure Act.
a. Observations in bold fail the consistency test and are dropped from the estimation sample.
b. LP spread > HMDA spread.
c. LP spread ≤ HMDA spread.

spreads of at least three percent. We divide this cell into two groups: those in which the HMDA spread exceeds the LP spread (right-hand side, or RHS) and those in which the HMDA spread is less than the LP spread (left-hand side, or LHS). Those mortgages in the LHS also fail this consistency check. For the cell in the northeast corner, all of the mortgages have a HMDA spread that equals or exceeds the LP spread so they pass the consistency check. Finally, for the mortgages in the northwest corner cell, the HMDA spread is censored, and the LP spread is also less than 3 percent. However, we are not able to apply our consistency check on these mortgages (that is, we could not verify whether the HMDA spread is at least as large as the LP spread) since the HMDA spread is censored. For our estimation sample, we delete the mortgages that fail this consistency check.

Data Description

Our merged HMDA-LP dataset provides new information on subprime loan characteristics and demographic indicators. Table 2 reports unconditional mean characteristics of owner-occupant borrowers who took first-lien subprime hybrid 2/28 loans during August 2005. Several features of the data merit discussion. First, comparison of the "Female" and "Overall" columns indicates that loans with a female primary applicant are generally quite similar to those with a male primary applicant. We do, however, observe some differences by race and ethnicity.

The characteristics of the neighborhoods in which the collateral properties are located vary by type of borrower. Black borrowers generally secured their loans with properties located in areas that are more heavily black, that experienced lower rates of house price appreciation during 2004, and that had a lower rate of new housing permits. Collateral for loans made to Asian and Hispanic borrowers tended to be in neighborhoods that, on average, had experienced recent, much higher house price appreciation and, for Hispanics, higher permit rates, presumably a reflection of the concentration of these borrowers in high-growth areas like Florida and California, where house prices also experienced some of the fastest appreciation rates. Unemployment rates in the counties where all borrowers lived were around 5 percent, although they were slightly higher for black and Hispanic borrowers.

The typical first-lien mortgage in our data was for a principal amount of about $217,000, but the average loan made to black borrowers was about 12 percent smaller, while those made to Hispanic, and especially Asian, borrowers tended to be larger. Origination loan-to-values (LTVs) for these borrowers were broadly similar, although Asian borrowers were more likely to have LTVs of 95 or more, implying that the value of the house was the main source of this variation.

A substantial majority of the loans made to Asian and Hispanic borrowers were for the purchase of a new property, as opposed to a refinance, and these borrowers provided full documentation less than half the time. Black borrowers provided full documentation nearly 70 percent of the time.

Debt-to-income ratios were broadly similar across these demographic groups; black borrowers had lower credit scores, while Asian and Hispanic borrowers' scores tended to exceed the overall average. Black borrowers were more likely to have very low FICO scores (below 560) and less likely to have very high scores (above 719). In light of this, it is perhaps unsurprising that initial interest rates received by black borrowers averaged approximately 20 basis points higher than the overall average, while Asian and Hispanic borrowers' rates were 25 to 36 basis points lower than average. Margins for 2/28 loans, which is the amount added to the six-month LIBOR rate to determine the adjustable rate in the future, follow a similar pattern, although the differences are smaller than they are for origination rates.

While these unconditional differences are of interest, they are very difficult to interpret on their own. The interest rate and margin charged on a given loan should be functions of the loan terms, the borrower's characteristics, and the collateral property and its location. We next turn to a multivariate analysis of the determinants of the initial interest rate and reset margin.

Table 2. Mean Characteristics, by Borrower Race, Ethnicity, and Gender[a]

		Primary borrower identified as—			
	Overall	*Female*	*Black*	*Asian*	*Hispanic*
Observations	75,744	28,489	12,892	2,655	15,647
Borrower characteristics					
Asian	3.51	3.92	0	100	0.47
Hispanic	20.66	19.19	2.18	2.79	100
Female	37.61	100	51.66	42.11	34.95
Loan characteristics					
Initial interest rate	7.32	7.37	7.53	6.96	7.06
Margin over six-month LIBOR	5.88	5.90	5.96	5.76	5.81
FICO	618.95	617.04	606.41	645.01	618.97
Percentage < 560	15.57	16.96	19.17	7.72	10.88
Percentage > 719	5.16	5.10	2.99	10.88	8.21
LTV	87.43	86.70	88.47	89.40	88.39
Percentage < 80	19.64	21.58	17.48	12.84	17.55
Percentage ≥ 95	42.74	41.21	45.59	49.11	48.13
DTI[b]	40.88	41.62	41.24	41.77	41.64
Percentage < 40	54.47	52.08	53.24	45.72	46.92
Percentage ≥ 50	7.98	8.47	9.06	7.61	6.65
Percentage full documentation	60.81	57.87	68.52	43.46	43.01
Percentage purchase	49.59	48.79	51.54	61.66	58.01
Loan amount ($10,000)	21.69	20.87	19.01	32.88	25.30
Percentage with prepayment penalty	74.03	73.04	67.28	75.59	80.98
Months penalty in effect[c]	24.04	24.10	23.94	23.23	23.67
Neighborhood characteristics					
Average credit score	736.46	733.27	706.58	750.62	724.68
Percentage Asian	3.84	3.91	3.06	11.00	5.07
Percentage black	14.66	17.32	37.79	10.09	11.42
Percentage Hispanic	16.42	16.15	11.17	21.14	35.14
Homeownership rate	63.59	62.95	60.49	62.45	59.25
House price appreciation in prior year	10.19	10.12	8.74	14.06	14.58
House price risk[d]	0	0.012	−0.046	−0.109	−0.002
Unemployment rate	5.12	5.13	5.27	5.07	5.23
Lagged permits in county per 100 units	3.14	2.99	2.45	2.87	3.60

Source: Authors' calculations.
DTI: debt-to-income; LIBOR: London Interbank Offered Rate; LTV: loan-to-value.
a. Subprime 2/28 mortgages for owner-occupants only.
b. Back-end ratio. Missing for 25.97 percent of loans—generally low and no-doc loans.
c. For loans with prepayment penalties.
d. Standardized (two-year) variance of Office of Federal Housing Enterprise Oversight (OFHEO) index.

Empirical Specification and Results

We investigate the pricing of subprime fixed-rate and adjustable-rate mortgages using the following regression specification:

$$r_{ijk} = X_i\beta_1 + Y_i\beta_2 + Z_j\beta_3 + \alpha_k + \varepsilon_{ij}.$$

The dependent variables are the initial interest rate and the reset margin. The interest rate and margin always refer to the first-lien mortgage. While we know if a second lien exists, we do not know the rate on the second-lien mortgage. In addition, neither LP nor HMDA report any up-front points that may be paid by the borrower. As a result, we have an incomplete picture of the full price of the mortgage(s).[5] Our sample includes rates only for mortgages that were approved, and we do not control for any variation in denial rates across different locations. The vector X_i contains a set of indicators for the characteristics of the ith borrower. We focus on two racial indicators (Asian and black), one ethnic indicator (Hispanic), and an indicator for the gender of the primary applicant.

The vector Y_i captures the risk profile of the ith borrower. The basic risk characteristics we control for are the borrower's credit score (FICO score), the initial combined loan-to-value and debt-to-income ratios, level of documentation used in the underwriting, whether the mortgage is for a purchase or a refinance, the loan amount, the presence and duration of a prepayment penalty, the type of property used as collateral, and the loan type. We follow Haughwout, Peach, and Tracy (2008) in allowing the FICO, LTV, and DTI variables to have nonlinear pricing effects. We include indicators for different intervals for each variable. In cases where a second lien is present, the pricing may differ between the first-lien and second-lien mortgages. Ideally, we would like an average interest rate weighted by the relative loan amounts. However, lacking information on the interest rate for the second lien, we interact the LTV and DTI variables for the presence of a second lien. The coefficients on the LTV and DTI variables, then, refer to cases where only a first-lien mortgage is present, and the coefficients on the second-lien interactions show the degree to which differential pricing exists between mortgages with and without a second lien.

Finally, vector Z_j contains controls for the characteristics of the geographic area where the house is located. We follow Mayer and Pence (2007) and control at the zip code level for the average credit score (Vantage credit score), percentage Asian, percentage black, percentage Hispanic, and the homeownership rate. At the MSA level we control for the extent of house price

5. In future work, we will try to back out the points and fees by comparing the reported APR from HMDA with a zero-points-and-fees APR calculated from LP.

appreciation during the prior year, house price risk, the unemployment rate and the degree of new building activity as proxied by the issuance of building permits relative to existing housing units. The α_k represents any location error components that remain after controlling for the observed borrower, mortgage, and neighborhood characteristics. We report specifications that include MSA and zip code fixed effects to sweep out the α_k.

Summary statistics are provided in appendix table A-1. The results for pricing the initial interest rate are provided in table 3. Specification (1) includes only borrower characteristics (X_i). Specification (2) adds controls for the risk profile of the mortgage (Y_i). Specification (3) adds controls for the neighborhood characteristics (Z_j). Finally, specification (4) checks for robustness by adding MSA fixed effects, while specification (5) replaces the MSA fixed effects with zip code fixed effects.[6] We follow the same format when reporting the results for pricing the reset margin in table 4.

In our sample of subprime 2/28 mortgages, we find modest differences in the average initial interest rates paid by different groups of borrowers. Interest rates for Asian and Hispanic borrowers on average were 41 and 31 basis points *lower* than for our left-out group of borrowers (specification (1) of table 3).[7] In contrast, interest rates for black borrowers were on average 16 basis points higher than our left-out group. In the case of women who are the primary applicant, the data indicate a 5-basis-point higher average initial interest rate relative to the left-out group. In all cases, these differences are smaller for the reset margins (specification (1) of table 4).

These unconditional differences in average interest rates could reflect systematic differences in the risk profiles of the mortgages underwritten for these different groups of borrowers, or differences in the characteristics of the geographic locations of these loans which might affect pricing, or both. The extent to which these factors can explain the rate differences can be seen from expanding the estimation to include controls for these factors. We see in specification (2) of table 3 that controlling for differences in the observed risk profiles of the mortgages significantly reduces the unexplained differences in average initial interest rates across our demographic groups. The 41-basis-point lower rate for Asians is eliminated, while the 31-basis-point lower rate for Hispanics is reduced to 11 basis points. Similarly, the 16-basis-point higher average rate for blacks and the 5-basis-point higher average rate for women are both reduced

---

6. Specifications (2) through (5) contain three property type fixed effects and six loan product type fixed effects. Details are given in the table footnotes.

7. The left-out group of borrowers consists of primary applicants who are male, non-Asian, non-black, and non-Hispanic living in a single-family home and who took out a standard 2/28 mortgage.

to zero. Controlling for the geographic characteristics in specification (3) of table 3 further reduces the average rate difference for Hispanics from −11 basis points to −3 basis points. Adding MSA or zip code fixed effects, while improving the overall fit of the empirical specification, has minimal further impact on these results.[8]

The reset margin is a less transparent feature of the mortgage's price than the initial rate. Lenders who wanted to charge specific groups of borrowers different prices that did not correspond to verifiable risk factors might choose to do so with the margin.[9] The data, however, do not provide any evidence that differential pricing by demographic characteristics of the borrower emerge in the determination of the reset margin. Specifications (2) through (5) of table 4 show the same pattern that we saw for the initial interest rate. As we control for the characteristics of the mortgage as well as the geographic area, the average residual differences in margins for our different types of borrowers become quite small in magnitude.

The results in tables 3 and 4 indicate similar pricing of 2/28 subprime mortgages in terms of initial rates and reset margins for Asians, blacks, Hispanics, and females as for our left-out group of borrowers. We carried out several checks for robustness on these results. The results reported in tables 3 and 4 are based on means of the pricing distributions. It is possible that disparate pricing practices, if they exist, may not be evident at the means but may only manifest themselves when we look further out in the tails of the rate distributions.[10] To check for this, we estimated quantile regressions for the initial rate and the reset margin for the 75th and 25th percentiles. The results from the quantile regressions are broadly similar to those from the mean regressions. The data provide no evidence that disparate pricing by demographic groups occurs for mortgages with high or low residual rates.

A concern might be that any differential pricing faced by women when securing a mortgage may be mitigated if she has a male coapplicant. To check for this possibility, our second robustness check was to restrict the female indicator to those women borrowers with *no* coapplicant on the mortgage. This does not significantly change our earlier findings of no positive residual price differences for women borrowers.

---

8. Including MSA fixed effects increases the R squared from 0.469 to 0.489, while including zip code fixed effects increases the R squared to 0.572.

9. In auto financing, disparate pricing practices have tended to manifest themselves in the dealer "markup" over the risk-adjusted rates quoted to the dealers by the lending companies. See Cohen (2006).

10. For example, Charles, Hurst, and Stephens (2008) found evidence of racial disparities in pricing of auto loans by finance companies at the 75th percentile but not at the median or 25th percentile.

Table 3. Initial Interest Rate: Subprime 2/28 Mortgages, Owner-Occupied[a]

			Specification		
	(1)	*(2)*	*(3)*	*(4)*	*(5)*
Borrower characteristics					
Asian	−0.413**	−0.016	0.027*	0.030*	0.019
	(0.021)	(0.016)	(0.016)	(0.016)	(0.017)
Black	0.157**	0.006	−0.026**	−0.026**	−0.017*
	(0.010)	(0.008)	(0.009)	(0.009)	(0.009)
Hispanic	−0.315**	−0.106**	−0.029**	−0.026**	−0.029**
	(0.010)	(0.007)	(0.008)	(0.008)	(0.009)
Female	0.055**	−0.002	−0.002	−0.004	−0.008
	(0.008)	(0.006)	(0.006)	(0.006)	(0.0060
Loan characteristics					
FICO: missing		2.376**	2.344**	2.279**	2.213**
		(0.088)	(0.087)	(0.086)	(0.093)
< 560		1.854**	1.838**	1.820**	1.788**
		(0.016)	(0.016)	(0.016)	(0.016)
560–589		1.113**	1.096**	1.082**	1.058**
		(0.015)	(0.015)	(0.015)	(0.016)
590–619		0.717**	0.699**	0.689**	0.675**
		(0.015)	(0.014)	(0.014)	(0.015)
620–649		0.419**	0.406**	0.402**	0.395**
		(0.014)	(0.014)	(0.014)	(0.015)
650–679		0.232**	0.225**	0.221**	0.215**
		(0.015)	(0.015)	(0.014)	(0.015)
680–719		0.082**	0.078**	0.078**	0.078**
		(0.016)	(0.016)	(0.015)	(0.016)
LTV: 80–84		0.117**	0.060**	0.035**	0.033**
		(0.010)	(0.010)	(0.010)	(0.010)
85–89		0.392**	0.326**	0.298**	0.290**
		(0.012)	(0.012)	(0.012)	(0.013)
90–94		0.568**	0.486**	0.452**	0.449**
		(0.011)	(0.011)	(0.011)	(0.012)
95+		1.092**	0.988**	0.932**	0.916**
		(0.012)	(0.012)	(0.012)	(0.013)
95+ * second lien		−0.993**	−0.961**	−0.911**	−0.887**
		(0.012)	(0.012)	(0.012)	(0.012)
DTI: missing		−0.056**	−0.056**	−0.053**	−0.040**
		(0.008)	(0.008)	(0.008)	(0.008)
40–44		−0.028**	−0.023**	−0.012	0.003
		(0.010)	(0.010)	(0.010)	(0.011)
45–49		−0.034**	−0.025**	−0.013	0.002
		(0.010)	(0.010)	(0.010)	(0.010)
50+		−0.091**	−0.084**	−0.064**	−0.047**
		(0.013)	(0.013)	(0.013)	(0.014)
40–44 * second lien		0.096**	0.098**	0.097**	0.088**
		(0.016)	(0.016)	(0.016)	(0.017)
45–49 * second lien		0.061**	0.062**	0.063**	0.056**
		(0.015)	(0.015)	(0.015)	(0.016)

Table 3. Initial Interest Rate: Subprime 2/28 Mortgages, Owner-Occupied (continued)[a]

	Specification				
	(1)	*(2)*	*(3)*	*(4)*	*(5)*
50+ * second lien		0.019	0.018	0.012	−0.003
		(0.023)	(0.023)	(0.023)	(0.024)
Limited documentation		0.516**	0.532**	0.539**	0.547**
		(0.006)	(0.006)	(0.006)	(0.007)
No documentation		0.562**	0.585**	0.596**	0.609**
		(0.063)	(0.063)	(0.062)	(0.065)
Refinance–cash out		−0.169**	−0.148**	−0.124**	−0.118**
		(0.007)	(0.007)	(0.007)	(0.008)
Refinance–no cash out		−0.204**	−0.211**	−0.196**	−0.178**
		(0.013)	(0.013)	(0.013)	(0.014)
Loan amount ($10,000)		−0.017**	−0.011**	−0.008**	−0.008**
		(0.000)	(0.000)	(0.000)	(0.000)
Prepayment penalty		−0.220**	−0.177**	−0.172**	−0.198**
		(0.018)	(0.018)	(0.018)	(0.020)
Months penalty in effect		−0.003**	−0.004**	−0.008**	−0.009**
		(0.001)	(0.001)	(0.001)	(0.001)
Neighborhood characteristics					
Average credit score (× 10)			−0.017**	−0.012**	
			(0.001)	(0.001)	
Percentage Asian (× 10)			−0.040**	−0.006	
			(0.006)	(0.006)	
Percentage black (× 10)			−0.007**	−0.004	
			(0.002)	(0.003)	
Percentage Hispanic (× 10)			−0.028**	−0.025**	
			(0.002)	(0.003)	
Homeownership rate (× 10)			−0.002	−0.012**	
			(0.002)	(0.003)	
House price appreciation in prior year			−0.014**		
			(0.000)		
House price risk			0.001		
			(0.003)		
Unemployment rate			−0.010**		
			(0.002)		
Lagged permits in county / 100 units			−0.002**		
			(0.001)		
R squared	0.026	0.458	0.469	0.489	0.572
MSA fixed effects	No	No	No	Yes	No
Zip code fixed effects	No	No	No	No	Yes

Source: Authors' calculations.
DTI: debt-to-income; LTV: loan-to-value.
**Significant at the 5 percent level; *significant at the 10 percent level.
a. Number of mortgages = 75,744. Specifications (2)–(5) contain three property-type fixed effects: condo (8.1 percent), 2-4 units (5.2 percent), and townhouse (0.4 percent); and six product-type fixed effects: two-year interest only (IO) (7.4 percent), three-year IO (0.02 percent), five-year IO (21.2 percent), ten-year IO (0.2 percent), IO unknown period (0.07 percent), and ARM balloon (5.6 percent).

Table 4. Margin to 6-month LIBOR: Subprime 2/28 Mortgages, Owner-Occupied[a]

	Specification				
	(1)	*(2)*	*(3)*	*(4)*	*(5)*
Borrower characteristics					
Asian	–0.123**	0.005	0.019	0.036**	0.025
	(0.020)	(0.018)	(0.018)	(0.018)	(0.019)
Black	0.071**	–0.010	–0.017*	–0.015	–0.001
	(0.010)	(0.009)	(0.010)	(0.010)	(0.011)
Hispanic	–0.081**	–0.057**	–0.050**	–0.030**	–0.030**
	(0.009)	(0.008)	(0.009)	(0.009)	(0.010)
Female	0.028**	–0.008	–0.008	–0.012*	–0.010
	(0.007)	(0.007)	(0.007)	(0.006)	(0.007)
Loan characteristics					
FICO: missing		1.279**	1.252**	1.211**	1.101**
		(0.098)	(0.097)	(0.096)	(0.105)
< 560		1.140**	1.131**	1.113**	1.081**
		(0.018)	(0.018)	(0.017)	(0.018)
560–589		0.701**	0.696**	0.681**	0.659**
		(0.017)	(0.017)	(0.017)	(0.018)
590–619		0.462**	0.455**	0.443**	0.427**
		(0.016)	(0.016)	(0.016)	(0.017)
620–649		0.231**	0.226**	0.224**	0.207**
		(0.016)	(0.016)	(0.016)	(0.016)
650–679		0.118**	0.114**	0.113**	0.097**
		(0.016)	(0.016)	(0.016)	(0.017)
680–719		0.019	0.017	0.024	0.014
		(0.017)	(0.017)	(0.017)	(0.018)
LTV: 80–84		0.146**	0.137**	0.126**	0.120**
		(0.011)	(0.011)	(0.011)	(0.012)
85–89		0.204**	0.192**	0.185**	0.171**
		(0.013)	(0.013)	(0.013)	(0.014)
90–94		0.290**	0.275**	0.265**	0.255**
		(0.012)	(0.012)	(0.012)	(0.013)
95+		0.705**	0.688**	0.660**	0.636**
		(0.013)	(0.014)	(0.014)	(0.015)
95+ * second lien		–0.732**	–0.725**	–0.698**	–0.672**
		(0.013)	(0.013)	(0.013)	(0.014)
DTI: missing		–0.363**	–0.363**	–0.362**	–0.350**
		(0.009)	(0.009)	(0.009)	(0.009)
40–44		–0.029**	–0.030**	–0.021**	–0.016
		(0.012)	(0.012)	(0.011)	(0.012)
45–49		–0.011	–0.017	–0.009	–0.003
		(0.011)	(0.011)	(0.011)	(0.012)
50+		–0.038**	–0.039**	–0.022	–0.019
		(0.015)	(0.015)	(0.015)	(0.016)
40–44 * second lien		0.095**	0.095**	0.101**	0.097**
		(0.018)	(0.018)	(0.018)	(0.019)
45–49 * second lien		0.105**	0.106**	0.115**	0.108**
		(0.017)	(0.017)	(0.017)	(0.017)

Table 4. Margin to 6-month LIBOR: Subprime 2/28 Mortgages, Owner-Occupied (continued)[a]

	(1)	(2)	Specification (3)	(4)	(5)
50+ * second lien		−0.036	−0.035	−0.039	−0.042
		(0.026)	(0.026)	(0.025)	(0.027)
Limited documentation		0.401**	0.398**	0.404**	0.402**
		(0.007)	(0.007)	(0.007)	(0.008)
No documentation		0.463**	0.459**	0.454**	0.432**
		(0.071)	(0.070)	(0.069)	(0.073)
Refinance—cash out		−0.166**	−0.164**	−0.137**	−0.134**
		(0.008)	(0.008)	(0.008)	(0.009)
Refinance—no cash out		−0.211**	−0.204**	−0.186**	−0.179**
		(0.015)	(0.015)	(0.015)	(0.016)
Loan amount ($10,000)		−0.008**	−0.006**	−0.005**	−0.005**
		(0.000)	(0.000)	(0.000)	(0.000)
Prepayment penalty		−0.110**	−0.113**	−0.091**	−0.103**
		(0.020)	(0.020)	(0.020)	(0.022)
Months penalty in effect		0.005**	0.005**	−0.000	−0.001
		(0.001)	(0.001)	(0.001)	(0.001)
Neighborhood characteristics:					
Average credit score (× 10)			−0.018**	−0.011**	
			(0.001)	(0.002)	
Percentage Asian (× 10)			−0.015**	−0.005	
			(0.007)	(0.007)	
Percentage black (× 10)			−0.021**	−0.011**	
			(0.003)	(0.003)	
Percentage Hispanic (× 10)			−0.019**	−0.011**	
			(0.002)	(0.003)	
Homeownership rate (× 10)			−0.002	−0.003	
			(0.003)	(0.003)	
House price appreciation in prior year			−0.000		
			(0.001)		
House price risk			0.041**		
			(0.003)		
Unemployment rate			−0.022**		
			(0.002)		
Lagged permits in county / 100 units			−0.003**		
			(0.001)		
R squared	0.003	0.221	0.226	0.263	0.372
MSA fixed effects	No	No	No	Yes	No
Zip code fixed effects	No	No	No	No	Yes

Source: Authors' calculations.

DTI: debt-to-income; LIBOR: London Interbank Offered Rate; LTV: loan-to-value.

**Significant at the 5 percent level; *significant at the 10 percent level.

a. Number of mortgages = 75,744. Specifications (2)–(5) contain three property-type fixed effects: condo (8.1 percent), 2-4 units (5.2 percent), and townhouse (0.4 percent); and six product-type fixed effects: two-year interest only (IO) (7.4 percent), three-year IO (0.02 percent), five-year IO (21.2 percent), ten-year IO (0.2 percent), IO unknown period (0.07 percent), and ARM balloon (5.6 percent).

Another possibility is that first-time homebuyers are less skilled at negotiating mortgage rates (see Avery, Brevoort, and Canner 2006; Bucks and Pence 2008). If in the subprime mortgage market blacks and Hispanics are overrepresented as first-time buyers, then the estimated coefficients on the indicators for these two groups would suffer from a positive left-out-variable bias. Neither the LP nor the HMDA data contain information on whether the applicant is a first-time buyer. However, we can identify a subset of applicants that definitely are *not* first-time buyers—refinances. We interacted the Asian, black, Hispanic, and female indicators with an indicator for a refinance. In each case and for both outcome rate measures, the interaction is negative and significant. For Hispanics, the data indicate that the initial rate (reset margin) is on average 14 (9) basis points lower for a refinance as compared with a purchase. However, even with purchase mortgages, Asians and Hispanics pay only 3 to 4 basis points higher initial rates and reset margins as compared with white male borrowers.[11]

Mayer and Pence (2007) found that subprime mortgage originations were more prevalent in locations with high concentrations of black and Hispanic residents. One possible explanation is that these same neighborhoods were the most credit constrained by the conforming mortgage market, so the development of the subprime market had a differential impact in these areas.[12] An alternative possible explanation is that deceptive practices were used to entice borrowers to take out subprime mortgages and that these practices were relatively more effective in heavily minority neighborhoods. The first explanation is essentially a shift out in the supply of credit, while the second explanation is an induced shift out in the demand for credit.

Mayer and Pence (2007) could not investigate the merits of either of these explanations for their finding since their data did not permit controlling for the race and ethnicity of the individual borrower. Although we cannot provide a definitive explanation for the Mayer and Pence finding, our data shed some light on the relative merits of the different possible explanations. Specifications (3) and (4) of tables 3 and 4 report the pricing effects from neighborhoods with higher concentrations of black and Hispanic residents holding constant the race and ethnicity of the primary applicant and the risk profile of the subprime mortgages. The data indicate that increases in the percentage black and the percentage Hispanic are generally associated, ceteris paribus, with lower interest rates and reset margins. Given that Mayer and Pence found positive quantity effects, the

11. There is no significant difference in the initial rate or in the reset margin on purchase mortgages for black borrowers.
12. See Ladd (1998); Charles and Hurst (2002); Gabriel and Rosenthal (2005).

negative price effects are consistent with a shift in the supply of mortgage credit. That is, the development of subprime lending may have resulted in a differential expansion of mortgage credit in neighborhoods with high concentrations of minorities.

Our findings regarding the pricing of risk characteristics of the mortgages are also of interest, and we briefly summarize these findings now. Specification (2) of table 3 shows how the initial interest rate on a 2/28 varies with the characteristics of the mortgage. The results line up well with the findings in Haughwout, Peach, and Tracy (2008) on how these same characteristics affect early default rates. Haughwout, Peach, and Tracy (2008) reported that early defaults rise in a nonlinear fashion as the FICO score deteriorates and as the LTV increases, but they are relatively insensitive to DTI.[13] These patterns in early default risks are reflected in the upfront pricing based on the mortgage's FICO and LTV. The pricing effects of variation in DTI are inconsistent with intuition but are small in magnitude compared with the FICO and LTV effects. The interaction between the LTV and an indicator for the presence of a second lien suggest that the first-lien mortgage is priced at a discount to what would be indicated by the combined LTV across both mortgages.[14] This is true for both the initial interest rate as well as the reset margin.

Turning to the remaining loan characteristics, Haughwout, Peach, and Tracy (2008) reported that early defaults are higher for mortgages with limited documentation, and lower for refinances as compared to mortgages for new purchases. This again matches the pattern in pricing of the initial interest rates on 2/28 mortgages. Mortgages with limited documentation are assessed around 50 basis points in higher interest rates, and a higher reset margin of around 40 basis points. Similarly, controlling for observed risk characteristics, interest rates are lower for refinances—both cash-out and no cash-out—as compared to mortgages for new purchases. The magnitudes range from 12 to 21 basis points for the interest rate and reset margin depending on whether geographic controls are included.[15]

The final two attributes of the mortgage are the loan balance and the presence of prepayment penalties. For 2/28 mortgages, the interest rate as well as

13. Haughwout, Peach, and Tracy (2008) controlled for the updated LTV, which is a function of the initial LTV and the house price appreciation since the mortgage was underwritten.

14. A typical example would be that the first-lien mortgage has an LTV of 80, and the second-lien mortgage can bring the combined LTV to well in excess of 95. The data indicate that the first-lien mortgage in this case is typically priced comparable with an 80 LTV mortgage that does not have a second lien present.

15. We do not know whether the refinanced mortgage is with the same lender, in which case the reduced rate may also reflect the value of an ongoing business relationship. Alternatively, the refinance effect may reflect better negotiating skills as discussed earlier.

reset margin decline with the size of the loan. Each additional $10,000 in principal balance reduces the interest rate from around 0.8 to 1.7 basis points. The data indicate that borrowers who are willing to accept a prepayment penalty can reduce the interest rate by 27 to 41 basis points.[16] Mortgages with prepayment penalties will be more attractive to borrowers who expect to keep the mortgage for a longer period of time. Haughwout, Peach, and Tracy (2008), though, found that early default rates are higher for mortgages with prepayment penalties. The optimal pricing for a prepayment penalty, then, depends on the relative trade-off between lower prepayment risk and higher default risk.

The pricing of 2/28 mortgages is influenced by the house price dynamics in the local housing market. The initial interest rate is lower in markets that experienced a greater degree of house price appreciation during the prior year. If lenders expect these areas to continue to outperform on price appreciation, then the rate of future equity buildup will be higher for these mortgages, which could justify the lower initial interest rate. Holding constant the degree of past house price appreciation, increases in the within-market dispersion of two-year house price changes lead to higher reset margins.[17]

One final note is that for 2/28 mortgages the degree of risk-based price differentiation for the initial interest rate tends to be higher than for the reset margin. It is possible that lenders price the reset margin based on the expected risk profile of the mortgage given that it survives the first two years. If the borrower's FICO score improves and house price appreciation reduces the current LTV, then the lender may take this factor into account when setting the reset margin. This would result in smaller coefficients in the margin regression as compared with the initial interest rate regression. Further progress on this issue will require working with the lender identification information.

Conclusion

In a sample of more than 75,000 2/28 subprime mortgages, we were able to merge LP and HMDA data to provide a more detailed picture of loan pricing. Our results provide no evidence of adverse pricing by race, ethnicity, or gender of the borrower in either the initial rate or the reset margin. If any pricing

---

16. This assumes that the duration of the prepayment penalty is twenty-four months—that is, it covers the period up to the first rate reset. The LP data do not contain information on the points involved in the prepayment penalty.

17. Our two-year house price risk is derived from the variance estimate produced by the MSA-specific repeat-sale analysis. We have standardized this variable to have a zero mean and unit standard deviation across MSAs.

differential exists, minority borrowers appear to pay slightly lower rates. We also find that borrowers in zip codes with a higher percentage of black or Hispanic residents or a higher unemployment rate actually pay slightly lower mortgage rates. Mortgage rates are also lower in locations that experienced higher past rates of house price appreciation.

These results suggest appreciable scope for additional research. First and foremost, it is important to determine whether mortgages originated to minority borrowers had higher up-front costs. In future work, we plan to use the reported APR in HMDA and the initial interest rate, reset margin, and interest rate caps reported in LP to infer the up-front points and fees charged on these mortgages. We also plan on using information about the names of the lenders in the HMDA data to consider the role of regulated lenders and also unregulated mortgage brokers in the origination process.

Finally, these results suggest the possibility that subprime lending did serve as a positive supply shock for credit in locations with higher unemployment rates and minority residents. These results are consistent with economies of scale in subprime lending. We believe that further research is needed to understand better how this additional credit impacted these locations. Policy responses today often consider how to limit subprime lending in the future, but it is important to understand any positives that may also have occurred along with the downsides of subprime lending.

Appendix: Matching LP to HMDA

We match LP data into HMDA data in multiple stages as described below.

Stage 1

Only those loans in the LP dataset with nonmissing originators are considered. LP loans are matched to HMDA loans with the same purpose, occupancy, and lien status. The HMDA loan must be within ± $1,000 of the LP loan for it to be considered. For LP loans with nonimputed dates only, HMDA loans within ± 5 working days are considered; for loans with imputed dates, HMDA loans within the same month of origination are considered. LP loans are only matched to HMDA loans with the same first 4 digits of the LP loan's zip code. Last, if an LP loan matches to multiple HMDA loans, a tie breaker is attempted using the subprime variable.

Table A-1. Summary Statistics: Subprime 2/28 Mortgages, Owner-Occupied[a]

Statistic	Mean	Std. Dev.	Min.	Max.
Borrower characteristics				
Asian	0.035	0.182	0	1
Black	0.170	0.376	0	1
Hispanic	0.207	0.405	0	1
Female	0.376	0.484	0	1
Loan characteristics				
Initial interest rate	7.323	1.063	4.25	12.75
Interest rate margin over six-month LIBOR	5.878	0.988	1.25	11.35
FICO: missing	0.001	0.033	0	1
< 560	0.156	0.362	0	1
560–589	0.151	0.358	0	1
590–619	0.205	0.404	0	1
620–649	0.205	0.404	0	1
650–679	0.140	0.347	0	1
680–719	0.090	0.287	0	1
LTV: 80–84	0.176	0.381	0	1
85–89	0.083	0.276	0	1
90–94	0.117	0.321	0	1
95+	0.427	0.495	0	1
95+ * second lien	0.320	0.467	0	1
DTI: missing	0.260	0.438	0	1
40–44	0.172	0.377	0	1
45–49	0.204	0.403	0	1
50+	0.080	0.271	0	1
40–44 * second lien	0.065	0.246	0	1
45–49 * second lien	0.081	0.273	0	1
50+ * second lien	0.024	0.155	0	1
Limited documentation	0.390	0.488	0	1
No documentation	0.002	0.045	0	1
Refinance–cash out	0.450	0.497	0	1
Refinance–no cash out	0.054	0.226	0	1
Loan amount ($10,000)	21.694	13.436	1.25	154
Prepayment penalty	0.740	0.438	0	1
Months penalty in effect[b]	24.036	4.882	5	60
Neighborhood characteristics				
Average credit score	736.46	44.94	600.9	873.0
Percentage Asian	3.84	5.63	0	65.09
Percentage black	14.66	20.98	0	98.18
Percentage Hispanic	16.42	19.66	0	97.87
Homeownership rate	63.59	15.48	0	99.27
House price appreciation in prior year	10.19	7.98	−1.69	29.11
House price risk (standardized, two year)	0	1	−2.54	7.12
Unemployment rate	5.12	1.37	2.3	16
Lagged permits in county / 100 units	3.14	3.07	0	30.07

Source: Author's calculations.

APR: annual percentage rate; FICO: borrower's credit score; LIBOR: London Interbank Offered Rate.

a. Number of mortgages = 75,744.

b. Conditional on an existing prepayment penalty.

After finding all possible HMDA matches for each LP loan, the LP loans are then classified as nonmatches, one-to-one matches, or multiple matches. Any LP loan that has no corresponding HMDA loans using the above criteria is a *nonmatch*. Any loan that matches to either multiple HMDA loans or to a HMDA loan that another LP loan also matches to is a *multiple match*. Finally, any LP loan that matches to a HMDA, with no other LP loans matching to the given HMDA loan, is a *one-to-one match*.

After stage 1 all LP loans classified as one-to-one matches, and their corresponding HMDA loans, are set aside and not considered in future matches. All other loans are then considered in future stages.

Stage 2

Stage 2 is exactly like stage 1, except that the originator name field is ignored. This means LP loans both with and without originator name information are considered. As well, LP loans can match to HMDA loans with any originator name. As with stage 1, all one-to-one matches are set aside and not considered in future stages.

Stage 3

Stage 3 is exactly like stage 1 except that the zip code is matched to five digits not just four digits, and the origination amounts for the LP and HMDA must be exactly the same. This stage tries to break multiple matches that may have occurred in stage 1.

Stage 4

Stage 4 is exactly like stage 2, except that the zip code is matched to five digits not four digits and origination amounts for the LP and HMDA must be exactly the same. This stage tries to break multiple matches that may have occurred in stage 2.

Stage 5

Stage 5 is exactly like stage 1, except that the origination amount is matched to within ± 2.5 percent of the LP origination amount.

Stage 6

Stage 6 is exactly like stage 2, except that the origination amount is matched to within ± 2.5 percent of the LP origination amount.

The one-to-one matches from each of the six stages above are aggregated into a dataset for further analysis in our paper.

Comments

Dwight M. Jaffee: There has been long-standing concern for discriminatory lending in U.S. mortgage markets. By discriminatory lending I mean lending that provides disadvantageous loan terms to minority borrowers, even when controlling for the observable measures of their creditworthiness. Concern for discriminatory lending led to the Home Mortgage Disclosure Act, which requires important classes of lenders to report application and loan data, including the minority status of the borrower. HMDA data have indicated high rates of loan rejection for minority borrowers, in some cases beyond the amount that could be explained by the borrowers' creditworthiness.

Subprime lending significantly reversed this situation, making loans available to minorities and in zip codes that previously had high rates of loan rejection.[1] Subprime mortgage data thus provide an exceptional opportunity to study the extent to which discriminatory lending continues in U.S. mortgage markets. In particular, it may be possible to evaluate whether subprime lending usefully expanded borrowing opportunities to subprime borrowers or whether it simply replaced discriminatory rejections with discriminatory lending.

The paper by Andrew Haughwout, Christopher Mayer, and Joseph Tracy starts by generating a unique dataset by combining information from the HMDA data with information from the LoanPerformance data, the latter representing the most extensive loan data available for subprime loans. In particular, they are able to match individual loans between the two sources, an impressive feat. Furthermore, the paper makes use of the annual percentage rate data available from the HMDA source. This allows the analysis to distinguish the contract rate on the one hand from the points and closing fees on the other hand as two distinct aspects of a loan's cost.

There are, however, notable data limitations. First, the HMDA data are collected only for major lenders in MSAs. Second, the quality of the LP data has

1. See Mian and Sufi (2008).

been questioned in some aspects. Finally, the data cover only the category of 2/28 subprime loans made during the month of August 2005. These factors necessarily limit the generality of the results. Nevertheless, I believe these data can provide useful results regarding possible discrimination in subprime mortgage markets.

The most important result of the paper is the lack of any evidence of direct discrimination against minority borrowers on subprime loans. Indeed, minority borrowers received loans with initial contract rates that were 2.5 basis points (bps) lower and margins (the spread used when the rate adjusts) that were about 2 bps lower. To be sure, the up-front fees and points were higher (equaling about $1,200 on a $200,000 loan), so the APR on minority loans was about 5.6 bps higher. It remains an open question whether the higher fees and points simply represent the higher cost of originating minority loans or whether they indicate discriminatory prices. Haughwout, Mayer, and Tracy properly place further work on this question at the top of their to-do list.

There is one perplexing pair of results: nonminority borrowers receive a lower mortgage rate when their property is located in a minority zip code, and minority borrowers receive a higher rate when taking out a mortgage in a nonminority zip code. In other words, more favorable lending terms were actually available in minority zip codes (after controlling for borrower creditworthiness). This result is possible if lenders, using the new technology available to evaluate subprime mortgages, competed for market share in the minority zip codes and thereby reduced the interest rate below what the same loan would have been charged in a nonminority zip code.

The discriminatory lending discussed in this paper should not be confused with the predatory lending that has been identified with some subprime lending. By predatory lending, I mean lending that induces borrowers to take out loans against their own best interest. Because subprime lending was focused in geographic areas with large concentrations of minority borrowers, it has also been frequently assumed that subprime lending represented discriminatory lending. While predatory lending and discriminatory lending may coincide if the predatory loans are directed only to minority borrowers, this paper does not find this to be the case. In other words, while predatory subprime lending surely occurred, the predatory loans seem to have been imposed on minority and nonminority subprime borrowers alike. It is also worth emphasizing that important revisions were made in July 2008 by the Federal Reserve to its truth in lending regulations (Regulation Z). These changes make future predatory subprime mortgage lending highly unlikely.

Tomasz Piskorski: The paper by Andrew Haughwout, Christopher Mayer, and Joseph Tracy is an empirical study investigating the impact of race, ethnicity, and gender on loan pricing in the subprime mortgage market. The authors focus on so-called 2/28 mortgages originated in August 2005. The 2/28 loan contract is a hybrid adjustable rate mortgage in which borrowers are charged an initial mortgage rate for two years, followed by biannual rate resets based on a margin over a short-term rate. The authors take advantage of newly merged data that provide demographic information on subprime borrowers (HMDA data) as well as the rich data on mortgage characteristics that they extracted (LoanPerformance data). In a sample of more than 75,000 adjustable rate subprime mortgages, they find no evidence of adverse pricing by race, ethnicity, or gender of the borrower in either the initial rate or the reset margin. If any pricing differential exists, minority borrowers appear to pay slightly lower rates. They also find that borrowers in zip codes with a higher percentage of black or Hispanic residents or a higher unemployment rate actually pay slightly lower mortgage rates. Mortgage rates are also lower in locations that experienced higher past rates of house price appreciation.

This is a very timely and policy-relevant study. The recent unprecedented housing market crisis has brought attention to the subprime mortgage market, which experienced exponential growth over the past few years. Because of high default rates among subprime borrowers and big losses to subprime investors in the declining housing market, subprime lending has lately caused a storm of controversy. Many critics accuse subprime lenders of predatory lending practices that exploit naïve borrowers who do not fully understand mortgage terms. According to these arguments, minority groups have been particularly liable to this kind of abuse. Consequently, these critics contend that subprime loans do not make economic sense and should be banned, especially among the most vulnerable class of borrowers.

Empirical investigation of the efficiency and fairness of subprime lending is not straightforward. For example, let us consider the following two hypotheses.

Hypothesis 1: The subprime lending was efficient for borrowers and lenders, at least from the ex-ante perspective (given their beliefs).[1]

Hypothesis 2: The subprime lending was predatory, allowing at least some of the lenders to profit at the expense of unsophisticated borrowers.

The task of distinguishing between these competing hypotheses is a hard one. Many observed features of subprime lending are consistent with both hypotheses. The high concentration of new mortgage products among the most risky unsophisticated borrowers could be viewed as evidence for hypothesis 2.

1. Here we leave aside the question of subprime lending's potential externalities.

However, one could make an argument that during the housing boom many homes were bought with little or no money down and initial teaser rates because both buyers and lenders bet on additional home price appreciation to create equity. These bets, while risky, gave less creditworthy borrowers a chance at homeownership, benefiting them as well as the lenders (at least from the ex-ante perspective).[2]

Haughwout, Mayer, and Tracy do not attempt to investigate whether subprime lending was predatory. Recognizing the difficulty of this task, they investigate the more modest question of whether subprime lending was discriminatory based on race, ethnicity, or gender. A lack of evidence for discrimination would suggest that under hypothesis 1, the benefits of subprime lending were equally spread among borrowers of similar risk. Under hypothesis 2, this evidence would suggest that lending was equally abusive among groups of similar risk irrespective of their minority status.

As the authors point out, there are at least three dimensions along which mortgage lenders may treat similar groups of borrowers differently. First, they may simply refuse to offer credit at all. Second, they may steer accepted applicants into less attractive or more costly products, such as subprime loans. Finally, they may simultaneously price a given product differently for different borrowers. Among these, the authors focus on the third dimension—price discrimination—and examine the determinants of both the initial interest rate as well as the margin used to adjust the rate after two years in a 2/28 loan category.

The authors find no evidence of adverse pricing by race, ethnicity, or gender of the borrower in either the initial rate or the reset margin. The primary goals of the Home Mortgage Disclosure Act of 1975 are to determine whether financial institutions are meeting the housing credit needs of their communities and to identify possible disparities in lending patterns. The law, which has been broadened in scope several times during its thirty-year history, requires lenders to collect and report data on the race, gender, income, and ethnicity of loan applicants by geography to determine whether the nation's fair lending and antidiscrimination goals are being met. The presented evidence could thus suggest that the current fair lending and antidiscriminatory laws have been successful.

One important limitation of this interpretation of the evidence, which the authors fully recognize, is that they do not observe the points and fees paid

2. See the discussion by Piskorski and Tchistyi (2008) that shows that many features of subprime lending observed in practice are consistent with rational behavior of both borrowers and lenders. In particular, when house prices are expected to rise, it is optimal to provide the risky borrowers with a lower initial rate, which is to increase over time, and to increase the borrowers' access to credit.

when the borrower initially took out the mortgage. So in principle, it is possible that they miss data that might show disparate treatment in loan origination costs. The HMDA reports the difference between the APR on each loan and the rate on comparable maturity Treasuries for all loans in which this spread is at least 300 basis points (3 percent). The APR, which is calculated by the institution reporting the HMDA data, is based on the full cost of the loan, including both interest costs and such up-front charges as points and fees, amortized over the full loan term. Thus an omission of origination fees might seem innocuous at first, at least for high-cost loans. One could claim that any discrimination based on race, gender, or ethnicity would be reflected in higher APR, exposing lenders to potential regulatory action. However, this view ignores the realties of the subprime mortgage market and the shortcomings of the APR measure for its stated objective of providing a measure of a cost of credit.

There are at least two problems with this measure and the current regulatory framework. First, most of the subprime mortgages have much shorter effective maturity than the term of the loan, because of the high prepayment rates or defaults. The fact that the APR reported in the HMDA data amortizes interest costs and such up-front charges as points and fees over the full term of the loan could result in the incorrect measure of the true cost of the loan. More precisely, given a much shorter effective maturity than the loan term, loans with higher origination costs would be costlier compared with loans with lower origination costs despite having the same APR. The failure of regulators to recognize this reality might provide the lenders with the opportunity to abuse a certain subset of risky borrowers in a way that would be difficult to detect. For example, within the same risk group, the lenders could offer less sophisticated borrowers lower interest rates and higher origination fees, while more sophisticated borrowers would be offered lower origination costs and higher interest rates—resulting in the same APR based on costs amortized over the full term of the loan but a higher cost of credit to less sophisticated borrowers. The authors provide evidence that if any differential pricing exists, minority borrowers appear to pay slightly lower rates. This might suggest that some form of discriminatory pricing described above might be actually taking place, warranting further investigation.

Second, the HMDA reports the difference between the APR on each loan and the rate on comparable maturity Treasuries for all loans in which this spread is *at least* 300 basis points (3 percent). At first it seems reasonable, as one could claim that the degree of financial sophistication correlates with the credit quality and minority status and so the borrowers with the highest cost of credit are the most prone to abuse and thus have the additional reporting requirement. However, this argument ignores the fact that low credit quality might also protect these borrowers from abusive practices. This is because the likelihood of default, which is typically costly to the lender, is much more sensitive to the cost of credit for the less creditworthy borrowers. So while it is true that the lenders could impose a higher cost of credit on less creditworthy and minority borrowers because of their lack of financial sophistication, doing so creates an extra cost since it substantially increases the likelihood of foreclosure for these borrowers, thereby endangering lender profits. As a result, the group of borrowers who are most likely to suffer from abuse might actually consist of minority borrowers with *better* credit quality, a group missed by the APR reporting requirement.

In future research, the authors could try to back up the implied origination costs from the reported APR measure and investigate pricing in the most risky mortgages, taking into account these costs. Furthermore, it would be worthwhile to investigate the potential for discriminatory pricing among minority borrowers of better credit quality, a group that might arguably be the most liable to discriminatory pricing.

References

Avery, Robert B., Kenneth P. Brevoort, and Glenn B. Canner. 2006. "Higher Priced Home Lending and the 2005 HMDA Data." *Federal Reserve Bulletin* 92 (September): A123–A166.

———. 2007. "The 2006 HMDA Data." *Federal Reserve Bulletin* 93: A73–A109.

Bucks, Brian, and Karen Pence. 2008. "Do Borrowers Know Their Mortgage Terms?" *Journal of Urban Economics* 64 (2): 218–33.

Canner, Glenn B., Stuart A. Gabriel, and J. Michael Wooley. 1991. "Race, Default Risk and Mortgage Lending: A Study of FHA and Conventional Loan Markets." *Southern Economics Journal* 58 (1): 249–62.

Charles, Kerwin Kofi, and Erik Hurst. 2002. "The Transition to Homeownership and the Black-White Wealth Gap." *Review of Economics and Statistics* 84 (2): 281–97.

Charles, Kerwin Kofi, Erik Hurst, and Melvin Stephens Jr. 2008. "Rates for Vehicle Loans: Race and Loan Source." *American Economic Review* 98 (2): 315–20.

Cohen, Marc A. 2006. "Imperfect Competition in Auto Lending: Subjective Markup, Racial Disparity, and Class Action Litigation." Vanderbilt Law and Economics Research Paper 07-01. Vanderbilt University Law School (December).

Gabriel, Stuart, and Stuart Rosenthal. 2005. "Homeownership in the 1980s and 1990s: Aggregate Trends and Racial Gaps." *Journal of Urban Economics* 57 (1) (January): 101–27.

Haughwout, Andrew, Richard Peach, and Joseph Tracy. 2008. "Juvenile Delinquent Mortgages: Bad Credit or Bad Economy?" *Journal of Urban Economics* 64: 246–57.

Ladd, Helen. 1998. "Evidence on Discrimination in Credit Markets." *Journal of Economic Perspectives* 1 (Spring): 223–34.

Mayer, Christopher, and Karen Pence. 2007. "Subprime Mortgages: What, Where, and To Whom." Working Paper 14083. Cambridge, Mass.: National Bureau of Economic Research.

Mian, Atif R., and Amir Sufi. 2008. "The Consequences of Mortgage Expansion: Evidence from the U.S. Mortgage Default Crisis." University of Chicago School of Business (December 12, 2008). Available at SSRN (http://ssrn.com/abstract= 1072304).

Munnell, Alicia H., Geoffrey M. B. Tootell, Lynne E. Browne, and James McEneaney. 1996. "Mortgage Lending in Boston: Interpreting HMDA Data." *American Economic Review* 86 (1): 25–53.

Piskorski, Tomasz, and Alexei Tchistyi. 2008. "Stochastic House Price Appreciation and Optimal Mortgage Lending." Mimeo. Columbia University Business School.

Ravina, Enrichetta. 2008. "Love & Loans: The Effect of Beauty and Personal Characteristics in Credit Markets." Working Paper Series. New York University Department of Finance (July).

Sherlund, Shane. 2008. "The Past, Present and Future of Subprime Mortgages." Finance and Economics Discussion Series 2008-63. Washington: Federal Reserve Board, Divisions of Research & Statistics and Monetary Affairs.

GERALD CARLINO
Federal Reserve Bank of Philadelphia

ROBERT HUNT
Federal Reserve Bank of Philadelphia

What Explains the Quantity and Quality of Local Inventive Activity?

In models of endogenous growth, knowledge, rather than tangible assets, plays a central role in the economic growth of nations. The model of Romer (1990) assumes that economic agents everywhere have free access to the stock of knowledge. Agrawal, Kapur, and McHale (2008), among many others, point out that immediate accessibility to knowledge is likely to depend on the geographic proximity of agents. This intuition has been verified in empirical studies of patterns of patent citations (Jaffe, Trajtenberg, and Henderson 1993) and in studies of knowledge spillovers among advertising agencies in New York City (Arzaghi and Henderson 2005) and, more generally, in manufacturing (Rosenthal and Strange 2001).

In earlier research, we found additional evidence of such spillovers. In particular we found that the rate of patenting per capita—or *patent intensity*—is about 20 percent higher in a metropolitan area with twice the *employment density* (jobs per square mile) of another metro area (Carlino, Chatterjee, and Hunt 2007). In addition to a number of other interesting results, we documented the importance of local research and development (R&D) inputs, in particular human capital, in explaining the inventive productivity of cities.

The authors especially thank Kristy Buzard, Jake Carr, and Bob O'Loughlin for excellent research assistance. Thanks also to Annette Fratantaro for her work on the Compustat variables. Thanks to Colin Webb and Dominique Guellec of the OECD for sharing their patent citations data and answering our many questions. Thanks to Jim Hirabayashi of the U.S. Patent and Trademark Office for his gracious responses to our many questions. We also thank Jordan Rappaport, Gilles Duranton, and Matt Turner for sharing data with us. This paper has benefited from comments from Edward Coulson, Gilles Duranton, Vernon Henderson, Robert Inman, Janet Pack, Tom Stark, and Bruce Weinberg. We alone are responsible for any remaining errors.

The views expressed here are those of the authors and do not necessarily represent the views of the Federal Reserve Bank of Philadelphia or the Federal Reserve System.

In this paper, we extend our analysis in a number of important dimensions. First, we introduce a measure of the quality of local inventions—the number of citations a patent receives in patents obtained by subsequent inventors. These *forward citations* have been demonstrated to be correlated with a variety of indicators of value, and they have been used to document the highly skewed distribution in the value of patented inventions. We rely on a relatively new, and underutilized, source of citations—the Organization for Economic Cooperation and Development–European Patent Office (OECD–EPO) Patent Citations database. Using these data, we can determine whether our earlier results are sensitive to these adjustments for the quality of local inventions.

Second, we decompose our data on local academic R&D in a number of important dimensions, including the sources of R&D funding, R&D performed in different fields of science, and the mix of basic and applied R&D that is funded. This permits us to test whether the results of academic R&D are indeed homogenous. Third, we incorporate data on congressional earmarks for R&D that is largely performed by colleges and universities. We are able to compare these earmarks to the overall patterns of federal funding for academic R&D and to test for inefficiencies introduced by the allocation of funds through that process.

Adjusting for the quality of patents does not dramatically change most of the results we found using our simple measure of patents per capita. For example, regardless of whether we use an unweighted or weighted measure of patent intensity, the elasticity associated with employment density is about 0.22. In other words, doubling the employment density of a metropolitan area raises the per capita output of patents by 22 percent.

But some of our results do change. Using unweighted patents per capita, scale (that is, total employment) is not statistically significant in the regressions unless we allow for diminishing returns. With citation-weighted patents per capita, however, the implied elasticity of scale is 0.12 and statistically significant. If we do allow for diminishing returns and we adjust for the quality of inventions, we find that metro areas enjoy increasing returns to scale over a much larger range than we estimated previously. In that case, these returns are exhausted at a population of about 1.8 million. In contrast, when we do not employ citation weighting, our estimates suggest these returns to scale are exhausted for populations around 720,000.

The presence of an educated workforce is the decisive factor that explains the inventive output of cities, even after controlling for the historical mix of industries and technologies invented. Evaluated at the mean, a 10 percent increase in the share of the workforce with at least a college degree raises our measures of patent intensity by about 10 percent. All else equal, a 1 standard deviation increase in our human capital variable is associated with a 30 percent higher patent intensity.

As we found in our earlier research, once we account for local human capital, the effects of incremental increases in local R&D intensities (among private labs, government labs, and academia) are relatively modest. For example, evaluated at the mean, a 10 percent increase in the ratio of private labs to total private establishments raises citation-weighted patent intensity by about 1 percent. A comparable increase in academic R&D intensity has a somewhat smaller effect.

We find very modest variations in the contributions of academic R&D in certain scientific fields. Two exceptions are mathematical and life sciences, which produce fewer patents than other fields (the implied elasticities at the mean are –0.03 and –0.06, respectively). The effect is particularly striking for computer science, especially given the rapid growth in software patenting during this period (Bessen and Hunt 2007). But these results do not necessarily imply fewer inventions; they may simply reflect less reliance on patenting in those fields.

We find that increases in the share of academic R&D funded by the federal government reduces patent intensities relative to R&D funded by the university itself. This effect is relatively large (the elasticity at the mean is about –0.14). In contrast, academic R&D financed by other sources, perhaps including private foundations, is more productive. Although it is not clear why federal funds for academic R&D tend to produce fewer patents, it should be remembered that generating patents is not the primary objective of making those funds available.

To further explore this effect, we decomposed the federally funded academic R&D into basic and applied shares. Using these measures, we only found a statistically significant negative effect for the applied portion of federal R&D funding to universities. But the difference in the coefficients on the basic and applied R&D is not statistically significant. While admittedly weak, these results are surprising, given our initial expectation that applied R&D is more closely related to final products, and thus more conducive to patenting.

Finally, we find evidence that most academic R&D allocated through a congressional earmark (in 1990, at least) did not seem to come at the expense of the major programs that allocate research funds by some form of peer review. Nevertheless, we do find a small negative effect associated with more earmarked academic R&D in metro areas (the elasticity at the mean is about –0.05). There are small variations in this effect depending on which federal agency's budget has been earmarked. Perhaps these funds distract researchers from more promising agendas. Alternatively, it is possible that the projects funded are not ones that rely on the patent system.

The remainder of this paper is organized as follows. The next section reviews the literature. The third section introduces our data. The fourth section describes the regression strategy and some of our main results. The fifth presents our new results for academic R&D and for academic earmarks. The penultimate section reviews some robustness checks, including tests for unobserved heterogeneity, endogeneity, and spatial dependence. The final section reviews a number of policy implications and concludes.

Literature

Much of the theoretical literature on urban agglomeration economies has focused on externalities in the production of goods and services rather than on invention itself. Nevertheless, the three mechanisms primarily explored in this literature are also relevant for the invention of new goods and services: input sharing, matching, and knowledge spillovers.[1] The first of these points to the sharing of indivisible factors of production, or the benefits of increased variety of differentiated inputs, that occurs in areas with a large number of final-goods producers.[2] A second theory argues that denser urban agglomerations improve learning and the quality of matches among firms and workers.[3] The third strand of theory argues that the geographic concentration of people and jobs in cities facilitates the spread of tacit knowledge. For example, denser locations can hasten learning about new technologies.[4] But there can be too much density in the sense that it may be harder to maintain trade secrets in

1. These themes are developed in the excellent survey by Duranton and Puga (2004). Recent surveys of the empirical literature on agglomeration economies include Eberts and McMillen (1999); Rosenthal and Strange (2004).

2. For example, Ciccone and Hall (1996) showed how density can give rise to increasing returns in production because of the greater variety of intermediate products that are available in denser locations. They argued that the positive correlation between employment density and productivity implies that agglomeration economies dominate the congestion effects. See also Helsley and Strange (2002); Sedgley and Elmslie (2004).

3. Models of this sort include Glaeser (1999); Wheeler (2001); Helsley and Strange (2004); Berliant, Reed, and Wang (2006); and the refinement of Berliant, Reed, and Wang's model in Hunt (2007). In the latter two models, workers in dense locations are more selective in their matches because the opportunity cost of waiting for a prospective partner is lower. That is because even though agents are more selective, on average they form matches more quickly. As a result, the average output from matches is higher, and a higher share of the workforce is engaged in productive matches.

4. See, for example, Glaeser (1999). Some authors argue that local creativity (Florida 2002) and local entrepreneurship (Acs 2002) are also conducive to innovation.

more dense locations. This potential for poaching may force firms in dense areas to rely on patenting to a greater extent.

In this paper we are agnostic about the precise mechanism by which density affects innovative activity. That is, we do not expect our regressions to be able to sort among the various mechanisms (input sharing, matching, and knowledge spillovers) that likely matter for the innovation process in cities. Our goals are to demonstrate that local job density is empirically relevant in explaining the quality-adjusted volume of local innovative activity; to test for increasing returns to scale (urbanization economies) in cities' output of quality-adjusted innovation; to more precisely quantify the contributions made by the available local R&D inputs, including human capital; and to discuss the implications of these results for public policy.

A full review of the empirical literature on the geographic extent of knowledge spillovers is beyond the scope of this paper, but we will touch on a few especially relevant papers.[5] Several studies have found convincing evidence that spatial proximity mediates knowledge spillovers. Rosenthal and Strange (2001), for example, found that the effects of knowledge spillovers on the agglomeration of manufacturing firms tend to be quite localized, influencing agglomeration only at the zip code level.

Looking at innovative activity, Jaffe, Trajtenberg, and Henderson (1993) and more recently Agrawal, Kapur, and McHale (2008) found that nearby inventors are much more likely to cite each other's inventions in their patents, suggesting that knowledge spillovers are indeed localized. In the latter paper, the authors reported that every 1,000-mile increase in the distance between two inventors reduces the probability of knowledge flow (as measured by patent citations) by about 2 percent. Arzaghi and Henderson (2005) found that the density of advertising agencies in New York City contributes to information spillovers that enhance productivity, but those spillovers dissipate rapidly with distance among agencies.

Ciccone and Hall (1996) looked at the relation between county employment density and productivity at the state level. They found that a doubling of employment density in a county results in about a 6 percent increase of average labor productivity. More recently, Combes and others (2008) revisited the relationship between productivity and density using French data. In addition to using standard historical instruments to deal with endogeneity between productivity and density, they introduced a new set of geological instruments—for example, depth to bedrock, dominant parent material (the material from which soil

---

5. See Audretsch and Feldman (2004) for a review of the literature on the geography of knowledge spillovers.

forms), topsoil water capacity, among others. The idea is that geological characteristics should be fundamental drivers of population settlement patterns. They found that simultaneity bias between density and productivity is relatively small, reducing the impact of density on productivity by about 20 percent. Their preferred estimate for the elasticity of total factor productivity with respect to density is around 3.5 percent.

But why is density important for productivity? Carlino, Chatterjee, and Hunt (2007) showed that density is important in explaining innovative output, and this may explain the pattern in productivity found in both Ciccone and Hall (1996) and Combes and others (2008). Specifically, Carlino, Chatterjee, and Hunt found that, all else equal, a metropolitan area with twice the employment density (jobs per square mile) of another metropolitan area will exhibit a patent intensity (patents per capita) that is 20 percent higher.

Several authors found that patent activity increases with metropolitan area size.[6] But most of these studies do not explain how other city characteristics, such as local density, influence the production of these spillovers. And because these studies do not control for local inputs into the innovation process, such as R&D, or the educational attainment of the labor force, they cannot clearly distinguish between spillovers that are external to individual workers or firms. Carlino, Chatterjee, and Hunt found that after controlling for many local inputs into the R&D process, the benefits of urban scale are realized for cities of moderate size. In fact, with the exception of San Jose, the top 5 percent of metropolitan areas ranked in terms of patent intensity had populations below 1 million.

In addition to returns to scale (that is, urbanization economies), researchers have also investigated whether there are increasing returns to the size of an industry in a city (localization economies). Although we do not touch on that question here, Carlino and Hunt (2007) tested for urbanization and localization economies in patenting rates in more than a dozen industries. They found evidence of both effects in most industries, and the estimated localization economies were typically comparable with the estimated urbanization economies. This suggests that interindustry spillovers are often just as important as intra-industry spillovers in explaining local rates of innovation.

A number of studies have looked at the role that local inputs into R&D activity play in the innovative process. For example, Jaffe (1989), Audretsch and Feldman (1996), and Anselin, Varga, and Acs (1997) found evidence of localized knowledge spillovers from university R&D to commercial innovation by private firms, even after controlling for the location of industrial R&D. Car-

6. See, for example, Feldman and Audretsch (1999); Ó hUallacháin (1999).

lino, Chatterjee, and Hunt found that local R&D inputs, especially human capital, contribute to higher patent intensities.

Andersson, Quigley, and Wilhelmsson (2005) found evidence that the expansion of the number of university-based researchers in a local labor market is positively associated with an increase in the number of patents granted in that area. Agrawal and Cockburn (2003) argued that local academic R&D is likely to be more productive, in terms of its contribution to additional patents, in the presence of a large research-intensive firm located nearby—the "anchor tenant" hypothesis. Taking this effect into account, they reported a significant positive correlation between local patents and academic publications in the fields of medical imaging, neural networks, and signal processing.

Economists debate the effects of an area's market structure on the rate of innovation and growth. Chinitz (1961) and Jacobs (1969) argued that the rate of innovations is greater in cities with competitive market structures. Glaeser and others (1992) argued that the Marshall-Arrow-Romer (MAR) view implies that a local monopoly may foster innovation because firms in such environments have fewer neighbors who imitate them. The empirical literature tends to favor the Chinitz and Jacobs view over the MAR view. Feldman and Audretsch (1999) and Carlino, Chatterjee, and Hunt found that local competition is more conducive to innovative activity than is local monopoly. Glaeser and others (1992) found that local competition is more conducive to city growth than is local monopoly.

Our Data and Some Descriptive Statistics

As in Carlino, Chatterjee, and Hunt (2007), we continue to measure innovations (imperfectly) by using counts of patents obtained by a city's inventors over the years 1990–99. We also employ a rich set of controls for the historical mix of industries and technologies present in a city (see below). These controls help us to address both concerns about the heterogeneity of cities and biases associated with using patents as a proxy for innovation.[7] Since we are primarily interested in explaining variations in inventive productivity, all of our regressions normalize the left-hand-side variable by population. We thus refer to our dependent variable as *patent intensity*.

One concern about using patents as an innovation indicator is that the value of patents is very highly skewed. Most are not worth very much, while some have values that are higher by several orders of magnitude (see, for example,

---

7. For a general discussion on the use of patents as indicators, see Griliches (1990).

Harhoff and others 1999). Fortunately, there are ways to introduce an adjustment for quality into these counts, just as is done for journal articles—by counting the number of citations a patent receives in subsequent patents. A number of empirical studies document a strong positive correlation between these forward citations and the economic value these patents contribute to the firms that own them. For example, Hall, Jaffe, and Trajtenberg (2005) showed that a one citation increase in the average patent in a publicly held firm's portfolio increases its market value by 3 percent.[8] In addition, these citations present a concrete illustration of knowledge spillovers.[9]

We regress both patent intensity and citation-weighted patent intensity in a metropolitan area on measures of city size, the density of jobs, local market structure, and a set of variables that capture the availability of local R&D inputs. To mitigate any bias induced by endogeneity or reverse causation, all the independent variables are lagged—none reflect economic activity after 1990. In a later section of this paper, we investigate these potential biases more closely and find that if any exist, they exert a downward bias on our OLS estimates. In that sense, our OLS estimates can be viewed as conservative. Before presenting the exact specification, we will describe the variables used in our regressions.

The sample consists of 280 metropolitan areas (MAs). Included in this sample are 264 primary metropolitan statistical areas (PMSAs), and nine consolidated metropolitan statistical areas (CMSAs) as they were defined by the Census Bureau in 1983 (we employ a lagged definition of metropolitan areas to rule out another potential source of bias in our results). The remaining seven MAs were constructed by aggregating twenty-one separate PMSAs.[10] We do this because we locate our patents on the basis of a unique match of addresses to a county or city and there is a tendency for a higher number of nonunique matches to occur when cities are nearby.

---

8. For further evidence from U.S. patent data, see Trajtenberg (1990). For results correlating survey data to highly cited European patents, see Harhoff, Scherer, and Vopel (2003); Gambardella, Harhoff, and Verspagen (2008).

9. In a survey of 1,300 inventors, Jaffe, Trajtenberg, and Fogarty (2000) found that approximately one-half of the patent citations refer to some sort of knowledge spillovers, of which 28 percent correspond to a very substantial spillover. Jaffe, Trajtenberg, and Henderson (1993) provided evidence that these spillovers are at least initially localized.

10. See the appendix to Carlino, Chatterjee, and Hunt (2007) for a list of MSAs that were combined. In that paper, we verified that our results did not depend on the inclusion of the ad hoc MAs in the regression sample.

Figure 1. Patent Intensity across Metropolitan Areas

Patents per 10,000 population

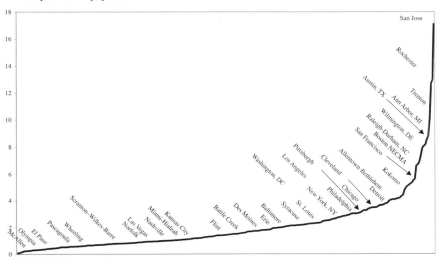

The Patent Data

We assign patents to a metropolitan area using the residential address of the first inventor named on the patent.[11] We are able to locate more than 581,000 patents granted from 1990 to 1999 to inventors living in the United States to either a unique county or MA, a match rate of 96 percent. Just over 534,000 (92 percent) of these patents are associated with an urban county.

Figure 1 reproduces the distribution of patents per capita over the 1990s reported in Carlino, Chatterjee, and Hunt (2007). In terms of frequencies, the figure implies our data are highly left skewed.[12] The average number of patents per 10,000 of population during the 1990s in our data is about 2. But this varies from as few as 0.07 in McAllen, Texas, to as many as 17 in San Jose, California, a center of the U.S. semiconductor industry.

Our patent citation counts are constructed from the OECD–EPO Patent Citations database. These are data developed by the European Patent Office (EPO) and the Organization for Economic Cooperation and Development's Patent Sta-

---

11. In Carlino, Chatterjee, and Hunt, we verified that our results were not sensitive to the choice of the first inventor on the patent.

12. When analyzing these data in Carlino, Chatterjee, and Hunt we could not reject the null hypothesis of a log normal distribution.

tistics Task Force.[13] The underlying data tables span all patent applications published by the EPO, WIPO, and Patent Cooperation Treaty (PCT) countries from 1978 to 2001.[14] There are some 6.2 million citations to patent and nonpatent prior art in this dataset. More than 3.4 million patents have been cited at least once in these data (Webb and others 2005). U.S. patents account for about a third of this total. We match the U.S. patents in these data to our geo-located patents and extract the total number of citations received by each of these patents.

We rely on this source, rather than the citation data in the National Bureau of Economic Research (NBER) U.S. Patent Citations Data File (see Hall, Jaffe, and Trajtenberg 2001), because the OECD–EPO dataset includes counts of citations to a U.S. patent made in patents obtained in the United States and abroad. In other words, it represents a measure of the worldwide influence of a patent. The NBER dataset is an excellent resource, but its counts of patent citations are only those made in other U.S. patent documents—citations in foreign patents are not included. For our analysis, we were concerned that such an omission could be problematic, in particular for industries in which a significant share of R&D is performed outside the United States. If those industries or technologies are dispersed nonrandomly across our MAs (and we believe they are), it is possible that censoring of relevant citations might lead to spurious results.

We are able to match essentially all of our patents to ones contained in the OECD–EPO citation data. Figure 2 plots the distribution of citations in our patent data. As other researchers have found, this distribution is very highly left skewed. About half (49 percent) of patents in our data had not received any forward citations at the time the OECD compiled its data. Almost a quarter (24) of the patents had received only one citation. More than 95 percent of our patents had received five or fewer citations. One-half of 1 percent of our patents have received a dozen or more citations. These are likely the most valuable patents in our data.

Scale, Industrial Composition, and Density

Our primary measure of city size is total civilian employment in 1989 as measured in the data used in the payroll employment survey. These are counts of jobs based on the location and sector of the establishment. In addition to

---

13. We thank Dominique Guellec and Colin Webb for technical assistance with the data. For additional details on these and other OECD patent data, see Webb and others (2005) and the OECD website for the Directorate for Science, Technology and Industry.

14. WIPO is the World Intellectual Property Organization.

Figure 2. Forward Citations

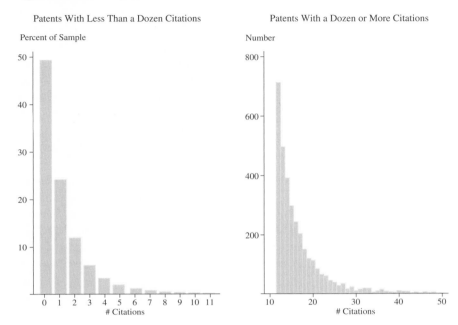

Source: Authors' tabulations of the OECD–EPO Patent Citations Database.

total employment, we compute the shares of jobs falling into seven one-digit SIC industry groups, plus federal and local government employment shares.[15]

To investigate the potential effects of local market structure on inventive output, we construct a variable similar to one suggested in Glaeser and others (1992)—the number of establishments per worker in the metropolitan area in 1989. These data are derived from the 1989 edition of *County Business Patterns*.[16]

Our measure of job density relies on estimates of the built-up areas of urban counties in 1990. Specifically, we use the land area of the urbanized areas (UAs) contained in our MAs. These are defined as an area with a population of 50,000 or more, composed of at least one place, and the adjacent settled surrounding

15. We construct these variables from county-level data contained in the 1999 vintage of the Bureau of Economic Analysis' Regional Economic Information System (REIS). SIC stands for Standard Industrial Classification.

16. County Business Patterns is an annual series that provides subnational economic data by industry. These data are based on administrative records at the level of individual establishments. For details, see U.S. Census Bureau (1991) (www.census.gov/epcd/cbp/index.html).

area with a population density of at least 1,000 per square mile (U.S. Census Bureau 1994). While UAs are not bounded by county lines, we were able to collect data on urbanized-area land area in nearly every urban county, and we used these to construct our measure of the relevant land area in our MAs.

We use this measure of land area because it is a better proxy for the space in which urban labor markets function than is total county land area (Mills and Hamilton 1994). This is especially true for counties in the western United States. For example, in the 1990 census only 12 percent of the 580,000 square miles of land in MSA counties was categorized as urban in nature. In that year, the urban share of MSA land area varied from less than 1 percent in Yuma, Arizona, to 65 percent in Stamford, Connecticut.

But there is a trade-off in this choice of land area, since we use our county-level counts of employment to construct our density measures. To the extent that we are picking up employment occurring outside urbanized areas, our job density measure will be somewhat overstated. In Carlino, Chatterjee, and Hunt (2007), we explored this question in detail and concluded that the degree of overstatement is relatively small and is only likely to bias our results downward.[17]

R&D Inputs

We are especially interested in the contribution of local inputs to the rate of innovation in our MAs. In our earlier work, we identified four of these inputs: local human capital plus the R&D activity of universities, private firms, and any nearby government laboratories.[18] Because these variables are all highly correlated with the size of cities, we include them in intensity form in our regressions. For example, local human capital is measured as the share of the population older than 25 years of age with a college degree in 1990. Private R&D is captured with a count of the number of private research labs in 1987 divided by the total number of private establishments.[19] Federal government lab R&D in the years 1987–89 is normalized by the number of federal civilian employees in the MA. R&D performed by academic institutions during the

---

17. In that paper, we ran all of our regressions with an alternative measure of size and density using a residence-based employment variable linked to urbanized areas and found very similar results. We did not rely on such a measure, however, because it significantly understates employment in urbanized areas.

18. We also controlled for the influence of having many nearby universities, a possible college-town effect, by including in our regressions the ratio of college enrollment to population in the years 1987–89.

19. We geocoded the location of 1,800 private sector research labs using the 23rd edition of the *Directory of American Research and Technology*.

years 1987–89 is normalized by total full-time enrollment at colleges and universities in the MA in those years.

In this paper, we retain three of the four measures as they were constructed in Carlino, Chatterjee, and Hunt (2007). But we have reconstructed the academic R&D variable and derived a number of new variables based on those data. The new variables decompose academic R&D into as many as twenty-six separate fields of study, as defined by the National Science Foundation (or NSF, 2006). We are also able to identify the sources of funding for academic R&D, and we decompose federally funded R&D into basic and applied R&D according to the composition of academic R&D funded by different federal agencies.[20] These new data permit us to explore variations in the effects along each of these dimensions.

Some Facts about Academic R&D in Our Data

The total amount of R&D performed by universities from 1987 to 1989 in our data was $40.5 billion. By comparison, again according to NSF, private industry funded about $200 billion of R&D during those years. Approximately 600 separate campuses reported a positive amount of R&D in our data. The leading institution, Johns Hopkins University, performed about $1.7 billion in R&D during that period. MIT, the University of Wisconsin, and Stanford each performed more than $800 million. The twenty largest performers accounted for about one-third of the total.

One complication in geocoding academic R&D is that about twenty institutions report their R&D at the system level, but they have active research campuses in more than one location. It is not uncommon, for example, for a teaching hospital of a large university to be located well away from its main campus. Collectively these institutions account for about $5 billion in R&D— an eighth of the total. More than ten of these institutions performed at least $150 million in R&D in the 1987–89 period. In our earlier paper, we allocated R&D for these institutions to specific campuses on the basis of the shares of all advanced degrees awarded at those locations.[21] For this paper, we refined our technique by allocating the R&D in each field of science according to the university's geographic distribution of degrees awarded in that field.

---

20. These data were constructed from various datasets downloaded from the NSF's WebCaspar server (http://webcaspar.nsf.gov).

21. These are the sum of doctorates, master's degrees, and first professional degrees awarded in the 1987–89 period of study. The latter require at least six years of college work and two years of professional training.

In terms of the sources of funding for academic R&D, the federal government was by far the largest provider of support for academic R&D ($25 billion, or 60 percent of the total) from 1987 to 1989. Institutions themselves funded over $7 billion in academic R&D (18 percent). State and local governments contributed more than $3 billion (8 percent) and private industry about $2.6 billion (7 percent). Other sources, which we believe include private foundations, accounted for another $2.8 billion (7 percent).[22]

The NSF tabulates the mix of federal funding for academic R&D by various federal agencies in terms of basic or applied R&D. Over the fiscal years 1987–89, slightly more than two-thirds (68 percent) of federal agency R&D funds allocated to universities were categorized as basic. There was considerable variation across agencies. The basic R&D share was highest at NSF (94 percent) and lowest in the Department of Health and Human Services, excluding the National Institutes of Health (39 percent). There was also considerable variation across fields of science: 98 percent of all federal academic R&D funds for astronomy are categorized as basic, while in economics it is less than 40 percent. The share of basic R&D tends to be higher in the physical sciences and somewhat lower in the life and medical sciences.

We are also interested in the effects of variations in the quality of academic research departments. To do this, we coded the ratings of universities in four fields (engineering, physical sciences, mathematical sciences, and life sciences) from the National Research Council's (NRC's) Survey of Scholarly Quality of Faculty for 1982.[23] We took the sum of these ratings over universities in an MA and included this as a control in some of our regressions.

Congressional Earmarks of Agency Funds for Academic R&D

An additional question we wish to explore is the effect, if any, of how federal funding for academic R&D is allocated. In particular, we will test for any differences in inventive productivity that are associated with congressional earmarks of R&D funds.[24] We do this by coding a dataset of those earmarks published by

---

22. According to NSF (2006), this category of funds includes grants for R&D from nonprofit organizations and voluntary health agencies and gifts from private individuals that are restricted by the donor to the conduct of research, as well as all other sources restricted to research purposes not included in the other categories.

23. These data were downloaded from NSF's WebCaspar database in 2004. For additional information and a copy of the survey instrument, see Jones, Lindzey, and Coggeshall (1982).

24. For studies of the political economy of these earmarks, see Savage (1999); de Figueiredo and Silverman (2006). Savage identified as the first modern academic earmark a $10 million grant for a veterinary school (from the 1977 appropriations for the Department of Agriculture).

Figure 3. Academic Earmarks

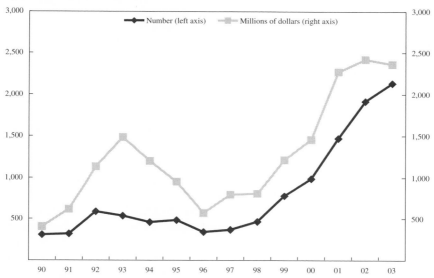

Source: Authors' calculations based on data from the *Chronicle of Higher Education.*

the *Chronicle of Higher Education.*[25] Our data span the years 1990–2003. During those years, according to this source, there were about 11,000 items allocated to one or more academic institutions in appropriations acts, and the total amount of funds authorized to be spent was about $17.6 billion.

The aggregate pattern of earmarks is depicted in Figure 3. Academic earmark activity seems to follow the overall pattern of annual appropriations. During the period of binding annual appropriations caps, academic earmarks either fell or remained stable. When those caps expired in the late 1990s, academic earmarks surged. In the final year of our data, academic earmarks had increased fivefold from the 1990 level ($2.1 billion as opposed to $404 million).[26] This surge in earmarks has prompted concerns about the effects of this form of allocation on research output.

Table 1 shows that in 1990 nearly half of the dollar value of academic earmarks (47 percent) was found in the budget for the Department of Agriculture (USDA). This is not surprising given this agency's long history of funding uni-

25. These data were downloaded from the *Chronicle*'s website (http://chronicle.com/stats/pork/) in July 2007.
26. Savage (1999) offered an alternative explanation—the collapse of collective attempts by universities to refrain from seeking academic earmarks around 1993.

versity research. The idea of allocating R&D funds via some form of peer review took hold only shortly after World War II. Before that time, most federal research funding was done in the form of agricultural research grants to support the extension service, for example (Savage 1999).[27]

The other notable concentrations appeared in the appropriations for the Energy (DOE) and Defense (DoD) departments and NASA, which accounted for 18, 7, and 4 percent, respectively, of the dollar value of earmarks. In the later years of our data, earmarks in the defense appropriations increased dramatically. As a consequence, academic earmarks on DoD budgets account for nearly a third (31 percent) of all earmarked funds from 1990 to 2003.[28]

Table 1 also reports the R&D spending of various federal agencies in 1990.[29] If we compare the NSF R&D numbers to the earmarks data, two patterns seem clear. First, the distribution of aggregate federal resources for R&D is very different from the distribution of those resources to academic institutions. For example, compare the shares of federal R&D accounted for by the Department of Defense and the National Institutes of Health (NIH). In terms of aggregate R&D spending, R&D in the DoD budget was 4.5 times larger than that for NIH. But in terms of R&D allocated to academia, the NIH allocated an amount almost four times greater than that allocated by DoD.

Second, while only about 4 percent of federal agency R&D support to academia was earmarked in 1990, there was considerable variation across agencies. For example, a majority of academic R&D in the USDA budget was allocated via earmark. At DOE, 15 percent of academic R&D funding was allocated via earmarks.[30] In contrast, while two-thirds of federal support ($6.1 billion) for academic R&D was funded through the NSF and the NIH in 1990, there were no earmarks in their appropriations in that year. In fact, in all of the years of our data, there were no earmarks of NSF funds and only twelve earmarks, for a total of $30 million, of NIH funds (in fiscal year 1996–97).[31]

27. For a fascinating description of the institutional details and history of R&D earmarks affecting USDA, see Law and Tonon (2006).

28. For a description of the research performed by centers created with two of the largest (and earliest) earmarks of USDA and DOE budgets, see Mervis (2008).

29. These are federal R&D obligations for universities and colleges in the 1990 budget, as tabulated by NSF and downloaded from WebCaspar in the summer of 2008.

30. These shares are simply the ratio of the number for agency earmarks from the *Chronicle of Higher Education* data divided by the R&D funds provided to universities by the federal agency, as reported by NSF. These percentages should be treated as very approximate since our measures of earmarks and total R&D funding are derived from different sources. Nor is it clear that NSF counts all of these earmarks as R&D in its data.

31. Earmarks are not the only means of directing federal research funding, however. See, for example, Payne (2006), who describes the NSF's set-aside program, EPSCoR, and its effects on research output. And in a detailed analysis of NIH grants, Hegde and Mowery (2008) found that

Table 1. Federal Spending on R&D and R&D Earmarks, 1990

Agency	R&D outlays (millions of dollars)				Academic earmarks (millions of dollars)	
	Total	Percent	Allocated to universities	Percent	Total	Percent
Agriculture Dept.	1,108	1.7	348	3.8	189	46.7
Defense Dept.	37,268	58.6	1,213	13.3	29	7.2
Energy Dept.	5,631	8.9	500	5.5	74	18.2
NASA	6,533	10.3	471	5.2	17	4.2
NIH	7,979	12.6	4,779	52.3	0	0.0
NSF	1,690	2.7	1,321	14.5	0	0.0
Other	3,344	5.3	505	5.5	96	23.6
Total	63,553		9,138		404	

Source: *Chronicle of Higher Education*, "Congressional Earmarks for Higher Education"; National Science Foundation, "Federal R&D Obligations for Universities & Colleges"; and authors' calculations.

One conclusion that could be drawn from the table, then, is that most R&D earmarks represent a reallocation of federal funds in addition to the vast majority of R&D funds allocated to university researchers according to some form of peer review.[32] The efficiency implications of these earmarks are thus less clear than might first appear. For example, the funded research may simply be directed to questions that are not particularly relevant for private markets. Nevertheless, there might still be an effect on inventive productivity, if earmarked funds divert academic manpower from more promising pursuits.

There is some evidence of such effects in terms of research publications. Payne (2002) found that $1 million in R&D earmarks resulted in an increase of twenty-two publications among the recipient universities, but it also reduced the average number of citations to articles published by researchers at those universities. In other words, while quantity increased, quality declined. Hegde and Mowery (2008) found that the geographic composition of the relevant House appropriations subcommittee has some effect on the funding of biomedical research performers (for example, specific scientists) in the lowest two quartiles of the distribution of research grants funded by the same NIH institute in earlier years. Earlier studies were unable to establish a systematic relationship

about $1.7 billion of $37 billion in research grants to institutions in 2002–03 were influenced by the geographic composition of the relevant House appropriations subcommittee.

32. But plentiful earmarks could eventually lead to an unraveling of political support for the major programs that use peer review (for a discussion, see de Figueiredo and Silverman 2007). Our regressions cannot measure such effects.

between a university's success in obtaining academic earmarks and subsequent changes in their academic rankings (de Figueiredo and Silverman 2007).

To test for any effects on local rates of patenting, we include in some of our regressions academic earmarks, again normalized by full-time college enrollment, and similarly normalized values for earmarks from the primary agencies involved.

Additional Control Variables

Since we are limited to cross-sectional regressions, it is extremely important to control for differences across our MAs that are relevant to explaining either potential measurement error or other variations in inventive productivity. As noted earlier, we include in our regressions a set of controls for the historic mix of industries (employment shares). In addition, we include a set of controls for the historic mix of technologies developed in an MA. We include shares of patents obtained in each MA during the 1980–89 period of study that fall into one of six technology groups as defined in Hall, Jaffe, and Trajtenberg (2001).[33] We also include the share of patents obtained in the 1980s by firms in R&D-intensive industries.[34]

In our earlier paper, we considered the possibility that firms that relied more on trade secrets might be less likely to locate in dense cities where greater worker mobility might undermine the effectiveness of trade secrets in protecting innovations. In that case, a correlation between patent intensity and job density might reflect selection of firms or industries that rely more heavily on patents. To test for this possibility, we constructed a variable, using survey results in Cohen, Nelson, and Walsh (2000), that captures the relative importance of trade secret protection across different manufacturing industries. We did this by constructing a weighted average of those ratings using the mix of industrial R&D facilities located in our MAs as weights. We include that variable in the analysis here.

We include a number of other control variables. We control for variations in demographics by including the share of the population in 1990 that is of working age. We also include the percent change in employment over the years 1980–89 as a control for the effects of unobserved differences in local economic opportunities on inventive activity. We also include seven dummy variables based on the Bureau of Economic Analysis (BEA) economic region in which the MA is located (the Rocky Mountain region is omitted).

33. The categories are chemicals, computers, medical, electrical, mechanical, and all other. We included shares of the first five in our regressions. We construct these shares using the NBER Patent Citations Data File (www.nber.org/patents/).
34. See Carlino, Chatterjee, and Hunt (2007) for details on the construction of that variable.

Table A-1 (see appendix) presents the descriptive statistics of the variables used in the analysis to follow. We also examined the correlation coefficients among these variables. The vast majority of the correlations among the variables are well below 0.50. One exception, as should be expected, is MA employment and its square. Despite the high correlation between these variables, there is no evidence of a collinearity problem in our regressions—the coefficients on all other variables are not affected by the inclusion or exclusion of the square of MA employment. Given that we believe there is nonlinearity in scale, we prefer a regression that includes employment size and its square.[35]

Some Results

We begin by summarizing our estimation strategy. We regress the log of either patents or citation-weighted patents per 10,000 of population during the 1990s on the log of MA size and MA density (both measured in terms of jobs), the log of the inverse of average establishment size, the share of the adult population with a college degree, and our measures of local government, academic, and private R&D input intensities. In addition, we include controls for the historical mix of local industries and patented technologies, BEA region dummies, and a number of other control variables. All the right-hand-side variables are lagged or beginning-of-period values to minimize the possibility of endogeneity bias.

The main regression results for our two dependent variables are reported in table 2. The standard errors reported are corrected for potential heteroskedasticity.[36] The results in column 1 can be compared with tables 2 and 3 in Carlino, Chatterjee, and Hunt (2007). The only other difference in the data used in this research compared with that of Carlino, Chatterjee, and Hunt (2007) is that here we are using an improved measure of academic R&D intensity. There is also one difference in the specification: here we include share of the adult population with a college degree in log form.

---

35. A table showing these correlations is available from the authors. A Ramsey RESET test (not shown) for omitted variable bias reveals that the null hypothesis of no omitted variables is only rejected when we exclude the square of MA employment in our main regressions.

36. A Breusch-Pagan test (not shown) indicates that this is an issue for our regressions. Our regressions are performed using STATA 10. Unless otherwise mentioned, we use robust standard errors (White correction).

Table 2. Main Regressions[a]

Independent variable	Dependent variable (in logs)			
	1 Patents per 10,000 pop.		2 Citation-weighted patents per 10,000 pop.	
	Coef.	Std. error	Coef.	Std. error
Scale, density, and local market structure				
Job density, 1990†	0.2210	(0.0867) **	0.2168	(0.1102) **
Employment (10,000), 1990†	0.3810	(0.1472) ***	0.5168	(0.1698) ***
Employment squared†	−0.0494	(0.0177) ***	−0.0563	(0.0207) ***
Establishments per employee, 1989†	1.5814	(0.3418) ***	1.4209	(0.3913) ***
Local R&D inputs				
College education (percent), 1990†	0.9651	(0.1796) ***	1.0535	(0.2546) ***
College enrollment / population, 1990	0.3800	(1.0549)	0.1066	(1.0852)
Academic R&D per student, 1987–89	0.0693	(0.0263) ***	0.0649	(0.0263) **
Federal lab R&D / federal civilian jobs, 1987–89	0.0062	(0.0018) ***	0.0078	(0.0022) ***
Private R&D labs / establishements, 1989	0.3302	(0.0723) ***	0.4180	(0.0931) ***
Historical mix of industries and technologies				
Trade secrets index (lab weighted)†	0.3685	(0.2440)	0.0847	(0.3463)
Manufacturing employment (percent), 1989	2.1975	(0.6889) ***	3.2456	(0.8618) ***
Construction employment (percent), 1989	0.0262	(3.0434)	0.2303	(3.4430)
Transportation employment (percent), 1989	−1.9562	(2.7307)	−4.1986	(3.2903)
Wholesale employment (percent), 1989	−3.4096	(3.2619)	−2.6607	(3.8066)
Retail employment (percent), 1989	−3.7987	(2.2025) *	−1.6757	(2.4747)
Services employment (percent), 1989	0.1370	(0.9385)	1.3665	(1.1328)
Finance and real estate employment (percent), 1989	0.4545	(1.8083)	0.8305	(1.9221)
Federal civilian employment (percent), 1989	−2.1846	(1.4451)	−1.5148	(2.1050)
Local government employment (percent), 1989	−3.2298	(1.2936) **	−1.7624	(1.3473)
High-tech patents (percent), 1980–89	0.8496	(0.1898) ***	0.8629	(0.2075) ***
Chemical patents (percent), 1980–89	1.7397	(0.3946) ***	1.7287	(0.4850) ***
Computer patents (percent), 1980–89	3.3144	(0.6041) ***	3.7179	(0.6502) ***
Medical patents (percent), 1980–89	−0.3111	(0.5845)	0.6480	(0.6293)
Electrical patents (percent), 1980–89	0.9356	(0.4613) **	1.1309	(0.5932) *
Mechanical patents (percent), 1980–89	1.1009	(0.4424) **	1.3142	(0.4992) ***
Working-age population (percent), 1990	2.5352	(1.3948) *	3.5045	(1.6539) **
Employment growth (percent), 1980–89	0.3579	(0.2427)	0.4414	(0.2741)
Constant	−21.3111	(3.3309) ***	−21.2756	(3.9406) ***
Observations	280		280	
Adjusted R^2	0.7884		0.7968	

***Significant at 1 percent; **significant at 5 percent; *significant at 10 percent.
† = variable in logs.
a. Regressions include seven dummy variables for census regions. The dependent variable includes all patents and patent citations over the years 1990 to 1999. Standard errors are corrected for heteroskedasticity.

Table 3. Linear and Quadratic Specifications of Scale and Density[a]

Dependent variable: patents per 10,000 population, 1990–99†

	1	2	3	4
Job density, 1990†	0.2283	4.3558	0.2210	3.6225
	(0.0890)**	(1.7127)**	(0.0867)**	(1.7879)**
Job density squared†		–0.2816		–0.2320
		(0.1161)**		(0.1215)*
Employment (10,000), 1990†	0.0326	0.0350	0.3810	0.3473
	(0.0406)	(0.0398)	(0.1472)***	(0.1530)**
Employment squared†			–0.0494	–0.0444
			(0.0177)***	(0.0186)**
Optimal scale (1,000s)	n.a.	n.a.	473	500
Optimal density	n.a.	2,285	n.a.	2,458
n	280	280	280	280
Adjusted R^2	0.7829	0.7860	0.7884	0.7902

Dependent variable: citation-weighted patents per 10,000 population, 1990–99†

	1	2	3	4
Job density, 1990†	0.2251	6.0982	0.2168	5.2919
	(0.1133)**	(2.4232)**	(0.1102)**	(2.4627)**
Job density squared†		–0.4007		–0.3462
		(0.1639)**		(0.1668)**
Employment (10,000), 1990†	0.1197	0.1231	0.5168	0.4666
	(0.0474)**	(0.0460)***	(0.1698)***	(0.1729)***
Employment squared†			–0.0563	–0.0488
			(0.0207)***	(0.0211)**
Optimal scale (1,000s)	n.a.	n.a.	985	1,192
Optimal density	n.a.	2,017	n.a.	2,086
n	280	280	280	280
Adjusted R^2	0.7968	0.7968	0.7968	0.8002

***Significant at 1 percent; **significant at 5 percent; *significant at 10 percent.

n.a. = not applicable; † = log of the variable.

a. Regressions include all the other variables included in table 2. Standard errors are corrected for heteroskedasticity.

Results for (Unweighted) Patents Per Capita as the Dependent Variable

Not surprisingly, the coefficients reported here are very similar to our earlier results. For example, the coefficient on job density, which is the equivalent of an elasticity, is 0.22, as compared with 0.20 in the earlier paper. When we allow for a nonlinear relationship (see the top panel of table 3), the implied optimal job density is in the range of 2,300–2,500 per square mile.[37] These are slightly higher than the estimate (about 2,220) reported in our earlier paper.

Comparing the coefficients on the scale variables, the implied optimal city size is slightly smaller than we found before (473,000 jobs compared with 500,000 jobs). Assuming a labor force participation rate of 66 percent, the implied optimal population is about 720,000, a rather modest size. Recall that our dependent variable is already normalized by a measure of scale, so this result suggests that there is a range of city size in which increasing returns are operating, but those returns are exhausted at a relatively modest scale. Presumably above this city size, diminishing returns to scale have set in.

Relative to our earlier paper, the coefficient on the inverse of average establishment size hardly changes and remains highly significant (see table 2). The elasticity is quite large—a 10 percent decrease in average establishment size is associated with a 16 percent increase in patent intensity. Thus, for whatever reason, it appears that cities with a more competitive local market structure enjoy higher inventive productivity. Given the data we are using, we cannot distinguish between static (more competition) and dynamic (more new business formation) explanations.

As in our earlier work, local human capital remains the most important explanatory variable by far in our regressions. All else equal, a 10 percent increase in the share of the local adult population with a college degree raises the per capita rate of patenting by 9.7 percent. There is considerable variation in our human capital variable across cities. According to our estimates, a 1 standard deviation increase in the college educated share would increase the patenting rate by 30 percent.

Examining our other measures of local R&D inputs, the coefficients on federal and private lab R&D intensities are essentially the same as reported in our earlier paper (see table 2). The implied elasticities (0.01 and 0.10, respectively) are also very similar to our earlier results (see table 4). The estimated coefficient on academic R&D intensity is lower than we report in Carlino, Chatterjee, and Hunt (2007) (0.07 as opposed to 0.14 in the earlier paper), but the implied elasticities at the mean are essentially the same (0.07 as opposed to 0.08 before). The key point is that while these effects are quite precisely measured, they suggest relatively modest incremental contributions when compared with the effects

---

37. To facilitate comparisons with our earlier paper, we include all the variations with respect to scale and density in table 3. Note that the coefficients and standard errors for all the other variables in those regressions vary only slightly across specifications that include or exclude the square of density or scale.

of increasing local human capital.[38] This has important implications for policy, as we discuss later.

As with our earlier results, the historical mix of industries and technologies are important in explaining the inventive productivity of cities, at least as measured by patents (table 4). In some instances the implied elasticities are quite high: a doubling of the manufacturing share of jobs would imply a one-third increase in patenting per capita; a doubling of the historical share of chemical patents would imply a 30 percent increase.

In both of those examples, it is important to exercise care in interpreting the results since manufacturing firms, and chemical producers in particular, are relatively intensive users of the patent system. At least part of those effects reflects the measurement error associated with using patents as an indicator of innovations when there is differential reliance on patents across industries and fields of technology. But it is clear that we can soak up a good deal of this variation using our historical control variables.

Results for Citation-Weighted Patents Per Capita

With a few important exceptions, the general pattern of results using our new dependent variable is similar to what we found when using patents per capita as the dependent variable. For example, there is essentially no difference in the coefficients on employment density (0.22) in columns 1 and 2 of table 2. But when allowing for diminishing returns, we do find a difference in the implied optimal job density: adjusting for the quality of local inventions reduces our estimate by 200 to 400 jobs per square mile (compare columns 2 and 4 in the top and bottom panels of table 3).

But we do find some important differences in our results. For example, when adjusting for the quality of local inventions, we find a statistically significant linear effect of scale (total employment) on patent intensity. The implied elasticity of scale is about 0.12 (compare columns 1 and 2 in the top and bottom panels of table 3). That suggests there is at least some evidence of increasing returns to scale.

But as noted earlier, we found evidence of eventually diminishing returns to scale in our regressions on patents per capita. This is also true in the regressions adjusting for patent quality, but diminishing returns appear to set in much further into the tail of the city size distribution. Taking into account the labor force participation rate, the implied optimal scale in these regressions could be

---

38. These elasticities are not affected if we exclude the human capital variables from the regressions.

Table 4. Elasticities at Mean of Independent Variables[a]

| | Dependent variable (in logs) | | | |
| | Patents per 10,000 pop. | | Citation-weighted patents per 10,000 pop. | |
Independent variable	Coef.	Std. error	Coef.	Std. error
Local R&D inputs				
College education (percent), 1990	0.9651	(0.1796)***	1.0535	(0.2546)***
Academic R&D per student, 1987–89	0.0686	(0.0260)***	0.0642	(0.0260)**
Federal lab R&D / federal civilian jobs, 1987–89	0.0086	(0.0025)***	0.0109	(0.0031)***
Private R&D labs / establishements, 1989	0.1003	(0.0220)***	0.1269	(0.0283)***
Historical mix of industries and technologies				
Manufacturing employment (percent), 1989	0.3279	(0.1028)***	0.4842	(0.1286)***
Local government employment (percent), 1989	–0.3792	(0.1519)**	–0.2069	(0.1582)
High-tech patents (percent), 1980–89	0.1596	(0.0356)***	0.1620	(0.0390)***
Chemical patents (percent), 1980–89	0.2982	(0.0676)***	0.2963	(0.0831)***
Computer patents (percent), 1980–89	0.1887	(0.0344)***	0.2116	(0.0370)***
Medical patents (percent), 1980–89	–0.0200	(0.0375)	0.0416	(0.0404)
Electrical patents (percent), 1980–89	0.1353	(0.0667)**	0.1635	(0.0858)*
Mechanical patents (percent), 1980–89	0.2741	(0.1101)**	0.3272	(0.1243)***

***Significant at 1 percent; **significant at 5 percent; *significant at 10 percent.
a. Based on regressions reported in table 2. The dependent variable includes all patents and patent citations over the years 1990 to 1999. Standard errors are corrected for heteroskedasticity.

as high as 1.8 million people (compare columns 3 and 4 in the top and bottom panels of table 3). Here is clear evidence that the results depend in important ways on how inventions are counted.

Differences in the other coefficients are best examined in elasticity form (table 4). The elasticity of our human capital variable (1.05) is about 10 basis points higher than in our regression using unweighted patents. The elasticity for academic R&D intensity is about the same, but the elasticity on private lab R&D intensity rises about 3 basis points (an increase of 27 percent). Two elasticities in our historical control variables also rise significantly: the manufacturing share of jobs and the share of patents falling into the mechanical category.

We conclude that most of our earlier results are robust to controlling for the quality of inventions. But in some others (for example, estimates of returns to scale), the estimated effects vary significantly. And, adjusting for the quality of inventions, we find that local human capital and private R&D intensity are somewhat more important compared with what we found earlier.

Further Exploration of Academic R&D and Academic Earmarks

In this section we report new results using our additional variables related to the local academic R&D performed on our sample of MAs. In all of these regressions, the inclusion of additional variables or their interactions has little or no effect on the coefficients or standard errors of the other variables we have already discussed (and continue to include in the regressions). Thus, for the sake of brevity, we will not report those coefficients in the discussion and tables in this section.[39]

Controlling for the Quality of Academic Institutions

We added to our base specifications our controls for the quality of academic institutions in the MA. Recall that these are counts of quality rankings of academic departments in four areas of science as reported in a 1982 NRC survey of academics in the field. We explored a variety of regressions using these variables. In all of them the estimated coefficients on these quality variables are positive, but they are never statistically significant.

We suspect the reason for this lack of significance is that the quality of academic departments is already reflected in the academic R&D funding they receive from the federal government and other sources. As evidence, if we exclude our academic R&D intensity variable from the regression (not shown), the estimated elasticity of the aggregated quality measure is 0.04 and statistically significant. A similar result is obtained using our NRC measure of the quality of academic engineering departments. These results could be interpreted as evidence in support of the view that most academic R&D is allocated based on the quality of the researchers who seek funding.

Differences across Fields of Science

Our second set of results explores potential variation in the contribution of different fields of science to patenting rates across our sample of cities. We expected to find stronger effects associated with academic R&D in the areas

---

39. To be explicit, all of the regressions in this section include density, scale, and the square of those variables. None of the results reported are sensitive to how we include density or scale in the regressions.

Table 5. Elasticities at Mean for Fields of Science and Other (Select) Variables[a]

| | Dependent variable (in logs) | | | |
| | *Patents per 10,000 pop.* | | *Citation-weighted patents per 10,000 pop.* | |
Independent variable	*Coef.*	*Std. error*	*Coef.*	*Std. error*
Local R&D Inputs				
Academic R&D per student, 1987–89	0.0748	(0.0287)***	0.0708	(0.0282)**
Federal lab R&D / federal civilian jobs, 1987–89	0.0078	(0.0026)***	0.0101	(0.0032)***
Private R&D labs / establishements, 1989	0.0940	(0.0215)***	0.1171	(0.0265)***
Coarse fields of science				
Percent Academic R&D: all engineering sciences, 1987–89	−0.0144	(0.0152)	−0.0137	(0.0181)
Pct acad R&D: all physical sciences, 1987–89	0.0085	(0.0153)	0.0199	(0.0207)
Pct acad R&D: all earth sciences, 1987–89	−0.0055	(0.0087)	0.0069	(0.0108)
Pct acad R&D: all mathematical sciences, 1987–89	−0.0206	(0.0066)***	−0.0273	(0.0101)***
Pct acad R&D: all life sciences, 1987–89	−0.0593	(0.0305)*	−0.0622	(0.0309)**
Pct acad R&D: all social sciences, 1987–89	−0.0091	(0.0113)	−0.0060	(0.0125)
Observations	280		280	
Adjusted R^2	0.7923		0.8040	

***Significant at 1 percent; **significant at 5 percent; *significant at 10 percent.

a. The excluded field is "interdisciplinary and other science." Regressions include all the other variables reported in table 2. The dependent variable includes all patents and patent citations over the years 1990 to 1999. Standard errors are corrected for heteroskedasticity.

of engineering and in at least a few of the physical sciences (for example, chemistry). But we found little evidence to support this expectation.

Table 5 reports the important coefficients (in elasticity form) for our R&D intensity variables and a set of variables that reflect the shares of all academic R&D falling into six of seven major categories of science (interdisciplinary and other sciences, as defined by the NSF, are the excluded share). The elasticity of academic R&D intensity is slightly higher than reported in table 4. The coefficients for most of the fields of science shares, including social sciences, are quite small and are statistically insignificant. The two elasticities that are statistically significant, mathematical sciences and life sciences, take small negative values (−0.02 and −0.06, respectively).

We also ran our regressions using a much finer breakdown of the fields of science into as many as twenty-three separate categories (table 6). Including

40. This does not appear to be due to collinearity in the share variables. The maximum correlation between any two variables was 0.42 (between mechanical and electrical engineering); for most of the others, the correlation was much smaller.

Table 6. Elasticities at Mean for Fields of Science and Other (Select) Variables[a]

| | Dependent variable (in logs) | | | |
| | *Patents per 10,000 pop.* | | *Citation-weighted patents per 10,000 pop.* | |
Independent variable	*Coef.*	*Std. error*	*Coef.*	*Std. error*
Local R&D Inputs				
Academic R&D per student, 1987–89	0.0815	(0.0331)**	0.0802	(0.0328)**
Federal lab R&D / federal civilian jobs, 1987–89	0.0080	(0.0028)***	0.0100	(0.0034)***
Private R&D labs / establishements, 1989	0.0914	(0.0223)***	0.1151	(0.0287)***
Narrow fields of science				
Percent academic R&D: aeronautical engineering, 1987–89	−0.0044	(0.0044)	−0.0045	(0.0046)
Pct acad R&D: chemical engineering, 1987–89	0.0020	(0.0070)	0.0073	(0.0073)
Pct acad R&D: civil engineering, 1987–89	−0.0036	(0.0110)	0.0004	(0.0123)
Pct acad R&D: electrical engineering, 1987–89	−0.0060	(0.0127)	0.0016	(0.0129)
Pct acad R&D: mechanical engineering, 1987–89	0.0021	(0.0120)	0.0003	(0.0134)
Pct acad R&D: materials science and other, 1987–89	−0.0010	(0.0100)	−0.0123	(0.0132)
Pct acad R&D: astronomy, 1987–89	−0.0014	(0.0047)	−0.0023	(0.0059)
Pct acad R&D: chemistry, 1987–89	0.0117	(0.0123)	0.0135	(0.0154)
Pct acad R&D: physics, 1987–89	−0.0012	(0.0090)	0.0039	(0.0114)
Pct acad R&D: other physical sciences, 1987–89	0.0010	(0.0042)	0.0020	(0.0063)
Pct acad R&D: earth sciences, 1987–89	−0.0029	(0.0091)	0.0091	(0.0115)
Pct acad R&D: mathematics, 1987–89	−0.0066	(0.0105)	−0.0090	(0.0161)
Pct acad R&D: computer science, 1987–89	−0.0149	(0.0053)***	−0.0195	(0.0080)**
Pct acad R&D: agricultural sciences, 1987–89	−0.0151	(0.0116)	−0.0182	(0.0103)*
Pct acad R&D: biology, 1987–89	−0.0184	(0.0182)	−0.0214	(0.0173)
Pct acad R&D: medicine, 1987–89	−0.0293	(0.0180)	−0.0315	(0.0192)
Pct acad R&D: other life sciences, 1987–89	−0.0007	(0.0065)	−0.0011	(0.0084)
Pct acad R&D: psychology, 1987–89	−0.0171	(0.0083)**	−0.0167	(0.0099)*
Pct acad R&D: economics, 1987–89	−0.0007	(0.0125)	0.0034	(0.0147)
Pct acad R&D: political science and public admin., 1987–89	−0.0020	(0.0014)	−0.0030	(0.0017)*
Pct acad R&D: sociology, 1987–89	0.0067	(0.0036)*	0.0075	(0.0059)
Pct acad R&D: other social sciences, 1987–89	−0.0115	(0.0087)	−0.0087	(0.0087)
Observations	280		280	
Adjusted R^2	0.7846		0.7968	

***Significant at 1 percent; **significant at 5 percent; *significant at 10 percent.

a. The excluded field is "interdisciplinary and other science." Regressions include all the other variables reported in table 2. The dependent variable includes all patents and patent citations over the years 1990 to 1999. Standard errors are corrected for heteroskedasticity.

all of these variables has only a slight effect on the coefficients on human capital or the other local R&D intensity variables. But the estimated coefficients on nearly all of the R&D shares were statistically insignificant.[40]

The most robust coefficient was found for the computer science share and it is negative but quite small. This is an interesting result, given the patterns reported in Bessen and Hunt (2007). They found successful domestic applications for software patents increased at a 16 percent annual rate during the 1990s. But only 2.5 percentage points of this growth could be explained by growth in the employment of computer programmers or engineers, and only about 1 percent could be explained by increases in R&D intensity. Nor does it appear that this growth can be explained by the increase in academic R&D in computer science.[41]

It is possible that our controls for the share of patents obtained by high technology firms and the historical mix of patents falling into different categories of technology are masking the effects we expect to see from different categories for academic R&D. We checked this by rerunning the regressions described in table 6, but excluding those control variables. Excluding those controls does change some of the results. For example, if the dependent variable is patents per capita, the elasticities associated with two fields become positive and significant: electrical engineering (0.02) and other life sciences (0.01). In addition to computer science, two others become negative and significant: agricultural sciences (–0.02) and biology (–0.04). The coefficients on the share variables for other fields remain insignificant. If the dependent variable is citation-weighted patents per capita, a statistically significant positive elasticity was found only for electrical engineering (0.03). Negative (and statistically significant) elasticities were found in other engineering (–0.02), computer science (–0.03), agricultural sciences (–0.02), and biology (–0.04).

Effects by Source of R&D Funding and Basic versus Applied Research

Our third set of results documents the variation in inventive productivity, as measured by patenting, of academic R&D based on the source of funding. It is not necessarily clear why the funding source should matter, but we do find evidence that it does. Columns 1 and 3 of table 7 modify our standard specification by including the shares of academic R&D funded by the federal government, state and local governments, industry, and other sources (the omitted share is R&D funded by the university itself). We believe that the other category includes grants from private foundations.

41. Adjusting for inflation, the annual growth rate in computer science R&D performed by universities during the 1990s was only 3.5 percent.

Table 7. Elasticities at Mean for Sources of Academic R&D Funding[a]

	Dependent variable (in logs)							
	1		*2*		*3*		*4*	
	Patents per 10,000 pop.		Patents per 10,000 pop.		Citation-weighted patents per 10,000 pop.		Citation-weighted patents per 10,000 pop.	
Independent variable	*Coef.*	*Std. error*	*Coef.*	*Std. error*	*Coef.*	*Std. error*	*Coef.*	*Std. error*
Local R&D inputs								
Academic R&D per student, 1987–89	0.0795	(0.0272)***	0.0873	(0.0274)***	0.0786	(0.0274)***	0.0845	(0.0273)***
Federal lab R&D / federal civilian jobs, 1987–89	0.0079	(0.0024)***	0.0081	(0.0024)***	0.0100	(0.0030)***	0.0103	(0.0030)***
Private R&D labs / establishements, 1989	0.1061	(0.0203)***	0.1024	(0.0198)***	0.1311	(0.0262)***	0.1289	(0.0257)***
Source of R&D funding								
Percent academic R&D: federal funds, 1987–89	-0.1353	(0.0359)***			-0.1390	(0.0390)***		
Pct acad R&D: state and local funds, 1987–89	-0.0219	(0.0142)	-0.0213	(0.0142)	-0.0205	(0.0191)	-0.0200	(0.0192)
Pct acad R&D: industry funds, 1987–89	-0.0074	(0.0195)	-0.0042	(0.0194)	-0.0005	(0.0240)	0.0025	(0.0240)
Pct acad R&D: other sources, 1987–89	0.0383	(0.0109)***	0.0378	(0.0108)***	0.0488	(0.0145)***	0.0484	(0.0143)***
Pct acad R&D: federal funds—basic R&D			-0.0633	(0.0462)			-0.0619	(0.0498)
Pct acad R&D: federal funds—applied R&D			-0.0772	(0.0427)*			-0.0789	(0.0442)*
Observations	280		280		280		280	
Adjusted R^2	0.8035		0.8039		0.8108		0.8108	

***Significant at 1 percent; **significant at 5 percent; *significant at 10 percent.
a. The excluded share is internal funding. Regressions include all the other variables reported in table 2. The dependent variable includes all patents and patent citations over the years 1990 to 1999. Standard errors are corrected for heteroskedasticity.

Relative to R&D funded by internal funds, R&D funded by the federal government was less productive in terms of generating patented inventions. The elasticity at the mean (–0.14) is quite large relative to many of the other effects we estimate in our regressions. Second, R&D funded by other sources was modestly more productive relative to internally financed R&D. Evaluated at the mean, the implied elasticities are 0.04 and 0.05, using our two dependent variables. Finally, R&D funded by industry, or state and local governments, appears very slightly less productive, in terms of patenting at the MA level, than R&D funded internally. But those effects are too small to be statistically significant.

It is possible that our results for federal R&D support depend on the kind of R&D that is funded. We usually think of government-funded academic R&D as being more directed at basic rather than applied research.[42] If applied research is closer to final goods markets, we might expect $1 million of applied research to generate more patents than $1 million of basic research. Thus, one possible explanation for this result is that it is an artifact of the federal government funding primarily basic R&D at universities (see the section above, "Some Facts about Academic R&D in Our Data").

To check this possibility, we decompose federal funding for academic R&D into basic and applied shares on the basis of the variation in those shares across federal agencies and in the distribution of agency R&D funding across universities. This permits us to include in our regressions the basic and applied shares of academic R&D in an MA that are funded by the federal government.[43] We include these variables in the regressions reported in columns 2 and 4 in table 7.

In either specification, the coefficients on both variables are negative, but only the coefficient on the applied R&D share is statistically significant. The implied elasticity is small (–0.07). The basic and applied coefficients are quite similar, and the difference between them is not statistically significant. While this is admittedly a weak result, it is nevertheless surprising given our assumption that applied R&D is more closely tied to final goods markets, and thus to patents.

We explored one additional possibility—variation in the patent propensity of academic R&D funded by different federal agencies. We added to the spec-

42. The NSF (2006) defines basic research as "systematic study directed toward fuller knowledge or understanding of the fundamental aspects of phenomena and of observable facts without specific applications towards processes or products in mind." It defines applied research as "as systematic study to gain knowledge or understanding necessary to determine the means by which a recognized and specific need may be met."

43. These variables are the product of the basic and applied shares of federally funded academic R&D, at the MA level, constructed from the federal agency data and the share of all academic R&D in an MA that is funded by the federal government.

ifications described in columns 1 and 3 in table 7 the shares of federal academic R&D funding of the seven most important funding agencies (Agriculture, Defense, Energy, Health and Human Services, NASA, NIH, and NSF). The only statistically significant effect (not shown) was for the Defense share, with an elasticity of –0.02 at the mean.

The Effects of Academic Earmarks

Our final set of results explores the potential that academic R&D funded by federal earmarks may have different effects on patent intensity than might R&D allocated by other means. As discussed in the section on data and descriptive statistics, it is not obvious that such effects would occur, since it does not appear that, in 1990 at least, these earmarks were diverting resources directly from the primary programs (NIH and NSF) that allocate academic R&D via some form of peer review.[44] To test for such effects, we include in our regressions earmarks in the same form of intensity as we did for academic R&D, normalizing by full-time college enrollment in the area. We retain in these regressions our controls for the sources of R&D funding.

The initial results are reported in columns 1 and 3 of table 8. The estimated elasticities for earmarked funds are negative, but quite small. And when unweighted patents are used, the coefficient is not statistically significant (see column 1). Once we include in the regressions the earmarks associated with the primary agencies experiencing this activity, we find somewhat stronger results (columns 2 and 4 of the table). The elasticity for earmarks in general becomes more negative (about –0.05), at least two-thirds the size of the elasticities reported on academic R&D intensity. They are also statistically significant. These effects are consistent with the finding in Payne (2002) that institutions receiving earmarks increased the quantity of their research publications, but the quality of those publications fell.

In a few instances, there is a statistically significant difference in the elasticity of earmarks on particular agency budgets, relative to the effect for all other earmarks. These effects are generally positive and, with the exception of earmarks on the Department of Agriculture budget, are an order of magnitude smaller than the general effect. Thus, any negative effect associated with earmarks on USDA appropriations appear to be about a third smaller than the overall effect of congressional earmarks. All of these results are robust to the inclusion of our coarse field of science controls in our regressions (not shown).

44. As mentioned earlier, we recognize that high earmark activity might dilute support for larger NIH and NSF budgets. But our regressions cannot test for such effects.

Table 8. Elasticities at Mean for Academic Earmarks[a]

	Dependent variable (in logs)							
	1		2		3		4	
	Patents per 10,000 pop.		Patents per 10,000 pop.		Citation-weighted patents per 10,000 pop.		Citation-weighted patents per 10,000 pop.	
Independent variable	Coef.	Std. error	Coef.	Std. error	Coef.	Std. error	Coef.	Std. error
Local R&D inputs								
Academic R&D per student, 1987–89	0.0832	(0.0279)***	0.0742	(0.0271)***	0.0826	(0.0284)***	0.0739	(0.0270)***
Federal lab R&D / federal civilian jobs, 1987–89	0.0076	(0.0024)***	0.0077	(0.0024)***	0.0097	(0.0030)***	0.0098	(0.0030)***
Private R&D labs / establishements, 1989	0.1033	(0.0203)***	0.1026	(0.0207)***	0.1281	(0.0263)***	0.1293	(0.0265)***
Source of R&D funding								
Percent academic R&D: federal funds, 1987–89	-0.1385	(0.0360)***	-0.1429	(0.0368)***	-0.1415	(0.0398)***	-0.1522	(0.0392)***
Pct acad R&D: state and local funds, 1987–89	-0.0219	(0.0142)	-0.0222	(0.0146)	-0.0208	(0.0190)	-0.0183	(0.0196)
Pct acad R&D: industry funds, 1987–89	-0.0071	(0.0193)	-0.0059	(0.0191)	-0.0003	(0.0238)	0.0006	(0.0241)
Pct acad R&D: other sources, 1987–89	0.0373	(0.0111)***	0.0372	(0.0112)***	0.0471	(0.0147)***	0.0474	(0.0148)***
Federal academic earmarks per student #	-0.0068	(0.0057)	-0.0464	(0.0131)***	-0.0154	(0.0070)**	-0.0544	(0.0214)**
DoD academic earmarks per student #			0.0050	(0.0014)***			0.0070	(0.0021)***
DoE academic earmarks per student #			0.0050	(0.0033)			0.0063	(0.0047)
GSA academic earmarks per student #			0.0010	(0.0017)			0.0021	(0.0024)
NASA academic earmarks per student #			0.0080	(0.0026)***			0.0078	(0.0040)*
USDA academic earmarks per student #			0.0186	(0.0079)**			0.0109	(0.0094)
Observations	280		280		280		280	
Adjusted R^2	0.8033		0.8054		0.8123		0.8120	

***Significant at 1 percent; **significant at 5 percent; *significant at 10 percent.

= earmarks in 1990 x 3, divided by full-time enrollment in the metropolican area from 1987 to 1989.

a. The excluded share is internal funding. Regressions include all the other variables reported in table 2. The dependent variable includes all patents and patent citations over the years 1990 to 1999. Standard errors are corrected for heteroskedasticity.

Robustness Checks

Our regressions include a good many control variables, and we have taken considerable care in how we construct them. We have also been careful in how we define our metro areas to minimize issues associated with measurement error or the potential endogeneity of city size. Nevertheless, it is still possible that our techniques have introduced both errors of omission and commission. This section summarizes a number of additional analyses we used to assess the robustness of our results. In particular, we explore an alternative measure of job density, an additional check for potential omitted variable bias, and an instrumental variables (IV) estimation to address any remaining concerns about potential endogeneity bias, and we explicitly test for spatial dependence.

The Density of Knowledge Workers

To this point, our measures of employment density reflect the entire workforce of the MA. Very few of those jobs, however, are directly involved in the process of inventing new products or processes. So it is reasonable to ask whether it would be better to focus instead on a measure of occupations consisting of the knowledge workers in an MA. To do that, we reestimate our regressions using a measure of job density that counts only scientists and engineers living in the urbanized area in 1990.[45] The results are reported in table 9.

The overall patterns are similar, but there are also many differences in the estimated coefficients. In the first column, using unweighted patents as the dependent variable, the elasticity with respect to scientists and engineers (S&E) density is 0.20, just a bit lower than that reported for overall job density in table 2 (0.22). But the elasticity is higher (0.26) when we adjust for the quality of inventions. We find some evidence of eventually diminishing returns to S&E density, but the increasing returns would be exhausted at levels so high that they are not observed in our dataset.

Once again we find evidence of eventually diminishing returns to scale. In the first column, the coefficients (where the dependent variable is patents per capita) imply that these returns are exhausted for a city with about 340,000 jobs, or a population of about 515,000. This is somewhat smaller than the optimal size reported for unweighted patents in table 3. The coefficients in the second column (where the dependent variable is citation-weighted patents per capita) imply an optimal city size of about 710,000, or a population of about 1.1 million. This is roughly the same size as reported in table 2.

45. This variable is constructed from census data. See Carlino, Chatterjee, and Hunt (2007) for additional details.

Table 9. Regressions Using Density of Scientists and Engineers[a]

	Dependent variable (in logs)			
	---	---	---	---
	Patents per 10,000 pop.		Citation-weighted patents per 10,000 pop.	
Independent variable	Coef.	Std. error	Coef.	Std. error
Scale, density, and local market structure				
S&E job density, 1990†	0.2025	(0.0705)***	0.2646	(0.0829)***
Employment (10,000), 1990†	0.3204	(0.1473)**	0.4337	(0.1684)**
Employment squared†	–0.0455	(0.0174)***	–0.0509	(0.0202)**
Establishments per employee, 1989†	1.4616	(0.3312)***	1.2923	(0.3740)***
Local R&D inputs				
College education (percent), 1990†	0.8928	(0.1852)***	0.9483	(0.2611)***
College enrollment / population, 1990	0.4926	(1.0969)	0.2147	(1.0739)
Academic R&D per student, 1987–89	0.0681	(0.0259)***	0.0619	(0.0254)**
Federal lab R&D / federal civilian jobs, 1987–89	0.0043	(0.0018)**	0.0056	(0.0021)***
Private R&D labs / establishements, 1989	0.2730	(0.0714)***	0.3472	(0.0919)***
Observations	278		278	
Adjusted R^2	0.7973		0.8097	

***Significant at 1 percent; **significant at 5 percent; *significant at 10 percent.
S&E = scientists and engineers; † = variable in logs.
a. Except for the density variable, the regression is identical to the one reported in table 2. The dependent variable includes all patents and patent citations over the years 1990 to 1999. Standard errors are corrected for heteroskedasticity.

After controlling for scientists and engineers, the implied elasticities on local human capital are a bit lower than what we report in table 4. In the regression using unweighted patents, the elasticity at the mean is about 0.89; using citation-weighted patents, it is about 0.95. The elasticities on private lab intensities fall about 2 basis points. The elasticity associated with average establishment size is also a bit smaller than that reported in table 2: it is 1.46 in the regression using unweighted patents and 1.29 in regressions using citation-weighted patents.

Omitted Variable Bias

Given the many control variables included in our regressions, we are not particularly concerned about this form of bias.[46] But one way of soaking up any potential remaining bias of this sort is to include in our regressions a lagged value of the dependent variable. For the unweighted dependent variable we

46. As noted earlier, a Ramsey RESET test on our main specifications does not reject the null of no omitted variables.

Table 10. Main Regressions, with Lagged Dependent Variable[a]

	Dependent variable (in logs)			
	Patents per 10,000 pop.		*Citation-weighted patents per 10,000 pop.*	
Independent variable	*Coef.*	*Std. error*	*Coef.*	*Std. error*
Scale, density, and local market structure				
Job density, 1990†	0.1370	(0.0653)**	0.1856	(0.1005)*
Employment (10,000), 1990†	0.1430	(0.0950)	0.4113	(0.1237)***
Employment squared†	–0.0253	(0.0114)**	–0.0469	(0.0159)***
Establishments per employee, 1989†	0.1075	(0.2272)	0.5408	(0.3145)*
Local R&D Inputs				
College education (percent), 1990†	0.4692	(0.1173)***	0.7707	(0.1510)***
College enrollment / population, 1990	–0.1786	(0.7388)	–0.6548	(0.8651)
Academic R&D per student, 1987–89	0.0432	(0.0161)***	0.0400	(0.0184)**
Federal lab R&D / federal civilian jobs, 1987–89	0.0035	(0.0013)***	0.0058	(0.0019)***
Private R&D labs / establishements, 1989	0.0378	(0.0558)	0.2318	(0.0735)***
Other				
Patent intensity, 1980s† #	0.6877	(0.0527)***	0.3869	(0.0667)***
Constant	–7.5713	(2.2655)***	–8.3142	(3.4159)**
Observations	280		254	
Adjusted R^2	0.8889		0.8582	

***Significant at 1 percent; **significant at 5 percent; *significant at 10 percent.

† = variable in logs; # = the average of patents per 10,000 population from 1985 to 1989 or citation-weighted patents per 10,000 population from 1980 to 1989.

a. Regressions are identical to those reported in table 2, except for the addition of the lagged dependent variable. The dependent variable includes all patents and patent citations over the years 1990 to 1999. Standard errors are corrected for heteroskedasticity.

include (in logs) the average rate of patenting per 10,000 of population for the years 1985–89. For our quality-adjusted dependent variable we include (again in logs) the average rate of citation-weighted patents granted over the years 1980–89. Results are reported in table 10.

The inclusion of lagged values of the dependent variable has the expected effect of reducing the coefficients on both our scale and density variables. In the unweighted patent regressions, the coefficients on one of our scale variables is no longer statistically significant. The coefficients on our density variables are reduced by 4 to 8 basis points. Our other variables of interest continue to be statistically significant, although the size of the coefficients is typically lower. In general, there appears to be less of an effect on the coefficients when we use citations to adjust for the quality of patents. We conclude, according to this harsh test, that potential omitted variable bias does not seem to explain our results.

Potential Endogeneity

We now consider the possibility that the MA employment, MA employment density, and the share of the population with a college degree are endogenous variables. Recall that our main specification relies on lagged values of the independent variables, and even lagged (and fixed) definitions of metropolitan areas, to minimize this possibility. Nevertheless, the concern remains.

As noted by Combes and others (2008), since Ciccone and Hall (1996) at least, it is standard practice to use long lags of population density (and population scale) as instruments for employment density (and employment size). We also use lags of the share of the population with a college degree as an instrument for the share of the MA population with a college degree. A good instrument must be correlated with the endogenous explanatory variable (instrument relevance), and the instruments must be contemporaneously uncorrelated with the residuals (instrument exogeneity).

As pointed out by Combes and others (2008), it is highly likely that spatial distribution of population, employment, and college share will exhibit persistence through time (instrument relevance), but that local determinants of current innovative activity will differ from those of the distant past (instrument exogeneity). The square of the log of MA job density in 1970 and a dummy variable for the significant presence of hills and mountains are used as instruments for MA employment density. Similarly, the 1940 population of the MA (in logs), and miles of planned highways in 1947 (in logs), and the square of those terms are used as instruments for MA employment size (and the square of employment size). The share of the 1940 population with a college degree is used as an instrument for human capital.

Table 11a shows the results of a variety of regressions when we instrument for MA employment density. Column 1 in the table reports the results of an IV estimation of the log of patents per capita on the log on employment density when no other endogenous or exogenous regressors (except for regional fixed effects) are included in the regression. Column 2 in the table shows the findings when the other exogenous variables are added to the IV regression, whereas column 3 gives the results when the other (potentially) endogenous variables are added to the IV estimation as well. The last three columns of table 11a are identical to the first three columns of the table, except the log of citation-weighted patents per capita replaces the log of patents per capita as the dependent variable.

As table 11a shows, the first-stage F statistics for our potentially endogenous regressors are well above the rule of thumb (F statistic of at least 10) for strong instruments suggested by Staiger and Stock (1997).[47] Table 11a reports the results on the log of employment density from the second-stage IV regressions. Note that we lose more than 50 observations because of the lack of historical data for our instruments.

The estimated coefficients on our employment density variable are somewhat larger than those reported in table 2 and remain statistically significant. Of course, if our instruments are also endogenous, our parameter estimates may still be biased. Since we have more instrumental variables than endogenous regressors, we use the Hansen J test to verify that the instruments are uncorrelated with the error term. The p values from those tests are well above 0.30. The endogeneity tests do not reject the null hypothesis of equality of our instrumented coefficients in the OLS (ordinary least squares) and IV regressions (the p values are 0.13 or greater in every instance) indicating that OLS estimations are unbiased and more efficient than the IV estimations.

The results reported in table 11b are similar to those reported in table 11a, except that we now instrument for MA employment size (and its square). The first-stage F statistics indicate that our instruments are strong. The estimated coefficients on our employment size variable are somewhat larger than those reported in table 2 and are only statistically significant in two of the six specifications.[48] The coefficients on the square of MA employment variable are significant in three of six specifications. This is not surprising given that the IV estimates are typically less efficient than those of OLS. For the most part, the tests for endogeneity bias for this variable do not indicate that the OLS coefficients are biased. Only in the most parsimonious specification is the null rejected, and in that case the results suggest our OLS coefficients are biased downward.

Finally, the results reported in table 11c are similar to those reported in table 11a, except that we now instrument for human capital. The first-stage F statistics indicate that instruments are strong. The estimated coefficient on the log of share of the population with a college degree variable is positive and significant in all cases. Since the regressions summarized in the table have a single instrument and a single included endogenous regressor, the coefficients reported in table 11c are exactly identified, and the Hansen J test is not applicable.[49]

---

47. These statistics also exceed the critical values of the size test for weak instruments and the small sample bias test for instrumental variables regressions in Stock and Yogo (2005). To conserve on space, we do not present the results of the first-stage regressions or the second-stage results for any variable other than the variable being instrumented for.

48. But the p values (not shown) for our scale variables in the specifications in columns 1 and 4 of the table are 0.12 and 0.13, respectively.

49. We also conducted overidentification tests in IV regressions by including a second instrument (log of inches of annual rain fall), and we never rejected the null hypothesis of exogenous

Table 11a. Instrumenting for Job Density (2SLS)[a]

	Dependent variable (in logs)					
	Patents per 10,000 pop.			*Citation weighted Patents per 10,000 pop.*		
	1	*2*	*3*	*4*	*5*	*6*
Second stage						
Job density, 1990† #	0.437	0.2900	0.2931	0.5477	0.3800	0.3603
	(0.229)*	(0.1379)***	(0.1091)***	(0.2861*)	(0.1807**)	(0.1426)**
Other exogenous variables	No	Yes	Yes	No	Yes	Yes
Other (potentially) endogenous variables	No	No	Yes	No	No	Yes
Overidentification test (*p* values)	0.9651	0.8642	0.5003	0.5718	0.4636	0.6950
Endogeneity test (*p* values)	0.2254	0.8470	0.3531	0.1282	0.5987	0.2456
First stage						
F statistic	51.06	61.53	62.75	51.06	61.53	62.75
Partial R^2	0.4707	0.5347	0.5316	0.4707	0.5347	0.5316
Observations	224	224	224	224	224	224

***Significant at 1 percent; **significant at 5 percent; *significant at 10 percent.

2SLS = two-stage least squares; † = variable in logs; # = variable is instrumented with the square of metropolitan area job density (in logs) in 1970 and a dummy variable for the significant presence of hills and mountains.

a. Standard errors are corrected for heteroskedasticity.

The endogeneity tests reject the null hypothesis of equality of our instrumented coefficients in the OLS and IV regressions (the *p* values are 0.08 or smaller in every instance) indicating that OLS estimations are biased. However, a comparison of the results for the human capital variable in the OLS regression (an elasticity of about unity) with those reported in table 11c (an elasticity of at least 2) indicates that to the extent that there is endogeneity bias, the bias works against the maintained hypothesis that high-skilled workers positively affect local innovative activity.

Spatial Dependence

There is a very high degree of spatial inequality in the distribution of patent activity. Patenting tends to be highly concentrated in the metropolitan areas of the northeast corridor, around the Research Triangle in North Carolina, and in California's Silicon Valley. Even though the coefficients on our regional dummy

---

instruments. However, the *F* statistics in the first-stage regression including the other exogenous variables are about 9.0. The coefficients are qualitatively similar to the ones reported in table 11c. Endogeneity tests consistently reject the null hypothesis of exogeneity for the human capital variable.

Table 11b. Instrumenting for Employment (2SLS)[a]

	Dependent variable (in logs)					
	Patents per 10,000 pop.			Citation-weighted patents per 10,000 pop.		
	1	*2*	*3*	*4*	*5*	*6*
Second stage						
Employment (10,000),	0.4382	0.4465	0.3057	0.4284	0.4798	0.3302
1990†#	(0.3377)	(0.2166)**	(0.1970)	(0.4041)	(0.2372)**	(0.2206)
Employment squared†#	–0.0302	–0.0570	–0.0393	–0.0931	–0.0527	–0.0339
	(0.0445)	(0.0262)**	(0.0239)*	(0.0689)	(0.0286)*	(0.0267)
Other exogenous variables	No	Yes	Yes	No	Yes	Yes
Other (potentially) endogenous variables	No	No	Yes	No	No	Yes
Overidentification test (*p* values)	0.4840	0.2309	0.4750	0.4859	0.1020	0.2600
Endogeneity test (*p* values)	0.0008	0.9757	0.8778	0.0000	0.5902	0.4740
First stage[b]						
F statistic	222.78	192.87	185.75	222.78	192.87	185.75
	286.87	214.93	212.72	286.87	214.93	212.72
Partial R^2	0.7695	0.7567	0.7567	0.7695	0.7567	0.7567
	0.8209	0.8093	0.8096	0.8209	0.8093	0.8096
Observations	277	277	277	277	277	277

***Significant at 1 percent; **significant at 5 percent; *significant at 10 percent.

† = variable in logs; # = variable is instrumented with the log of metropolitan area population in 1940 and the log of planned highway miles in 1947, and the square of those variables.

a. Standard errors are corrected for heteroskedasticity.

b. The first row of *F* statistics and partial *R* squared statistics refers to the first-stage regression for employment. The second row of those statistics refers to the first-stage regression for the square of employment.

variables are typically insignificant, this clustering of innovative activity suggests there could be strong spatial dependence at a more localized level and, if so, it should be controlled for in our empirical analysis.

The conjecture, then, is that patent intensity in one MA may be highly correlated with patent intensity in nearby MAs. The consequences of spatial autocorrelation are the same as those associated with serial correlation and heteroskedasticity: When the error terms across MAs in our sample are correlated, OLS estimation is unbiased but inefficient. However, if the spatial correlation is due to the direct influence of neighboring MAs, OLS estimation is biased and inefficient (Anselin 1990). The literature suggests two approaches to dealing with spatial dependence. In the first approach, spatial dependence is modeled as a spatial autoregressive process in the error term. The second approach models the spatial dependence in patenting activity via a spatially lagged dependent variable.

Table 11c. Instrumenting for Human Capital (2SLS)[a]

	Dependent variable (in logs)					
	Patents per 10,000 pop.			Citation-weighted patents per 10,000 pop.		
	1	2	3	4	5	6
Second stage						
College education (percent), 1990†#	1.9758 (0.2349)***	2.3566 (0.7458)***	2.0177 (0.7404)***	2.5871 (0.2665)***	2.7188 (0.8677)***	2.1731 (0.8368)***
Other exogenous variables	No	Yes	Yes	No	Yes	Yes
Other (potentially) endogenous variables	No	No	Yes	No	No	Yes
Overidentification test (*p* values)[b]	—	—	—	—	—	—
Endogeneity test (*p* values)	0.0049	0.0237	0.0777	0.0011	0.0142	0.0821
First stage						
F Statistic	186.95	13.17	12.04	186.95	13.17	12.04
Partial R^2	0.4775	0.0728	0.0653	0.4775	0.0728	0.0653
Observations	279	279	279	279	279	279

***Significant at 1 percent; **significant at 5 percent; *significant at 10 percent.
— = not applicable; † = variable in logs; # = variable is instrumented with the log of the share of the metropolitan area population with a college degree in 1940.
a. Standard errors are corrected for heteroskedasticity.
b. Overidentification tests, using the annual inches of rainfall (in logs) as a second instrument, do not reject the null hypothesis of instrument exogeneity. With two instruments, the F statistic in the first stage regression in columns 3 and 6 falls to just below 10. The second stage results are similar to those reported here.

Following Anselin and Hudak (1992), we perform three tests for spatial auto-correlated errors: Moran's I test, the Lagrange multiplier (LM) test, and a robust Lagrange multiplier test (robust LM). We also perform two tests for the spatial lag model (LM test and robust LM test). The Moran's I test is normally distributed, while the LM tests are distributed χ^2 with k and 1 degree of freedom, respectively.

We estimate each of the specifications previously reported in table 2 using these various tests for spatial dependence. The results are summarized in table 12. The null hypothesis of either a zero spatial error or zero spatial lag cannot be rejected in any specification (Moran's I test, the LM, or the robust LM test). Thus, spatial dependence does not appear to be a concern in our regressions.

Conclusions

A number of potentially important policy implications seem to follow naturally from our results. What, if anything, should local policymakers do to

Table 12. Tests for Spatial Dependence[a]

| | Dependent variable (in logs) | | | |
| | Spatial error | | Spatial lag | |
Test (null hypothesis)	Patents per 10,000 pop.	Citation-weighted patents per 10,000 pop.	Patents per 10,000 pop.	Citation-weighted patents per 10,000 pop.
Moran's I ($\lambda = 0$)	0.1583	0.2676	—	—
Lagrange multiplier ($\lambda = 0$)	0.2120	0.2698	—	—
Robust Lagrange multiplier ($\lambda = 0$)	0.6872	0.8940	—	—
Lagrange multiplier ($\rho = 0$)	—	—	0.1889	0.2158
Robust Lagrange multiplier ($\rho = 0$)	—	—	0.5654	0.5644

$N = 280$

— = not applicable.

a. *P* values are reported. Regressions use the specifications reported in table 2. The dependent variable includes all patents and patent citations over the years 1990 to 1999. Moran's I is based on standardized z values that follow a normal distribution. The Lagrange multiplier tests are distributed χ^2 with critical levels 3.84 ($p = 0.05$).

stimulate local innovative activity? The answer depends, in part, on who benefits from innovative activity. A metropolitan area might be highly innovative, but if the benefits of this innovation largely occur in other regions, local policymakers might have too little incentive to support local innovative activity. That would suggest a role for making policy at a national, rather than local level. But this begs the question—what policy instruments are important and who should decide how they should be used?

While this paper does not consider the extent to which patenting stimulates local growth, results found in Carlino and Saiz (2008) are instructive. Although measuring the effect of patenting on local growth was not the main purpose of that paper, the results do suggest that more patents obtained by local inventors are associated with more local job growth. Using the estimates reported in table 4 of that paper, if a city could double its rate of patenting per capita, the increase in local employment over a decade would be 1.9 percentage points higher. This is certainly an economically significant effect, but in itself, it does not tell us about the magnitude of any growth induced in other areas.

Returning to the results in this paper, the most significant policy lever policymakers at any level of government should consider are ones that influence the accumulation of human capital. It is by far the most important variable in explaining the overall rate of inventive activity in cities, even after controlling for other R&D inputs and other city characteristics. The estimated marginal effects of increasing local human capital are nearly an order of magnitude larger than almost any other variable in our analysis.

A second important finding (also reported in our earlier work) is an extremely robust inverse relationship between a city's patenting rate and the average size of its business establishments. The implied elasticities are again quite large. Unfortunately, the limitations of our data preclude us from speculating on the exact channel that explains this relationship. Is it the static benefits of more competitive local labor markets as suggested by Chinitz (1961) and Jacobs (1969)? Or are we identifying the effects of new business formation stimulated by drastic innovations? This is a very important question for future research and for policy design.

Third, we demonstrate that city size and job density are both empirically relevant in explaining the inventive productivity of cities. The marginal effects of density are of about the same magnitude as those for scale, or even larger. While these results are consistent with theories about matching externalities in labor markets (for example, Berliant, Reed, and Wang 2006; Hunt 2007), more theoretical and empirical work is required before precise policy implication can be suggested. And to identify the exact relationships at work, empirical studies almost certainly must be done using panel data and quite likely at the level of individual matches between workers and firms.

Nevertheless, labor markets do seem a very sensible focus for innovation policy. It is not uncommon for researchers to point to characteristics of U.S. labor markets to explain why U.S. labor productivity growth has outpaced that of many other developed countries over the last fifteen years. Part of those gains in productivity are almost certainly attributable to the development of new products and services—in other words, to innovation. Yet discussions about innovation policy are typically dominated by questions of how to allocate scarce public resources to particular regions to stimulate R&D or foster clusters. Such policies may prove complementary to, but are certainly not substitutes for, policies that encourage people to obtain education and for labor markets to put those skills to their best use.

Fourth, we find evidence of increasing returns to scale in the local rate of invention, but we also find that these returns are eventually exhausted. In our earlier work, which relied on unweighted patent counts, we found that these returns were exhausted at a relatively modest city size, roughly at the mean of cities in our data. In this paper, we find that adjusting for the quality of inventions using citation weights more than doubles our estimate of the city size at which increasing returns are exhausted. We suspect, however, that more precise and robust results can be obtained by working with panel rather than cross-sectional data. This is an important topic for future research.

Fifth, we continue to find that increases in local academic R&D generate a modest incremental contribution to the local rate of invention. With only one robust exception—computer science—we find remarkably little variation in the contribution of academic R&D in different scientific fields to local patenting. An increase in academic R&D in that field generates a relatively small increase in the patenting rate. This is likely a historical artifact of the field's lack of reliance on patents, but it stands in contrast to the very rapid growth in software patenting that occurred in the 1990s.

Sixth, we find that there are significant variations in the marginal contribution of academic R&D to patenting rates depending on the source of its funding. Interestingly, we find that "other" sources are the most productive, while federally funded R&D is the least productive, as measured by changes in the local invention rate. Of course we expect that government-sponsored R&D is more basic in character, perhaps several more steps removed from the creation of new products or processes. But our more disaggregated results showed that applied academic R&D funded by the federal government was no more productive than was the basic R&D and might even be less productive. Clearly there is room for further research on this question.

Finally, we are able to identify a modest negative effect associated with congressional earmarks of federal funds for academic R&D. To our knowledge, this is the first finding of an effect of these earmarks on research productivity as measured by the local rate of invention. This result is somewhat surprising since we could verify that the most important sources of academic R&D allocated via peer review (NIH and NSF) were largely immune to these earmarks during the period we studied. In other words, it appears that, for the most part, the earmarks represented a net addition of R&D funds, rather than a reallocation of funds. Nevertheless, our findings would be consistent with a less direct channel—the possibility that researchers are distracted from more productive activities. That would be consistent with the results for the quantity and quality of research publications reported in Payne (2002).

Appendix

Table A-1. Descriptive Statistics

	Mean	Std. Dev.	Min.	Max.
Patent variables				
Total patents 1990–99	1,907	4,638	7	42,702
Patents per 10,000 pop., 1990–99	2.06	2.11	0.07	17.14
Patents per 10,000 pop., 1985–89	2.76	2.23	0.16	15.65
Citations for patents granted, 1990–99	2,346	6,219	6	57,309
Citations per 10,000 pop, 1990–99	2.27	2.65	0.05	25.16
Citations per 10,000 pop., 1980–89	1.65	1.70	0	13.57
Scale, density, and market structure				
Payroll employment, 1989	392,480	862,483	37,375	9,665,015
UA land area 1990 census, sq. mi.	211	333	15	3,015
MSA employment / UA land area, 1990	1,728	689	408	5,021
Scientists and engineers / UA land area, 1990	26.15	21.57	1.17	195.04
Establishments per 100,000 workers, 1989	4,425	598	2,667	6,365
Local universities				
Full-time college enrollment, 1987–89	63,254	116,475	0	1,330,349
College enrollment / pop., 1987–89 (percent)	6.8	5.6	0	35.7
NRC faculty rating: S&E, 1983	3.75	8.78	0.00	84.60
Local R&D inputs				
Pop. with college degree, 1990 (percent)	19.5	6.2	8.1	45.4
Total acad. R&D / 1,000 enrollment, 1987–89	0.99	1.58	0	11.01
Fed. lab R&D ($1,000) / fed. civ. job, 1987–89	1.40	10.81	0	161.39
Private R&D labs per 1,000 estabs., 1987	0.30	0.39	0	2.71
Historical mix of industries				
Manufacturing employment, 1989 (percent)	14.9	7.4	1.8	46.1
Services employmt., 1989 (percent)	25.8	4.2	9.8	44.8
Construction employmt., 1989 (percent)	5.4	1.3	2.9	11
Transportation employmt., 1989 (percent)	4.4	1.5	1.6	11.9
Wholesale employmt., 1989 (percent)	4.3	1.4	0.7	9.2
Retail employmt., 1989 (percent)	17.7	1.9	12	24.8
FIRE employmt., 1989 (percent)	6.7	2	2.7	16.7
Local govt. employmt., 1989 (percent)	11.7	4.7	4.4	34.5
Federal civilian employmt., 1989 (percent)	2.3	2.4	0.3	20.8
Historical mix of technology				
High-tech patents, 1980–89 (percent)	18.8	19.5	0	88.9
Chemicals patents, 1980–89 (percent)	17.1	12.8	0	76.1
Computer patents, 1980–89 (percent)	5.7	6.5	0	48.2
Medical patents, 1980–89 (percent)	6.4	6.1	0	44.8
Electrical patents, 1980–89 (percent)	14.5	9.7	0	56.3
Mechanical patents, 1980–89 (percent)	24.9	10	5.6	62.4
Other controls				
Working-age pop., 1990 (percent)	64.4	3.1	53.8	74.8
Employment growth, 1980–89 (percent)	20.5	15.5	–25.8	77.7
Far West region dummy	0.13	0.33	0	1.00
Great Lakes region dummy	0.18	0.38	0	1.00
Mideast region dummy	0.12	0.32	0	1.00
New England region dummy	0.06	0.23	0	1.00
Plains region dummy	0.09	0.29	0	1.00
Southeast region dummy	0.28	0.45	0	1.00
Southwest region dummy	0.11	0.31	0	1.00

Table A-1. Descriptive Statistics (continued)

	Mean	Std. Dev.	Min.	Max.
Academic R&D, 1987–89				
Percent R&D: all engineering	9	15.2	0	87.1
Pct R&D: all physical sciences	9.1	14.4	0	81
Pct R&D: math & computer science	4	11.5	0	100
Pct R&D: all life sciences	29.5	31.7	0	100
Pct R&D: all social sciences	5.2	11.3	0	100
Pct R&D: aerospace engineering	0.6	3	0	35.4
Pct R&D: chemical engineering	0.8	2.8	0	28
Pct R&D: civil engineering	1	2.5	0	21.2
Pct R&D: electrical engineering	2.1	5.7	0	54.5
Pct R&D: mechanical engineering	1.3	3.3	0	29.8
Pct R&D: materials science and other	3.2	7.5	0	57
Pct R&D: astronomy	0.5	3.1	0	34.3
Pct R&D: chemistry	4.5	9	0	81
Pct R&D: physics	3.2	7.2	0	77.5
Pct R&D: other physical sciences	0.9	5.1	0	73.4
Pct R&D: all geosciences	5.2	10.8	0	85.9
Pct R&D: mathematics	0.9	1.9	0	15.6
Pct R&D: computer science	3.1	11	0	100
Pct R&D: agricultural science	4.1	11.9	0	100
Pct R&D: biology	12.9	17.3	0	100
Pct R&D: medicine	11.1	19.7	0	97.6
Pct R&D: other life sciences	1.4	5.2	0	67.9
Pct R&D: psychology	1.5	3.8	0	41.3
Pct R&D: economics	1.1	3.2	0	29.8
Pct R&D: polit. sci. and public admin.	0.9	6.3	0	100
Pct R&D: sociology	1.2	5.1	0	62.9
Pct R&D: other social sciences	1.9	6.6	0	62.8
Pct R&D: interdisciplinary and other science	1.4	4	0	36.8
Pct acad. R&D funded by industry	5.4	7.7	0	56.7
Pct acad. R&D funded by fed. govt.	34.4	31	0	100
Pct basic acad. R&D funded by fed. govt., 1987–90	24.2	23.2	0	76.7
Pct applied acad. R&D funded by fed. govt.	8.2	8.6	0	50.2
Pct acad. R&D funded by state and local govt.	6.4	11	0	62.8
Pct acad. R&D funded by university	13.2	16.1	0	95.8
Pct acad. R&D funded by other	5.2	9.6	0	93.6
Academic earmarks, 1987–89				
Academic earmarks, 90	985,302	2,680,645	0	21,000,000
Acad. earmarks, 90 x 3 / 1,000 enrollment	0.043	0.147	0	1.660
DoD earmarks, 90 x 3 / 1,000 enrollmt.	0.004	0.044	0	0.714
DoE earmarks, 90 x 3 / 1,000 enrollmt.	0.007	0.038	0	0.324
GSA earmarks, 90 x 3 / 1,000 enrollmt.	0.003	0.028	0	0.276
NASA earmarks, 90 x 3 / 1,000 enrollmt.	0.008	0.103	0	1.660
USDA earmarks, 90 x 3 / 1,000 enrollmt.	0.014	0.059	0	0.541
Instruments				
Jobs / UA land area, 1970	1,900	900	600	9,000
UA land area, 1970	156	263	12	2,425
1940 MA population	163,778	581,281	0	8,128,177
Planned highway miles, 1947	19	18	0	143
Population with college degree, 1940 (percent)	4.9	1.8	1.5	12.9

FIRE = Fire, Insurance, and Real Estate; MA = metropolitan area; MSA = metropolitan statistical area; NRC = National Research Council; UA = urbanized area.

Comments

Gilles Duranton: This paper is the second opus of Gerald Carlino and Robert Hunt's pioneering research on agglomeration effects in patenting. Let me say first that this paper goes much beyond revisiting the findings of Carlino, Chatterjee, and Hunt (2007). It does that for sure, but it does much more, including looking at two new first-order issues. Are better patents produced in bigger cities? Does the source of funding matter to explain local rates of patenting? In this brief discussion, I will not be able to do justice to the very rich set of findings provided by Carlino and Hunt. Instead, I will try to circumscribe my comments to a small number of core issues. In what follows, I mainly discuss the relatively small optimal city size for patenting, the fact that there appears to be a clear bell shape in the propensity to patent as a function of city size, and the result that the effect of city size seems to be downward biased when the estimation is conducted with ordinary least squares (OLS).

To understand the paper better, it is useful to focus on the following simple model. A representative research lab in city i produces new innovations, which are all patented, according to:

$$(1) \qquad y_i = A_i H_i^{\alpha,}$$

where A_i is a city-specific parameter to be developed further below and h_i is research labor. We assume $\alpha < 1$. Although it would be natural to interpret α as an inverse measure of decreasing returns, it is more insightful to think of this parameter as the share of local inputs in the production process. The production function in equation 1 is drastically simple. It considers only one factor of production, research labor, and a unique shifter to account for the effects of the local environment. For our purpose here, it is worth noting that other factors of production are going to be either like research labor and see their price increase with city size or, instead, like capital and have their price independent of city size. In the latter case, we ignore them.

Research labs maximize their profit:

(2) $$\pi_i = p_i y_i - w_i l_i,$$

with respect to the amount of research labor they hire and the location they choose. We consider a natural two-step maximization process where location is chosen before research labor is hired. For simplicity, we also normalize $p_i = 1$. The first-order condition with respect to research labor implies:

(3) $$h_i^* = \left(\frac{\alpha A_i}{w_i} \right)^{\frac{1}{1-\alpha}}.$$

Unsurprisingly, research inputs will be more intensively used and research output will be greater in places with a high productivity shifter for research, A_i, and low wages for research workers, w_i. Unfortunately, the predictive power of equation 3 is limited since we expect both A_i and w_i to increase with city size. As a result, the evolution of h_i and y_i as a function of city size is ambiguous, and further assumptions need to be made. A standard way to model the positive agglomeration effects of city size in the literature (Duranton and Puga 2004) is to assume $A_i = A_0 L_i^\varepsilon$, where L_i is the population (or employment) of city i and $\varepsilon > 0$. An equally standard way to model urban costs is to assume that workers all consume one unit of land and need to commute to a central business district to work. A city with a larger population implies more residential land being used and workers having to commute on average from further away. More specifically, assuming that the city is linear, that commuting is paid in units of time, that commuting speed is constant, and that land rent is redistributed to existing residents, it is easy to show that the equilibrium disposable income of research workers in city i is $w_i(1 - \tau L_i)$, where τ is a parameter that governs commuting costs. Workers are free to reside in the city or not. If they choose not to, they can get a disposable income of w_0 in the hinterland. It is then easy to show that the spatial equilibrium is such that we have $w_i = w_0/(1 - \tau L_i)$.

Equation 3 and the above expressions for A_i and w_i can be inserted into equation 2 to yield profit-maximized profit as a function of city size:

(4) $$\pi_i^* = \mathbf{Z} L_i^{\frac{\varepsilon}{1-\alpha}} \left(1 - \tau L_i \right)^{\frac{\alpha}{1-\alpha}},$$

where $\mathbf{Z}$ is a constellation of parameters. π_i^* is obviously concave in L_i. Taking the first-order condition of equation 4 with respect to L_i, the optimal city size for research is:

(5)
$$L_i^* = \frac{\varepsilon}{\tau(\alpha+\varepsilon)}.$$

The optimal research size for cities decreases with commuting costs. It also increases with the intensity of agglomeration effects, ε. With stronger agglomeration economies, it is indeed worthwhile to operate in a larger, and thus more costly, city. This trade-off between commuting costs and the intensity of agglomeration effects is very standard and has been routinely applied to all sorts of economic activity in cities (again, see Duranton and Puga 2004 for a survey). Optimal city size also decreases with α. This is because a larger α implies a greater share for inputs whose costs are sensitive to city size.

Taken literally, this model predicts that all research activity should take place in cities of population size given by equation 5. This prediction would be counterfactual since patenting appears to take place in cities of all sizes in the United States. This extreme and counterfactual result can be easily fixed by assuming that the total profit of a firm has a stochastic component and is actually given by:

(6)
$$\Pi_i = \pi_i^* + \mu_i,$$

where μ_i follows an appropriate *iid* (independent and identically distributed) extreme value distribution. In that case, the share of research firms located in city *i* is logistic and given by:

(7)
$$P_i = \frac{e^{\pi_i^*}}{\sum_j e^{\pi_j^*}},$$

where the summation at the denominator takes place across all cities. This would then predict a single-peaked distribution of research across city sizes taking a maximum for L_i^*.

Before going further into the interpretation of the results, I note that there is an ambiguity with respect to what the paper does. Carlino and Hunt do not estimate L_i^*, the optimal size for research, but instead consider as dependent variable the size that maximizes the research output relative to size. That is, they work with y_i/L_i. Simple algebra shows that the size that maximizes this quantity in equilibrium is:

(8)
$$L_i^{**} = \frac{(2-\alpha)\varepsilon - (1-\alpha)}{\tau[1+(2-\alpha)\varepsilon - (1-\alpha)]}.$$

Regressing patent per capita on population size and various powers of it (and absent the identification issues mentioned below) would lead to an estimate of L_i^{**} not L_i^*. Note that $L_i^{**} < L_i^*$. Whether introducing further controls for other research inputs actually leads Carlino and Hunt to estimate L_i^* is not entirely clear. In any case, this issue might be a moot point because L_i^{**} converges toward L_i^* as α converges to 1. Let me proceed as if Carlino and Hunt really estimate L_i^*.

The main finding of Carlino and Hunt is that L_i^* is relatively small regardless of whether they use a raw or a citation-weighted patent count. Since τ arguably applies to workers in research as well as workers in other forms of economic activity, the explanation must come from either α or ε. For research, we expect the share of revenue α that goes toward paying research labor to be large, possibly close to unity. However, this is also arguably the case for many other service activities like finance or advertising that seem to locate in bigger cities. Hence, I expect ε to do most of the work here. The relatively small optimal city size for research makes it hard to avoid the fact that the effects of city size on research are not large.

This is interesting because previous literature has focused on the other side of the relationship and looked at the effects of research on economic activity in cities. It is commonly believed that these effects are relatively large. All this suggests that research has large benefits for its local environment whereas it only gains modestly from it. If confirmed, this asymmetry would point to an interesting inefficiency. The privately optimal location for research is in medium-sized cities whereas its socially optimal location might be in very large cities. This conjecture deserves some serious scrutiny.

The second interesting result of Carlino and Hunt is that the bell-shaped distribution of research predicted by equation 7 is readily apparent in the data. Previous work on agglomeration economies for other sectors does not emphasize such bell shapes (see Rosenthal and Strange 2004, for a survey). Aside from Black and Henderson (2003) who show a tendency for sectors to cluster in cities of broadly similar size, the evidence is far from overwhelming. The existence of a clear pattern of a city size that maximizes some measure of efficiency for research and not for other sectors of economic activity is thus interesting. Especially because the model above could easily be adapted to other forms of economic activity. Hence, the problem is not with the fact that there is such a pattern for research; it is expected. The problem is more with the fact that the evidence for other sectors is so tenuous. Two conjectures can be offered here. The first is that for many activities, optimal city size is larger than what it is for research. With few very large cities, a bell-shaped pattern such as what Carlino and Hunt exhibit for research may become hard to detect in those activities. The second is that many sectors tend to spread across cities of all sizes because there is a significant local demand and their output is costly to ship. Relative to other forms of economic activity, research might be somewhat unique in that its output, patents, can be shipped at no cost. Yet, the literature on patenting argues that this may not be entirely true since patents are not self-contained and require human interaction for some learning to take place. This is correct, but the geographical bias evidenced by this literature is small (and this is discussed by Carlino and Hunt).

The third finding of Carlino and Hunt is that optimal city size for research is biased downward when using simple OLS. This type of finding can always be dismissed on the ground that the instruments used to show this are inappropriate. This is the usual caveat about instrumental variables (IV): the validity of instruments is in the eye of the beholder. However, this downward bias occurs for different sets of plausible instruments. Figure 1 in Carlino and Hunt is also very interesting. In the ranking of patenting cities, San Jose, California, is unsurprisingly at the very top. Interestingly, the other good patenters are Rochester, New York; Trenton, New Jersey; Detroit; Cleveland; and Buffalo, all in the top quartile. These cities are also at the bottom of the league for population growth over the last several decades. Hence, both IV and circumstantial evidence lead me to take this finding of a downward bias seriously for now. A downward bias implies that there is a negative feedback in the relationship between city size or density and patenting.

Such negative feedback is somewhat surprising since one would expect instead a positive feedback. Economic dynamism in a city can trigger both a high level of patenting and population growth, a form of positive feedback. Alternatively, successful patents can bring new economic activity, another form of positive feedback. Thus, a city with lots of patenting activity can naturally be expected to enjoy faster population growth and become larger, not the opposite. A distinct possibility is that successful patents need not be implemented locally. This could explain the absence of positive feedback but not a negative one. To explain this negative feedback, two conjectures are worth contemplating. The first is that research in a sector locates with economic activity that is related to it. New innovations might then be implemented elsewhere and thus take away economic activity. Duchess County, New York, is a possible example. A lot of the successful research on computers by IBM there might have allowed new generations of computers to be produced in Southeast Asia or in Mexico and led to the demise of IT employment in this suburb of New York. A second possibility is that successful innovations increase productivity but do not lead to proportional increases in sales. As a result local employment contracts. Research in many manufacturing cities may have been incredibly successful at raising productivity. However, this took place without much increase in demand. Hence, successful research may have led to the demise of production activities in those cities.

The interesting conjectures that arise from the paper will, I hope, receive some serious attention in the years to come.

Bruce A. Weinberg: At least since Romer (1990), economists have focused on the role of knowledge and knowledge production in economic growth. There is increasing evidence of a causal link between conditions believed to be important for knowledge production (such as population, human capital stocks, and the presence of educational and research institutions) on the one hand and knowledge production and local economic performance on the other. There is less evidence about the factors that matter for knowledge production and economic performance.

Gerald Carlino and Robert Hunt's piece is an ambitious study of two potentially important determinants of knowledge production in cities—the size and density of metropolitan areas and research and development performed by universities—and their impact on patents. I think it is useful to look at these two factors separately, and I will focus on the latter but will loop back to the former. One reason for focusing on research and development spending is that funding policies, which are controlled by the government to a large extent, are considerably easier to manipulate than population flows.

Carlino and Hunt's study of university-based research and development is particularly timely. Universities are believed to be an important source of knowledge production, are increasingly justifying public support by pointing to the economic benefits of the knowledge and students they produce, and are increasingly being looked to for these benefits. Carlino and Hunt's piece is a valuable contribution to our understanding of the role of universities in knowledge production and their local communities.

Carlino and Hunt contribute to our understanding of these important, policy-relevant questions in a number of ways. First, as is well known, measures of inventive activity based solely on counts of patents granted are, at least in principle, problematic because patents vary considerably in importance. To address this concern, Carlino and Hunt weight patents by the number of citations they receive. Although using citation-weighted patents does not change most of their results dramatically, it is an important validation of the results and is itself interesting insofar as it indicates that the places where a lot of innovations arise are similar (at least in terms of their characteristics) to the ones where important innovations arise.

Carlino and Hunt also break down research and development along a number of interesting dimensions. They consider the source of funding, the fields in which it is done, and whether it is basic or applied. They also look at congressional earmarks for research and development.

Their results are interesting and provocative. For instance, it is reassuring that academic research and development contributes to knowledge production. At the same time, Carlino and Hunt find that the population at which per capita patents are maximized is 720,000. I find this result surprising. It is interesting that the population at which citation-weighted per capita patents are maximized is 1.8 million, which squares better with my intuition.

In thinking about the estimates, it is worth thinking about the correct level of aggregation, and this theme will run through many of my comments. The paper focuses on metropolitan areas, but it is also worth thinking about what knowledge production locally can tell us about knowledge production at the individual level. Similarly, it is worth thinking about what knowledge production locally can tell us about knowledge production globally.

From the Individual to the Local Level

It is worth starting by thinking about the proper level at which to estimate the models, whether it is at the individual (or individual research group) level or the level of the local area. In the most simple model, in which there are no spillovers across individuals, a factor that increases innovation at the individual level by a certain amount increases local innovation by the same amount. If there are spillovers, activity by one person impacts others, and local knowledge output is greater than what the individuals involved would produce if they were acting in isolation.

Although it is interesting to know how activity is related to innovation, it is particularly important to know whether such spillovers are present. The presence of spillovers is naturally of interest for urban and regional economists. More generally, if spillovers operate, then decentralized decisionmaking will be suboptimal. Although the results on city size suggest external effects, it is not clear whether the estimated effects of university research and development on patenting reflect the effect at an individual level or whether there are spillovers.

From the Local to the Global Level

It is natural to think about the effect of universities on their local communities. Indeed, for some purposes it is the important question—local governments want to know how their support translates into benefits in their communities. Benefits received by neighboring or distant jurisdictions are external. At the same time, the regional, national, or global benefits may be quite large relative to the local benefits. While tacit knowledge may be more likely to be transmitted locally (Zucker, Darby, and Brewer 1998; Weinberg 2008), one feature of knowledge is that once it is reasonably well developed, it travels quite cheaply and quite far. It is believable that one of the reasons that the benefits do not continue to increase with size is because as populations increase, more of the benefits accrue to neighboring areas, and this factor may help understand some of the authors' results.

It is also possible that estimates of local knowledge production, especially as measured by patenting, overstate the wider benefits. Specifically, patents are allocated on the basis of a first-across-the-line criterion. It is also believable that the factors that increase patenting in one area increase patenting in part by "stealing" patents from areas that might not have been far behind. In the extreme, innovation may be almost entirely deterministic with a very small endogenous component, and yet local factors could have a large effect on local patenting by speeding up patenting in one area marginally relative to other areas. In this way, the estimates could be interesting from the perspective of a local authority but have little global significance.

Types of Research

Having laid out these two aspects of aggregation, the rest of my comments will discuss specific aspects of Carlino and Hunt's interesting piece. A nice aspect of their work is that it breaks down research and development along a number of valuable dimensions. It considers the source of funding, the fields in which it is done, and whether it is basic or applied. These findings are interesting and not entirely expected. For instance, Carlino and Hunt find that federally funded research and development is associated with fewer patents relative to the number of patents from research funded by other sources. One's initial reaction is that this might be due to a greater emphasis on basic research among federal funding agencies. Carlino and Hunt are able to address this possibility using their data, and when they do, the puzzle only deepens—it is federally funded applied research that is associated with fewer patents!

The answer to this puzzle is not immediately obvious, and I will weigh in with one possibility. The federal government has an incentive to focus on research that benefits the entire country, while state and local funders have an incentive to fund research that has local benefits (and it is plausible that industrial funders would focus on local universities). One explanation for the weaker effects of federally funded research and development is that federal funding agencies focus on projects that have national benefits, even if they have relatively small local benefits, while local funders focus on local benefits. Thus, federal projects may have benefits that are as large or larger than those of local projects, but those benefits accrue to the nation as a whole rather than to local areas and are missed in Carlino and Hunt's analysis.

Carlino and Hunt also look at congressional earmarks for research and development. Here the results are in keeping with one's intuition—funds allocated through earmarks are associated with fewer patents compared with the number of patents associated with other research funds. It is not clear, however, whether this indicates that research and development funded by earmarks is less productive at the individual level or whether it generates smaller spillovers.

Size, Density, and Patents

As indicated, Carlino and Hunt study how the size and density of metropolitan areas are associated with industrial innovation in addition to university-based research and development. Both sets of questions are interesting and they are interrelated.

The main issue is how the relationship between research and development varies with the size of a city. As cities become larger they are likely to include a wider range of activities. Thus, the same amount of research and development must be split among a wider range of activities. This might also explain the declining benefits of research and development.

Field of Research

Carlino and Hunt are to be commended for breaking down research and development into component fields. Here, their results are somewhat anomalous. Computer science appears to be the worst field for innovation, while sociology is the best.

More important, it is possible to break the patents into classes of technology, and I encourage the authors to probe such estimates further in future work. At a substantive level, it would be interesting to see if research in a field is particularly associated with patents in that field. In this way, it would be possible to construct an input-output matrix showing which fields patents draw on. This might also do something to address concerns with causality, which I will turn to next, insofar as one could check that research and development in a field is related to patents in the "right" fields.

Additional Thoughts

Carlino and Hunt are aware that there are causality issues with the analysis. To address causality concerns in their population and density estimates, they use instruments for employment and job densities based on lags of job density, education, and population, as well as miles of planned highways. The authors also do not address concerns with endogeneity in their research and development variables. I think that this component of the project is one of the most important, and I encourage them to think about instrumental variables strategies for addressing endogeneity in research and development in their framework.

One way in which academic institutions would affect innovation locally would be through their effect on the education of the population. The reported estimates control for the education of the population, giving the partial relationship between academic research and development and innovation while holding constant the education of the population. In private communication, the authors have indicated that estimates that do not control for the education distribution of the population are not substantially higher. This result is interesting in that it indicates that the primary effect of universities does not operate through the education of the population. Of course, highly educated workers are highly mobile, weakening the link between the presence of universities and the education of the local population (although Saha 2007 does find such a link). Also, it is not clear from these estimates whether there are spillovers from education or whether the estimates simply reflect the individual-level relationship between education and innovation.

Put together, Carlino and Hunt's piece represents a valuable contribution to our understanding of the factors that determine knowledge production locally. The analysis of university activity is particularly valuable and timely and ripe for additional work.

References

Acs, Zoltan 2002. *Innovation and the Growth of Cities.* Cheltenham, United Kingdom: Edward Elgar.

Agrawal, Ajay, and Iain Cockburn. 2003. "The Anchor Tenant Hypothesis: Exploring the Role of Large, Local, R&D-Intensive Firms in Regional Innovation Systems." *International Journal of Industrial Organization* 21 (9): 1217–153.

Agrawal, Ajay, Devesh Kapur, and John McHale. 2008. "How Do Spatial and Social Proximity Influence Knowledge Flows? Evidence from Patent Data." *Journal of Urban Economics* 64 (2): 258–69.

Andersson, Roland, John M. Quigley, and Mats Wilhelmsson. 2005. "Higher Education, Localization and Innovation: Evidence from a Natural Experiment." Working Paper 26. Stockholm: Centre of Excellence for Science and Innovation Studies.

Anselin, Luc. 1990. "Some Robust Approaches to Testing and Estimation in Spatial Econometrics." *Regional Science and Urban Economics* 20 (2): 141–63.

Anselin, Luc, and Sheri Hudak. 1992. "Spatial Econometrics in Practice: A Review of Software Options." *Regional Science and Urban Economics* 22 (3): 509–36.

Anselin, Luc, Attila Varga, and Zoltan Acs. 1997. "Local Geographic Spillovers between University and High Technology Innovations." *Journal of Urban Economics* 42 (3): 422–48.

Arzaghi, Mohammad, and J. Vernon Henderson. 2005. "Networking off Madison Avenue." Mimeo. Brown University.

Audretsch, David B., and Maryann P. Feldman. 1996. "R&D Spillovers and the Geography of Innovation and Production." *American Economic Review* 86 (3): 630–40.

———. 2004. "Knowledge Spillovers and the Geography of Innovation." In *Handbook of Regional and Urban Economics*, vol. 4: *Cities and Geography*, edited by J. V. Henderson and J-F. Thisse, pp. 2713–739. Amsterdam: North-Holland.

Berliant, Marcus, Robert R. Reed III, and Ping Wang. 2006. "Knowledge Exchange, Matching, and Agglomeration." *Journal of Urban Economics* 60 (1): 69–95.

Bessen, James and Robert M. Hunt. 2007. "An Empirical Look at Software Patents." *Journal of Economics and Management Strategy* 16 (1): 157–89.

Black, Duncan, and J. Vernon Henderson. 2003. "Urban Evolution in the USA." *Journal of Economic Geography* 3 (4): 343–72.

Bureau of Economic Analysis. 1999. Regional Economic Information System (REIS). Washington: U.S. Department of Commerce.

Carlino, Gerald A., Satyajit Chatterjee, and Robert M. Hunt. 2007. "Urban Density and the Rate of Invention." *Journal of Urban Economics* 61 (3): 389–419.

Carlino, Gerald A. and Robert M. Hunt. 2007. "Innovation across U.S. Industries: The Effects of Local Economic Characteristics." Working Paper 07-28. Federal Reserve Bank of Philadelphia.

Carlino, Gerald A., and Albert Saiz. 2008. "City Beautiful." Working Paper 08-22. Federal Reserve Bank of Philadelphia.

Ciccone, Antonio, and Robert E. Hall. 1996. "Productivity and the Density of Economic Activity." *American Economic Review* 86 (1): 54–70.

Chinitz, Benjamin. 1961. "Contrasts in Agglomeration: New York and Pittsburgh." *American Economic Review* 51 (2): 279–89, Papers and Proceedings of the Seventy-Third Annual Meeting of the American Economic Association.

Cohen, Wesley M., Richard R. Nelson, and John P. Walsh. 2000. "Protecting Their Intellectual Assets: Appropriability Conditions and Why U.S. Manufacturing Firms Patent (or Not)." NBER Working Paper 7552. Cambridge, Mass.: National Bureau of Economic Analysis.

Combes, Pierre-Philippe, Gilles Duranton, Laurent Gobillon, and Sébastien Roux. 2008. "Estimating Agglomeration Economies with History, Geology, and Worker Effects." Discussion Paper 6728. London: Center for Economic Policy Research.

De Figueiredo, John M., and Brian S. Silverman. 2006. "Academic Earmarks and the Returns to Lobbying." *Journal of Law and Economics* 49 (2): 597–625.

———. 2007. "How Does the Government (Want to) Fund Science? Politics, Lobbying and Academic Earmarks." NBER Working Paper 13459. Cambridge, Mass.: National Bureau of Economic Analysis.

Directory of American Research and Technology. 1988. 23rd ed. New York: R.R. Bowker.

Duranton, Giles, and Diego Puga. 2004. "Micro-Foundations of Urban Agglomeration Economies." In *Handbook of Regional and Urban Economics*, vol. 4: *Cities and Geography*, edited by J. V. Henderson and J.-F. Thisse, pp. 2063–117. Amsterdam: North-Holland.

Eberts, Randall W., and Daniel P. McMillen. 1999. "Agglomeration Economies and Urban Public Infrastructure." In *Handbook of Regional and Urban Economics*, vol. 3: *Applied Urban Economics*, edited by P. Cheshire and E. Mills, pp. 1455–495. New York: Elsevier Science.

Feldman, Maryann P., and David. B. Audretsch. 1999. "Innovation in Cities: Science-Based Diversity, Specialization and Localized Competition." *European Economic Review* 43 (2): 409–29.

Florida, Richard. 2002. *The Rise of the Creative Class: And How It's Transforming Work, Leisure, Community and Everyday Life.* New York: Basic Books.

Gambardella, Alfonso, Dietmar Harhoff, and Bart Verspagen. 2008. "The Value of European Patents." Discussion Paper 6848. London: Center for Economic Policy Research.

Glaeser, Edward L. 1999. "Learning in Cities." *Journal of Urban Economics* 46 (2): 254–77.

Glaeser, Edward L., Heidi D. Kallal, Jose A. Scheinkman, and Andrei Shleifer. 1992. "Growth in Cities." *Journal of Political Economy* 100 (6): 1126–152.

Griliches, Zvi. 1990. "Patent Statistics as Economic Indicators: A Survey." *Journal of Economic Literature* 28 (4): 1661–707.

Hall, Bronwyn H., Adam B. Jaffe, and Manuel Trajtenberg. 2001. "The NBER Patent Citations Data File: Lessons, Insights and Methodological Tools." NBER Working Paper 8498. Cambridge, Mass.: National Bureau of Economic Analysis.

———. 2005. "Market Value and Patent Citations." *RAND Journal of Economics* 36 (1): 16–38.

Harhoff, Dietmar, Francis Narin, F. M. Scherer, and Katrin Vopel. 1999. "Citation Frequency and the Value of Patented Inventions." *Review of Economics and Statistics* 81 (3): 511–15.

Harhoff, Dietmar, F. M. Scherer, and Katrin Vopel. 2003. "Citations, Family Size, Opposition and the Value of Patent Rights." *Research Policy* 32 (8): 1343–363.

Hegde, Deepak, and David C. Mowery. 2008. "Politics and Funding in the U.S. Public Biomedical R&D System." *Science* 322 (5909): 1797–798.

Helsley, Robert W., and William C. Strange. 2002. "Innovation and Input Sharing." *Journal of Urban Economics* 51 (1): 25–45.

———. 2004. "Knowledge Barter in Cities." *Journal of Urban Economics* 56 (2): 327–45.

Hunt, Robert M. 2007. "Matching Externalities and Inventive Productivity." Working Paper 07-7. Federal Reserve Bank of Philadelphia.

Jacobs, Jane. 1969. *The Economy of Cities*. New York: Vintage Books.

Jaffe, Adam B. 1989. "Real Effects of Academic Research." *American Economic Review* 79 (5): 957–70.

Jaffe, Adam B., Manuel Trajtenberg, and Michael S. Fogarty. 2000. "Knowledge Spillovers and Patent Citations: Evidence from a Survey of Inventors." *American Economic Review* 90 (2): 215–18, Papers and Proceedings of the Hundred Thirteenth Annual Meeting of the American Economic Association.

Jaffe, Adam B., Manuel Trajtenberg, and Rebecca Henderson. 1993. "Geographic Localization of Knowledge Spillovers as Evidenced by Patent Citations." *Quarterly Journal of Economics* 108 (3): 577–98.

Jones, Lyle V., Gardner Lindzey, and Porter E. Coggeshall. 1982. *An Assessment of Research-Doctorate Programs in the United States: Engineering*. Washington: National Academies Press.

Law, Marc T., and Joseph M. Tonon. 2006. "The Strange Budgetary Politics of Agricultural Research Earmarks." *Public Budgeting & Finance* 26 (3): 1–21.

Mervis, Jeffrey. 2008. "Building a Scientific Legacy on a Controversial Foundation." *Science* 321 (5888): 480–83.

Mills, Edward S., and Bruce W. Hamilton. 1994. *Urban Economics*. New York: Harper Collins College Publishers.

National Science Foundation (NSF). 2006. *Federal Funds for Research and Development: Fiscal Years 2003–05*. NSF 06-313. Arlington, Virginia.

Ó hUallacháin, Breandán. 1999. "Patent Places: Size Matters." *Journal of Regional Science* 39 (4): 613–36.

Payne, Abigail A. 2002. Do US Congressional Earmarks Increase Research Output at Universities?" *Science and Public Policy* 29 (5): 314–30.

———. 2006. "Earmarks and EPSCoR: Shaping the Distribution, Quality, and Quantity of University Research." In *Shaping Science and Technology Policy: The Next Generation of Research*, edited by David Guston and Daniel Sarewitz. University of Wisconsin Press.

Romer, Paul M. 1990. "Endogenous Technological Change." *Journal of Political Economy* 98 (5): S71–S102.

Rosenthal, Stuart S. and William C. Strange. 2001. "The Determinants of Agglomeration." *Journal of Urban Economics* 50 (2): 191–229.

———. 2004. "Evidence on the Nature and Sources of Agglomeration Economies." In *Handbook of Urban and Regional Economics*, vol. 4: *Cities and Geography*, edited by J. V. Henderson and J-F. Thisse, pp. 2119–171. Amsterdam: North-Holland.

Saha, Subhra B. 2007. "Economic Effects of Colleges and Universities." Working Paper. Ohio State University.

Savage, James D. 1999. *Funding Science in America: Congress, Universities, and the Politics of Academic Pork Barrel*. Cambridge University Press.

Sedgley, Norman, and Bruce Elmslie. 2004. "The Geographic Concentration of Knowledge: Scale, Agglomeration, and Congestion in Innovation across U.S. States." *International Regional Science Review* 27 (2): 111–37.

Staiger, Douglas and James H. Stock. 1997. "Instrumental Variables Regression with Weak Instruments." *Econometrica* 65 (3): 557–86.

Stock James H., and Motohiro Yogo. 2005. "Testing for Weak Instruments in Linear IV Regression." In *Identification and Inference for Econometric Models: A Festschrift in Honor of Thomas Rothenberg*, edited by J. H. Stock and D. W. K. Andrews, pp. 80–108. Cambridge University Press.

Trajtenberg, Manuel. 1990. "A Penny for Your Quotes: Patent Citations and the Value of Innovations." *RAND Journal of Economics* 21 (1): 172–87.

U.S. Census Bureau. 1991. "County Business Patterns, 1989." U.S. Government Printing Office.

———. 1994. *Geographic Areas Reference Manual* (www.census.gov/geo/www/garm.html).

Webb, Colin, Hélène Dernis, Dietmar Harhoff, and Karin Hoisl. 2005. "Analyzing European and International Patent Citations: A Set of EPO Patent Database Building Blocks." OECD STI Working Paper2005/9. Paris: Organization for Economic Cooperation and Development.

Wheeler, Christopher H. 2001. "Search, Sorting, and Urban Agglomeration." *Journal of Labor Economics* 19 (4): 879–99.

Weinberg, Bruce A. 2008. "Scientific Revolutionaries: Geography, Vintage, and Participation in Scientific Revolutions." Working Paper. Ohio State University.

Zucker, Lynne G., Michael R. Darby, and Marilynn B. Brewer. 1998. "Intellectual Human Capital and the Birth of U.S. Biotechnology Enterprises." *American Economic Review* 88 (1): 209–306.

ELEONORA PATACCHINI
University of Rome "La Sapienza"

YVES ZENOU
Stockholm University
Research Institute of Industrial Economics, IFN

Urban Sprawl in Europe

Changes in urban forms and development patterns are crucial to understanding the role of cities as engines of growth. Urban sprawl is usually defined as the spreading of a city and its suburbs over rural land at the fringe of an urban area. Urban planners emphasize the qualitative aspects of sprawl such as the lack of transportation options and pedestrian-friendly neighborhoods. Conservationists tend to focus on the actual amount of land that has been urbanized by sprawl.

Although urban sprawl has been extensively studied in the United States (see, for example, Brueckner 2000, 2001; Glaeser and Kahn 2001, 2004; Nechyba and Walsh 2004), very few empirical studies have been undertaken in Europe. Basic reasons for this lack of research are the conceptual divergences in the U.S. and European geographical definitions of cities and the limitations in the availability of actual data for Europe.

Urban sprawl is one of the most important types of land use changes currently affecting Europe. It increasingly creates major impacts on the environment (via surface sealing, emissions by transport, and ecosystem fragmentation), on the social structure of an area (by segregation, lifestyle changes, and neglect of urban centers), and on the economy (via distributed production, land prices, and issues of scale). It is therefore crucial to understand it better.

During the second half of the twentieth century, urban sprawl has become a mass phenomenon throughout the Western world. Although suburbanization took also place in Europe during the postwar period, its dimensions were by far less expansive than in the United States. In the 1950s, numerous European countries were concerned about reshaping their cities. Besides, a lot of countries had been decimated by the war, and many large cities such as Berlin,

We are grateful to participants in the 2008 Brookings-Wharton Conference on Urban Affairs and, in particular, to Jan Brueckner, Gary Burtless, Denis Epple, Vernon Henderson, and Janet Rothenberg Pack for valuable and helpful comments.

125

Vienna, Glasgow, and Birmingham were stagnating, or even lost population (Bruegmann 2005). The postwar period in the United States, on the contrary, was characterized by economic prosperity and a vast population growth (Burchfield and others 2006). Within less than twenty years, the U.S. population increased by 50 million people from 150 million in 1950 to 200 million in 1968 (Couch, Leontidou, and Arnstberg 2007). Some cities were even growing to a faster degree. In the same period, the Los Angeles area more than doubled from under 4 million to more than 8 million people. The Phoenix urbanized area grew almost fourfold, the San Jose area more than fivefold. In Europe, there was generally less growth in urban areas and therefore less pressure to develop the countryside. Besides, urban expansion was usually highly regulated. Planners and other government officials were able to intervene in city development more actively than their U.S. counterparts. In Paris, for example, large parts of suburban settlements consisted of high-density houses that were directly built by governmental bodies or were at least highly subsidized. This procedure was not common in the United States, where the private-market, single-family home was the norm.

As long as the American metaphor has not been replaced by a European one, it will shape the perception of many Europeans. In fact, remarkably little research has been done on the development of a "European" model (at least from economists). As stated above, this is mainly due to the scarce availability of data on indicators of urban performance such as urban amenities, housing, job opportunities, skills, and economic structure that limit the research possibilities in the European Union.

In this paper, we use a recently available dataset, the Urban Audit, which claims that it contains information on more than 300 variables for 258 towns and cities in the European Union's fifteen member states and its twelve eastern European candidate countries, measured at three different points in time: in 1991 (or in the period 1989–93), in 1996 (or in 1994–98), and in 2001 (or in 1999–2003).[1] Unfortunately, the effective information delivered is much more limited. Its coverage is rather poor. For several countries, many indicators are not provided, and missing values do not generally occur for the same cities across variables (even though data coverage does improve over the course of the decade). Nevertheless, collection of some evidence on urban differences is possible, in indicators such as population size, density, economic conditions, human capital, and amenities in the European context.

---

1. The Urban Audit is a rather new dataset from Eurostat, the statistical office of the European Union. For information on this dataset, see ⟨http://ec.europa.eu/regional_policy/conferences/urbanaudit2008/programme_en.htm⟩.

As will be discussed in the following section, there is no effective and standard definition of the concept of a city in Europe. We qualify the evidence contained in this paper as evidence on urban sprawl in Europe. Such an analysis, however, is by no means comparable with similar studies in the United States, as this would require standardized definitions and data not yet available in Europe. We use this terminology to document broad patterns of growth and decline of European cities and their correlation with factors considered as the main determinant of urban sprawls in the United States.

The plan of the paper is as follows. We will first discuss the differences between the U.S. and European geographical definitions of cities, highlighting the conceptual divergences and limitations in the availability of data for Europe (next section). Next, in the third section, we review the main theoretical mechanisms that cause urban sprawl, for the United States and for Europe. The fourth section presents some descriptive evidence on urban growth and decline in Europe. It also contains some simple regressions documenting correlations between the changes in population density and in variables typically advocated by the theory as the main determinants of urban sprawl. We continue our analysis in the fifth section with an investigation on the different characteristics of European cities using a principal component analysis. This exercise is based on the more comprehensive information provided by the Urban Audit for 2001. The final section concludes.

Comparing the European and U.S. City Definitions

Over the last few decades, a large number of comparable data on U.S. metropolitan areas have been produced. The U.S. metropolitan areas approach identifies a set of counties, known as central counties, that form an urbanized central "core," defined on the basis of population. A wider geographical entity is then defined as the core plus its connected urban areas, known as outlying counties. An outlying county is such that 25 percent of its employed workforce commutes into the central counties or 25 percent of the people that work in such an outlying county travel into it from the core or that both situations are occurring.

Conceptually the Urban Audit approach as conducted by Eurostat is similar to that of the U.S. metropolitan areas approach, but in practice there are fundamental differences on what a core and connected areas are. In the United States, the core is functionally defined by its level of population settlement; the European system, however, does not have an equivalent. The basic unit is the *administrative city*, which approximately corresponds to the U.S. *incorporated place*. The Urban Audit also defines a larger urban zone (LUZ) as the functional urban region containing one (or more) administrative cities, which, in principle, should correspond to the U.S. functional urban region (FUR). However, the rules of whether to include a region into a functional urban region are different from those in the United States. First, such an inclusion is defined only in terms of commuting into the administrative city (thus excluding out-commuting). Second, commuting thresholds are not well specified, thereby giving national statistical agencies considerable discretion in the data collection process. In addition, the actual rules used by the different countries are not known, thus introducing serious concerns about data comparability.

Another fundamental difference between U.S. and European urban statistics is that the U.S. metropolitan areas approach uniformly adopts the county as the statistical building block. The European standard for the definition of regions is called the Nomenclature of Territorial Units for Statistics (NUTS in French). NUTS is a hierarchical classification system that is the basis for collecting European regional statistics. The level of the largest regions is called NUTS1 and contains a number of NUTS2 regions, which, in turn, contain NUTS3 regions and so on down to NUTS5. Contrary to the system in the United States, the NUTS system cannot readily be used to construct LUZ data on a uniform basis because the data available for the different European countries are at different NUTS levels. The Urban Audit approach is thus forced to use a system mixing NUTS3, NUTS4, or NUTS5 areas as basic units for different countries. This introduces further concerns about the use of LUZ data.

In the United States, defining and collecting data about cities is part of the legal framework. The geographical definitions are established by federal law, are available to the public, and are the basis for clear rule-governed methods for calculated benchmarked statistics. The Urban Audit is not yet part of the legal European statistical framework, and its methods are not all fully available.

It is also important to observe that the U.S. definitions have changed over time and continue to evolve, suggesting that the task of standardization requires a great deal of work and time. When data collection on metropolitan areas began in the late 1940s, its core or central place was a city defined by its administrative boundary, as it is now in Europe. However, European cities are older, with longer traditions and with more complex political histories relative to U.S. cities. While U.S. economists now associate a city to a metropolitan area, the European economist still has in mind the political or administrative definition of the city.

The original aim of the Urban Audit project was to delineate cities according to their functional boundaries (irrespective of administrative units) and to give information on the relation between the city and its hinterland as well as on inner-city disparities. At the present time, however, only administrative units have sufficient data. As a result, in this paper, we define a city to be the equivalent of the core in the U.S. metropolitan area definition, on the basis of its administrative boundaries. A variation over time of the land area occupied by the city may thus reflect a redefinition of administrative units. Even though neither the rules nor the timing of such a process for the different European countries are clear, changes in the socioeconomic characteristics of the urban area are likely to be important, if not decisive, factors.

As clearly stated in the introduction, our investigation on urban sprawl in Europe contained in the next sections is by no means comparable to similar studies made in the United States, as this would require standardized definitions and data not yet available in Europe. Rather, we use this terminology to document broad patterns of growth and decline of core European cities and their correlation with factors considered as the main determinant of urban sprawl in the United States. Our conjecture is that such trends might also reflect changes in city decentralization processes in the European context. These issues, however, remain to be verified.

What Causes Urban Sprawl?

In the standard monocentric framework (Brueckner 1987; Fujita 1989; Zenou 2009), firms are all located in one location (the central business district, or CBD) while individuals and workers have to decide where to reside between the CBD and the city fringe. This creates a trade-off situation for workers between locations close to jobs where housing prices are high but commuting costs are low and locations far away from the CBD when the reverse occurs. In this model, urban sprawl is measured by population density or the city fringes or both, which are both endogenous and depend on the (endogenous) housing size. A clear implication of that model is that a reduction of commuting cost will cause urban sprawl. As a result, access to cars, which reduces commuting costs, could be a good predictor for urban sprawl. This line of research is strongly pushed by Glaeser and Kahn (2004). Also, as income rises, families desire to live in larger apartments or houses (if housing is a normal good) and will therefore reside at the periphery of the city. Similarly, since income is correlated to employment, a higher employment rate will also cause urban sprawl.[2]

2. For a formal analysis of the comparative statics results of the monocentric city model, see Wheaton (1974); Brueckner (1987).

The monocentric framework can be extended to incorporate racial segregation and crime. In the first case, black (or any other "visible" ethnic minority) and white workers will locate in different areas of the city depending on the assumptions of the model. If one considers the United States where ethnic minorities tend to reside in the city center (see, for example, Rose-Ackerman 1975; Yinger 1976), then the higher the percentage of ethnic minorities in a given area, the higher is urban sprawl. This is the result of the so-called white flight process when whites move to the suburbs to avoid living with the ethnic minority population. Thus, inner-city residents may wish to leave central cities not because they seek to form or join a particular (more homogeneous) suburb but rather to escape inner-city problems.

In a European monocentric-city model, in which ethnic minorities tend to live in the suburbs, this relationship between the percentage of ethnic minorities in a given city and urban sprawl will be negative (and not positive as in the U.S. case) because whites will, on the contrary, move to the city center to avoid living with ethnic minorities (see Selod and Zenou 2006, who analyze both the U.S. and the European cases).

One can also incorporate crime in the monocentric framework (see Freeman, Grogger, and Sonstelie 1996) with ethnic minorities (Verdier and Zenou 2004). The predictions will be the same and even more pronounced because ethnic minorities are overrepresented in criminal activities. This will result again in the "flight from blight," meaning that high-income white residents leave the central city in response to higher inner-city crime rates (but also lower quality schools and general fiscal distress within the central business district).[3] For example, Cullen and Levitt (1999) found that a 10 percent increase in crime corresponds to a 1 percent decline in central city population.

Introducing nonmonocentric cities (see Ogawa and Fujita 1982; Fujita, Thisse, and Zenou 1997; Henderson and Mitra 1999) will basically not change these results, even if the labor market is explicitly introduced (as in Smith and Zenou 1997; Coulson, Laing, and Wang 2001; Brueckner and Zenou 2003). For example, in the duocentric model of Brueckner and Zenou (2003), blacks tend mostly to reside close to the CBD because of housing discrimination, while whites tend to reside in the suburbs.

To summarize, there are five main causes of urban sprawl:

---

3. From a theoretical viewpoint, the impact of local property taxes on urban sprawl has been studied by Brueckner and Kim (2003) and Song and Zenou (2006) in a monocentric framework and by Song and Zenou (2009) in a duocentric model.

—Access to the automobile, by reducing commuting costs, allows individuals and workers to commute further away from jobs and thus causes urban sprawl.

—An increase in income induces families to live in larger housing and thus causes urban sprawl because land is cheaper in the suburbs.

—An increase in the employment rate increases urban sprawl because employment is positively correlated with income. Employment and income should therefore lead to the same results.

—An increase in the percentage of ethnic minorities in cities leads to more urban sprawl in the United States and less in Europe. Indeed, white families dislike residing close to ethnic minorities and thus desire to live further away from them. Since ethnic minorities mostly live in city centers in the United States and in the suburbs in Europe, an increase in the percentage of ethnic minorities will increase urban sprawl in the United States and reduce it in Europe.

—Higher crime rates increase urban sprawl in the United States but decrease it in Europe because white families move away from areas where crime is high. These high-crime areas are located in city centers in the United States and in the suburbs in Europe.

Observe that the first, second, and third cases lead to the same predictions for U.S. and European cities, while the fourth and fifth cases yield different predictions.

Evidence on Urban Sprawl in Europe

There are different ways of measuring urban sprawl (see, in particular, Galster and others 2001; Nechyba and Walsh 2004; Glaeser and Kahn 2004). The standard definition of sprawl is the "tendency towards lower city densities as city footprints expand" (Nechyba and Walsh 2004). Urban sprawl can take different forms. It may involve low-density residential developments. It can also take the form of planned communities. In any case, a common way to document the presence of urban sprawl over time is to look within urban areas at the evolving relationship between suburbs and central cities. As discussed in the previous section, the available LUZ data are limited, which prevents us from performing such a direct analysis in the European context. Therefore, we will adopt here a very narrow and limited view of urban sprawl. Indeed, we will essentially measure urban sprawl by the variation over time of the total land area and the population density of a given city. In the following sections, we exploit the Urban Audit dataset on the evolution of European cities, first to present some descriptive statistics, then to document some correlations between patterns of city growth and changes over time in specific variables, and finally to use a principal component analysis on the data from 2001, which is the year with the most extensive coverage.

Descriptive Statistics

We start by providing some simple evidence on the evolution of the cities of the European Union. We characterize broad patterns of growth and decline of European cities by using the following city-level indicators: "population," that is, the total population residing in a given city; "working-age population," that is, the total working-age population residing in a given city; "land area" (or urban size), which is the total land area in a given city; "population density," that is, the ratio of total resident population to total land area in a given city; and "working-age population density," the ratio of resident working-age population to total land area in a given city.

The variables are expressed in growth rates between 1991 and 2001.[4] Table 1 collects some descriptive statistics.[5]

Table 1 shows that the average growth in population size of European cities (around 0.34 percent) is much lower than that of U.S. cities (an average of 10 percent) during roughly the same period (Glaeser and Shapiro 2003). This is probably due to the lower mobility of European workers and the still-limited in-flows of non-EU citizens. This is also certainly due to the incredibly low (and declining) birth rate in most European countries.[6] Indeed, when the working-age population is considered instead of the total population then the average growth is higher, although it remains below 2 percent during the period 1991–2001. Despite such a limited growth in population size, the average EU city expanded in area size by about 7.5 percent during that period and decreased its population density by roughly 2.6 percent.

---

4. Missing values for the year 1991 have been replaced with values at 1996 in the cases where such information is available.

5. We will provide some evidence on the variables in levels (that is, not transformed in growth rates) in the fourth section below.

6. Urban growth in the EU appears to be largely driven by growth of the native-born population, and differences in birth rates between cities are found to be an important explanation of the observed differences in (native-born) population growth rates. Nonnative-European-born and non-European-born migrants contribute only marginally to urban growth differences (Bosker and Marlet 2006). The volume of U.S. interregional migration is 15 times higher than that in the EU (Cheshire and Magrini 2006).

Table 1. Urban Growth for all EU cities, 1991–2001

Variable in growth rate (percent)	Obs.	Mean	Std. Dev.	Min.	Max.
Population	263	0.34	8.28	−22.27	37.81
Working-age population	242	1.69	10.13	−23.23	44.79
Population density	160	−2.56	15.68	−79.55	85.04
Working-age population density	160	−2.08	15.47	−78.46	51.36
Land area	188	7.46	44.01	−29.73	497.18

Source: Authors' calculations of the Urban Audit (European Commission 2004) (http://ec.europa.eu/regional_policy/conferences/urbanaudit2008/programme_en.htm).

Table 2. Urban Growth for the Largest EU Cities, 1991–2001[a]

Variable in growth rate (percent)	Obs.	Mean	Std. Dev.	Min.	Max.
Population	76	−1.05	6.33	−16.14	16.90
Working-age population	69	−0.20	7.86	−17.71	17.75
Population density	48	−3.18	7.67	−34.80	12.96
Working-age population density	69	−0.20	7.86	−17.71	17.75
Land area	59	0.30	6.63	−25.72	39.97

Source: Authors' calculations of the Urban Audit (European Commission 2004) (http://ec.europa.eu/regional_policy/conferences/urbanaudit2008/programme_en.htm).
a. These EU cities are in the top quartile of population size.

Table 3. Urban Growth for the Smallest EU Cities, 1991–2001[a]

Variable in growth rate (percent)	Obs.	Mean	Std. Dev.	Min.	Max.
Population	57	2.47	10.59	−22.27	37.81
Working-age population	55	5.27	13.01	−23.23	44.79
Population density	38	−5.24	21.03	−79.55	19.04
Working-age population density	55	5.35	13.01	−23.23	44.79
Land area	39	23.28	89.90	−25.74	497.18

Source: Authors' calculations of the Urban Audit (European Commission 2004) (http://ec.europa.eu/regional_policy/conferences/urbanaudit2008/programme_en.htm).
a. These EU cities are in the bottom quartile of population size.

The feature of the urban growth experiences of European cities that is common to U.S. cities is their substantial heterogeneity. Indeed, table 1 shows that the fastest growing city saw almost a 40 percent increase in its population over the period 1991–2001, whereas the slowest growing city decreased by more than 20 percent

Given the heterogeneity of growth rates between cities, the relevant question is then what are the cities that spread more and why? If we split the cities according to their population size (tables 2 and 3), we find that urban sprawl is much stronger for cities at the bottom tail of the distribution than for the more populated ones. Table 2 indeed reveals that the largest European cities experienced, on average, a negative population growth and an extremely limited increase in urban land area. On the contrary, table 3, which focuses on the

Table 4. Urban Growth for the Top 5 percent of the Largest European Cities, 1991
Percent

City	Country	Population	Working-age population	Population density	Working-age population density	Land area
Prague	Czech Rep.	−3.71	2.41	−3.71	2.41	0
Berlin	Germany	−2.23	−0.26	−2.53	−0.56	0.30
Hamburg	Germany	2.22	1.82	2.18	1.78	0.04
Munich	Germany	−2.28	−4.40	−2.43	−4.54	0.15
Madrid	Spain	−2.38	n.a.	−2.25	2.40	−0.14
Barcelona	Spain	−8.41	n.a.	−8.16	−0.33	−0.27
Paris	France	−1.26	−0.30	n.a.	n.a.	0
Rome	Italy	−8.23	−13.23	7.03	1.20	−0.14
Milan	Italy	−8.25	−14.66	−8.47	−14.86	0.23
Budapest	Hungary	−11.83	−8.35	−11.85	−8.35	−0.002
Wien	Austria	0.67	2.24	0.66	2.24	0
Warsaw	Poland	2.03	5.45	0.18	3.53	1.86
Bucharest	Romania	−8.08	−5.62	n.a.	n.a.	n.a.
London	U.K.	5.02	6.86	n.a.	n.a.	n.a.

Source: Authors' calculations of the Urban Audit (European Commission 2004) (http://ec.europa.eu/regional_policy/conferences/urbanaudit2008/programme_en.htm).
n.a. Not available.

lower tail of the distribution of cities in terms of population, shows an average of 2.5 percent increase in population growth and a considerable land area growth of around 23 percent.

To better understand this simple evidence, we then look in more detail at the extent of urban growth for the top 5 percent of the largest European cities (table 4) and for the cities that grew most in area size (table 5).

Table 4 shows that half of the most populated European cities experienced no or even negative growth in area size, whereas table 5 reveals that the cities that spread more are less populated cities (most of them with a population below the median of the population distribution). Interestingly, more than half of those cities are located in Greece, and of the remaining four, two are in France and two in Lithuania). Most of these Greek cities are also the ones that display substantial population growth rates.

The distribution of European cities in terms of agglomeration has decreased in mean and dispersion during those ten years, although the decrease has not been substantial and the ordering remains almost the same.[7] Table 6 shows that the top 5 percent of the most dense cities in 1991 are still within the top 5 percent of the distribution of population density in 2001, with the addition of

7. The means and standard deviations (in parentheses) of population density are 2,444 (2893.631) and 2,233.38 (2629.09) for 1991 and 2001, respectively.

Table 5. Urban Growth for Cities that Grew the Most in Area Size
Percent

City	Country	Population	Working-age population	Population density	Working-age population density	Land area
Patras	Greece	10.22	15.55	−49.95	−47.53	20.21
Heraklion	Greece	18.02	25.57	−43.16	−39.52	107.64
Larissa	Greece	16.13	21.29	−16.38	−12.68	38.89
Kavala	Greece	18.56	22.81	−59.93	−58.49	195.88
Volos	Greece	5.62	4.05	−64.85	−65.38	200.54
Kalamata	Greece	22.11	28.62	−79.55	−78.46	497.18
Clermont-Ferrand	France	1.81	1.20	n.a.	n.a.	62.33
Grenoble	France	2.25	1.00	n.a.	n.a.	44.07
Panevezys	Lithuania	−6.77	−5.86	−45.10	−44.57	69.83
Vilnius	Lithuania	−8.74	−4.47	−34.800	−31.75	39.97

Source: Authors' calculations of the Urban Audit (European Commission 2004) (http://ec.europa.eu/regional_policy/conferences/urbanaudit2008/programme_en.htm).
n.a. Not available.

Table 6. Urban Agglomeration in EU Cities

5 percent of the cities with the highest population density		5 percent of the cities with the lowest population density	
1991	*2001*	*1991*	*2001*
Athens	Athens	Toledo	Toledo
Thessaloniki	Thessaloniki	Badajoz	Badajoz
Barcelona	Barcelona	Perugia	Perugia
Pamplona	Pamplona	L'Aquila	L'Aquila
Milano	Milano	Sassari	Sassari
Napoli	Napoli	Ponta Delgada	Ponta Delgada
Torino	Torino	Jönköping	Jönköping
Lisbon	Lisbon	Umeå	Umeå
	Brussels		Kalamata
	Geneva		Ajaccio
	Porto		

Source: Authors' calculations of the Urban Audit (European Commission 2004) (http://ec.europa.eu/regional_policy/conferences/urbanaudit2008/programme_en.htm).

Brussels, Geneva, and Porto and the least dense cities in 1991 remain within the bottom 5 percent, with the addition of Kalamata and Ajaccio.

Some Simple Regressions

In this section, we exploit our data as much as possible in an attempt to test the predictions highlighted in section two. Namely, we would like to see whether patterns of growth or decline in European cities (as measured here by the

Table 7. OLS Estimation Results[a]

Variable	(1)	(2)	(3)	(4)	(5)
Car access	−0.1281***				−0.2155***
	(0.0341)				(0.0317)
Non-EU population		0.0071*			0.0363***
		(0.0041)			(0.0098)
Crime rate			0.0142		0.0172
			(0.0220)		0.0298
Real GDP per capita	−0.0181	−0.0737*	−0.0566*	−0.0521	−0.2937***
	(0.0531)	(0.0425)	(0.0342)	(0.0332)	(0.0690)
Employment rate	−0.3495***	−0.1033	−0.0385	−0.0383	−0.5522***
	(0.1062)	(0.0728)	(0.0488)	(0.0453)	(0.1209)
Population size	0.5603***	0.8059***	0.8399***	0.8376***	0.6082***
	(0.1215)	(0.0846)	(0.0719)	(0.0701)	(0.1171)
Obs.	41	57	72	74	30
R^2	0.60	0.65	0.70	0.70	0.83

Source: Authors' calculations of the Urban Audit (European Commission 2004) (http://ec.europa.eu/regional_policy/conferences/urbanaudit2008/programme_en.htm).
OLS = ordinary least squares.
***Significant at the .01 level; **significant at the .05 level; *significant at the .10 level.
a. The dependent variable is "urban population density growth." Each column reports a separate OLS regression. Standard errors are in parentheses.

growth rate of population density) is positively correlated to an increase in car ownership, income, and employment and negatively correlated to an increase in the percentage of ethnic minorities (as measured by the percentage of non-European citizens) and in the crime rate.

Table 7 presents our regression analysis results. To prevent data loss, we first include each of the key variables in turn as explanatory variables of urban sprawl and then use all of them together.[8] Growth rate differences in population, income, and employment are accounted for in all regressions.

Table 7 documents evidence in line with our theoretical predictions for the European context (section 2). First, in line with the U.S. evidence, the estimated effect of income and employment is always negative. It is often also statistically significant. This means that richer people (either in terms of income or employment) tend to consume more land, which increases urban sprawl (and thus decreases population density). As predicted, the effect of car access is also in line with the U.S. evidence. Indeed, the higher the growth rate in the percentage of registered cars, the higher is urban sprawl (that is, the lower is the population density growth rate). This is clearly because workers are ready to accept jobs located further away because of a more rapid transportation mode. This may indicate that workers follow jobs when they decentralize. The effect

8. As mentioned in the introduction, missing values are a severe limitation of our dataset, in particular because they generally do not occur for the same cities across variables.

is statistically significant and nonnegligible in magnitude. Indeed, a 1 percent increase in the growth rate of car access is associated with an approximate 0.13 percent decrease in the growth rate of population density. Concerning the effect of ethnic minorities, we find that the higher the percentage of non-European residents is, the lower is urban sprawl, confirming our theoretical intuition about European cities. This is interesting since most U.S. studies obtain the opposite results (see, for example, Glaeser and Kahn 2004). We also obtain the same sign when considering growth rates in crime as explanatory variables of urban sprawl, even though the effect is not statistically significant. These results contradict U.S. studies (such as Cullen and Levitt 1999) but confirm our theoretical predictions in section two in the European context (see also Patacchini and Zenou 2008).[9]

It has to be clear, however, that *we are not claiming here any causal relationship*. Moreover, the number of observations is very small. Therefore, our evidence has to be taken only as suggestive of some possible correlations between different variables.

More Descriptive Evidence on Urban Growth in European Cities

Even though our dataset is quite limited, especially because of missing values, the information for 2001 has a relatively good coverage and allows us to appreciate urban differences in a large set of amenities and disamenities, economic opportunities, employment structure, human capital, transportation infrastructures, and accessibility by air.[10] Table 8 reports in the first four columns a list of such variables, together with our sample descriptive statistics.

The purpose of this section is to exploit the variation in these city characteristics to identify different city structures and then analyze which structure is more likely to experience an increase in city size (here measured by land area growth).

We adopt a principal component analysis (PCA hereafter). This technique uses the correlation between a set of observed variables to develop a smaller number of artificial variables (principal components), without losing much information. The reduction in variable "dimensions" helps to identify the obser-

9. The qualitative evidence remains roughly the same when country dummies are included. This indicates that the associations between urban sprawl and our variables of interest are not different when urban sprawl differences are investigated between and within countries.

10. Amenities play an important role in explaining urban sprawl; see Brueckner, Thisse, and Zenou (1999); Glaeser and Kahn (2004). These variables listed here were not used in the analysis of the previous section because they are typically not available for 1991 and 1996.

vations that are more similar or dissimilar along various characteristics. The PCA creates uncorrelated indicators or components, where each component is a linear weighted combination of the initial variables. The importance of each original variable in the determination of the principal components (that is, the weights or factor loadings) guides the interpretation of the results. The number of principal components is equal to the number of variables being analyzed. The number of retained components is based on the percentage of cumulative total variance explained. The components are ordered so that the first component (PC1) explains the largest possible amount of variation in the original data. The second component (PC2) is completely uncorrelated with the first component and explains additional but less variation than the first component. Subsequent components are uncorrelated with previous components; therefore, each component captures an additional dimension in the data, while explaining smaller and smaller proportions of the variation of the original variables. The higher the degree of correlation among the original variables in the data, the fewer are the components required to capture common information.

The principal component analysis is the optimal (in terms of mean squared error) linear scheme for compressing a set of high dimensional vectors into a set of lower dimensional vectors (principal components), thus enabling a more tractable organization of the data.

The output from a PCA is given by a table showing the eigenvectors of the correlation matrix of the original variables (that is, the factor loadings or weights for each variable in each component) with the associated eigenvalues, which give the percentage of total variance explained by each component. Because the original variables are standardized (that is, with a contribution of the total variance equal to one), a common method to select components is to retain those with eigenvalues greater than one. In our application, we find that the first two components account for roughly 79 percent of the total variance (both having eigenvalues much greater than one), whereas the remaining components account for only trivial amounts of variance (all of them having eigenvalues less than one). This implies that the information content of our different indicators of urban characteristics can be appropriately summarized by two derived variables, which can thus be interpreted as two different city structures.

Table 8 reports in the last two columns the importance of each original variable in the determination of these two artificial variables together with the absolute and cumulative percentage of the variance explained. Variables associated with positive (or negative) weights load positively (or negatively) to the components. The higher the magnitude of the weight is (in absolute terms), the higher is the contribution of the associated variable. Table 8 thus shows that

Table 8. Principal Component Analysis Results

Population size and density	Obs.	Mean	Std. Dev.	PC1	PC2
Total population	353	392,879.1	724,983.2	0.38	−0.26
Population density (per km²)	252	2,233.38	2,629.09	0.19	−0.30
Non-EU population	298	3.75	4.22	0.13	0.24
Amenities and disamenities					
Sun hours per day	231	5.28	1.38	−0.22	0.20
Rainy days per year	207	148.80	50.04	0.29	−0.35
Number of theaters	197	10.14	18.20	0.18	−0.03
Number of museums	221	13.81	21.20	0.15	0.02
Tourist hotel stays per resident population	245	3.48	4.99	0.04	0.21
Total crime rate	250	75.32	56.99	0.23	−0.20
Murders and violent death rate	255	0.06	0.08	0.16	−0.09
Economic opportunities, employment structure, and human capital					
Unemployment rate	300	12.14	7.21	−0.15	0.09
Share of new firms	248	12.40	7.70	0.03	0.31
Headquarters	172	202.17	1,812.38	0.21	−0.19
Share of employment in trade, hotels, and restaurants	279	21.57	8.25	0.41	−0.12
Share of industrial employment	280	25.50	9.73	0.10	−0.22
Share of highly educated people	177	0.20	0.06	0.18	0.33
Number of students	244	95.24	62.99	0.32	−0.16
Real GDP per head[a]	66	727,315.4	4,066,965	0.07	0.21
Transportation infrastructures and accessibility					
Registered cars per 1,000 pop.	246	358.37	145.80	0.09	0.40
Public transportation network to land area (km/km²)	171	8.36	68.98	0.34	−0.07
Number of arrivals in closer airport	197	3,773,899	7,629,137	0.18	−0.11
Eigenvalues				6.69	4.88
Percentage of explained variance				42	37

Source: Authors' calculations of the Urban Audit (European Commission 2004) (http://ec.europa.eu/regional_policy/conferences/urbanaudit2008/programme_en.htm).

PC1 = first principal component; PC2 = second principal component.

a. In euros.

the first principal component captures the variance given by the large European cities, which are associated with high levels of total population, high crime rates, high employment rates, large number of theaters and museums, efficient public transportation network, and high levels of employment in services. The weights associated with climatic variables suggest that we are mainly talking about cities in northern Europe.

The second principal component captures instead a different city structure. Those are cities with low population density, low crime rates, and high levels of human capital; rich in-tourists; with a high percentage of cars per capita; and

Figure 1. City Structures in the EU[a]

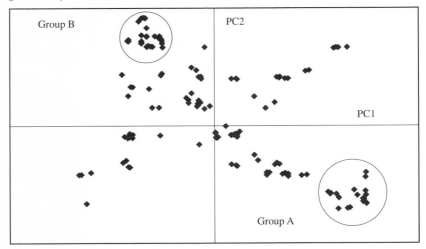

Source: Authors' calculations of the Urban Audit (European Commission 2004) (http://ec.europa.eu/regional_policy/conferences/
urbanaudit2008/programme_en.htm).
x-axis: PC1 = first principal component; *y*-axis: PC2 = second principal component.
a. See the text for descriptions of each component and the countries in each group.

which seem to have higher levels of GDP per capita. These cities also collect larger percentages of non-EU citizens. The weights associated with climatic variables indicate that cities with such structures are mainly located in southern Europe.[11]

To understand better what the European cities in those groups are, we plot in figure 1 our observations on the plane spanned by the first two principal components. The distance from the axes indicates how much each city is close to the characteristics captured by each principal component.

The scatter plot shows that the large majority of the cities are located in the northwest and southeast quadrants, confirming that the two principal components are roughly capturing the two different city structures of the European context. In the southeast quadrant, which contains cities positively correlated with the first principal component, we can clearly distinguish the large cities in northern Europe, namely London, Brussels, The Hague, Madrid, Berlin, Hamburg, Munich, Paris, Milan, and Rome (group A in figure 1). The northwest quadrant shows a distinct cluster of cities (group B) that contains small cities mainly located in southern Europe where the quality of life is high, includ-

11. Here, unemployment rates are higher with respect to those in northern Europe, which explains the positive sign of the weight for unemployment rate in this city structure.

Figure 2. Cities with a Fast Rate of Urban Area Growth in the EU[a]

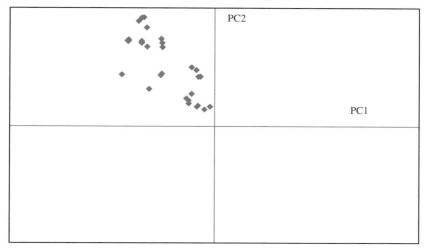

Source: Authors' calculations of the Urban Audit (European Commission 2004) (http://ec.europa.eu/regional_policy/conferences/urbanaudit2008/programme_en.htm).
x-axis: PC1 = first principal component; *y*-axis: PC2 = second principal component.
a. See the text for descriptions of each component and the countries in each group.

ing Florence, Perugia, Toulouse, Montpellier, Marseille, La Valletta, Toledo, and some cities in Greece. Those are cities that are positively and highly correlated with the second principal component and negatively with the first principal component.

If we look more closely at such a distribution of cities in terms of city size, we find that all the cities that experienced the more marked increase in land size (above the mean) are all located in the northwest quadrant (figure 2). This evidence thus indicates that an increase in urban size is positively associated with city characteristics captured by the second principal component (low population density, low crime rates, high levels of human capital, lots of tourists, high percentages of cars per capita, high levels of GDP per capita, good climatic conditions, large in-flows of non-EU citizens, high percentages of new businesses) and negatively with those determining the first principal component (high levels of total population, students, crime rates, employment rates, a large number of theaters and museums, an efficient public transportation network, and high levels of employment in services). Looking in more detail at the importance of the different variables in determining those city structures (the last two columns of table 8), it seems that an increase in urban size is more likely to be associated with a high percentage of high-skilled individuals, high car ownership rates, good climatic conditions, large in-flows of non-EU citizens, and a lively industrial structure. On the contrary, an efficient public transportation network, typically concentrated in big-city centers, large shares of employment in services, bad climatic conditions, and a high number of students seem to be factors preventing city expansion.

Concluding Remarks

In this paper, we have provided some evidence on patterns of growth and declines in cities of the European Union. We interpret our results as evidence for urban sprawl, acknowledging the limitation of this view. We have seen that there are basically two city structures with different growth experiences. Cities mainly located in northern Europe, which are typically bigger with old centers, have experienced lower declines in density than cities from southern Europe, which are smaller in size. Similarities and dissimilarities in the process of urban sprawl between Europe and the United States are highlighted. As in the United States, history has shown that there is a positive correlation between prosperity and the degree of urban sprawl. Our evidence suggests that as soon as people are affluent enough to be able to chose where they wanted to live and which transport mode they desire, they tend to live further away from the city centers. We have also shown that the predictions in terms of the percentage of ethnic minorities and crime rate are reverse for the European case and confirmed by our data. Even though our results are to be taken with caution, they reveal peculiarities of the European Union context that might be relevant to explain the different urban patterns between Europe and the United States.

Comments

J. Vernon Henderson: The paper by Patacchini and Zenou is entitled "Urban Sprawl in Europe," and much of the introduction and conceptual material deal with the topic of sprawl. The authors are the first economists to make use of a unique data set on European cities, and they make a number of key points about how and why urban development differs in many parts of Europe relative to the such development in the United States, helping to close a gap in our knowledge. My comments on the paper fall into two parts. First, I think it is important to distinguish sprawl from the more general notion of spatial deconcentration. Second, the paper in the empirical section does not really deal with sprawl per se, but rather two specific, related phenomena: loss of population from central cities of larger European urban areas and the decisions to redraw and expand city boundaries for smaller cities. This is useful information, but it is not directly about sprawl.

Sprawl and Deconcentration

Population deconcentration within cities, or declining densities of urban areas, is a process that has been going on for well over 100 years, spurred in large part by changes in transport technology—the development of intracity rail transport such as subways, the invention and then mass production of the automobile, and finally the development of regional highway systems running through cities as well as the development of radial and circumferential local highways. Economists study the deconcentration of both population and employment and the interaction between the two, and basic urban models examine the effect of reduced commuting and shipping costs on urban form.

Sprawl connotes something different. Certainly it may involve declining densities. But it involves a notion of excessive deconcentration and excessive use of land at the city fringes. It suggests that fringe development may not be compact. Rather, it may involve strip development along public roads and highways, leapfrogging, and socially wasteful destruction of local forests and agriculture. As such the implication is that there is either market failure of some sort or inappropriate government policies. Social underpricing of gasoline (as perhaps is the case in the United States relative to that in Europe) subsidizes the use of cars and long-distance commuting. Poor land use regulation may allow developers to strip-develop along state-funded roads, rather than absorb the full costs of construction of local road systems deep into residential developments. The social benefits of higher densities at the fringe, such as enhanced social interactions or preservation of green spaces, may not be incorporated into land use and development regulation. And there may be underconstruction of public transport facilities such as commuter rails.

Differences in densities overall and at the urban fringe between the "typical" American versus European city may be explained in part by differences in government policies regulating taxation of fossil fuels, the formulation and enforcement of land use regulations, and investment in public transport. And one can debate who over- and who underregulates and whether density is too high or too low in Europe. But there are also other fundamental differences. Central parts of European cities were constructed with high densities before the transport revolutions noted above; and there is considerable irreversibility, or persistence in prior high densities. With the exception of some of the largest East Coast cities, many U.S. cities were largely constructed after the start of these revolutions. Second, the United States has locally funded and operated school districts, while in Europe (or Canada), at least until recently, most school systems were operated at a national or regional level. In the United States, part of the rush to suburbanization in the 1950s was for higher-income households to escape central city school districts and to set up expensive, independent suburban districts, whereas in Europe or Canada a move to the suburbs leaves a family in the same school district.

The Empirics

Patacchini and Zenou utilize data on European cities, an accomplishment in itself. Unfortunately the data are rather limited. There seem to be two types of cities (at least at the extremes) in the data. First there are large European central cities, where the data cover the central city but not suburban areas of large European urban areas. One wishes Patacchini and Zenou had combined their data with, say, NUTS 3–level data so as to have information on the overall urban area as well as the data they have on central cities. In the data it appears the land area of these large central cities remains largely unchanged in Patacchini and Zenou's data (see table 4), so one can study the declining densities of these fixed area cities. That would definitely constitute evidence of deconcentration, although not sprawl per se.

The second type of cities is smaller stand-alone cities, where the city and urban area largely coincide. There seems to be a movement in countries like Greece to expand the boundaries of these cities; as they expand, they grow overall and deconcentrate. One wishes Patacchini and Zenou looked in more detail at these administrative decisions and treated them as political economy decisions, rather than as evidence of sprawl. That is, the vast expansion of land areas (for relatively modest population changes) is not evidence of sprawl per se, just incorporation of vast tracts of what probably remains rural land. A simple look at Google Earth could confirm this. A number of countries favor having one government for an urban area, rather than the jurisdictional fragmentation of urban areas that is common in the United States. To implement this, countries may either give central cities power to annex fringe areas or may simply redefine large tracts of yet to be developed rural fringe land as being within the city. Thus, as the urban area expands, it all remains under the governance of the original central city. These political economy decisions and differences in local governance arrangements across countries should be a subject of study themselves.

The paper makes key arguments that greater car access, smaller non-EU populations (who tend to live in the suburbs), and greater crime rates should spur deconcentration of central populations into suburban areas. Combining their data with NUTS-3 data would give a picture of what happens in larger European urban areas; the data Patacchini and Zenou have, however, are just on central cities. They find the interesting correlations that they hypothesized, albeit for small sample sizes. Of course, all the covariates they study are themselves endogenous; so, as they recognize, there can be no conclusions regarding causality. There is just evidence of the hypothesized correlations. Two items disappoint. First it would be helpful to have controls on overall urban area changes, so we would know the impact on central cities of overall urban area growth. Second it would be helpful in trying to interpret the results to know what cities remain in the final sample of thirty in table 7. Are these the central cities of large urban areas, the first type of city that I identified; or are they the second type, smaller, fully covered cities? Depending on which set of cities dominates gives a very different interpretation to the results.

Patacchini and Zenou raise a variety of relevant issues in studying urbanization in Europe and highlight the need for larger, integrated datasets. With such data we could better study the issues at hand and start to assess causality.

Dennis Epple: This paper seeks to contrast urban growth patterns in Europe and the United States. In doing so, the paper initiates study of a relatively new dataset for European cities titled the Urban Audit. Using this dataset, the paper undertakes a systematic portrayal of the characteristics of growing and declining cities in Europe.

As the authors carefully detail, this undertaking is hampered by the lack of a standard definition of *city* or *metropolitan area* in Europe. Indeed, the paper makes a valuable contribution in laying out the difficulties that arise in attempting a systematic cross-country comparison for Europe. This may in turn provide guidance for future designs of data collection efforts for urban areas in Europe. To that end, it may be useful to note here four key issues with respect to the data. One is that cities are defined by administrative boundaries rather than by a standardized definition of what constitutes an urban area. A second difficulty is that there are significant problems of missing data. A third is apparent absence of information about housing. A fourth is change over time in the definition of boundaries of administrative units.

The first and fourth problems pose a particular challenge for the type of investigation undertaken in this paper. The lack of a standardized definition of an urban area raises the possibility that apparent differences across urban areas are in fact due to definitional rather than actual differences. Changes over time in administrative boundaries create a similar problem for intertemporal comparisons. It is difficult to determine whether measured changes in population, density, or other variables arise simply because of a change in the boundaries or whether the measured changes reflect an actual change in the urban area. Evidence that the latter may be a problem can be seen in tables 1, 2, and 3. These tables show that, for various groupings of cities, there are one or more cities with a loss of land area of 25 percent or more during the period from 1991 to 2001. In particular, such declines are reported for EU cities in the top quartile by population size (table 2) and EU cities in the bottom quartile by population size (table 3). Housing and infrastructure investments tend to be long lived. Hence, one would expect declines in urbanized land area to occur slowly in a metropolitan area. Declines as large as 25 percent over a ten-year interval seem likely to be a consequence of redefinition of administrative boundaries rather than due to an actual shrinkage of the amount of land area that is urbanized.

Having carefully acknowledged the difficulties with the definition of cities, the authors proceed to provide summary evidence based on the data that are available. I think the paper is best viewed as providing us with interesting descriptive evidence on European cities rather than an analysis of sprawl. In part, this is because sprawl itself is an amorphous concept. The disparaging term *sprawl* was coined by observers who view suburbanization as bad per se, to be curtailed or prevented to the extent possible by restrictions on land use and other regulatory and planning tools.

From an economic perspective, sprawl is neither intrinsically good nor intrinsically bad. If some people prefer low density residential locations, and costs are internalized, then sprawl is a nonissue. Low density per se is not a culprit. If costs are not internalized, then policy should focus on internalizing the externalities with the best available instruments. If internalizing the externalities changes the density of development, then that is fine. If internalizing the externalities does not change the density of development, that is also fine. Most important, we should not accept measurement of density as a shortcut or substitute for the more challenging task of determining whether externalities have been internalized. The third paragraph of the introduction risks falling into this line of thinking in echoing the negative view of evolving land use patterns in Europe. Fortunately, the paper itself does not rest on such judgments about whether low density is good or bad. The Urban Audit is poorly suited to providing evidence about density at the urban fringe, and it is clearly not suited for making a judgment about whether the density of development is good or bad.

It would be quite interesting to pursue the linkage between evolving patterns of urban development in Europe and changing demographics in Europe, especially the declining birth rate and associated changes in the age distribution of the population noted in the section on descriptive statistics of the paper. Such an analysis would build on the strengths of the data. This paper marks a valuable step in providing a systematic portrayal of differences across European cities and in changes in European cities over time.

References

Bosker, Maarten, and Gerard Marlet. 2006. "Urban Growth and Decline in Europe." Discussion Paper Series 06-18. Utrecht, Netherlands: Utrecht School of Economics, Tjalling C. Koopmans Institute.

Brueckner, Jan K. 1987. "The Structure of Urban Equilibria: A Unified Treatment of the Muth-Mills Model." In *Handbook of Regional and Urban Economics,* vol. 2, edited by E. S. Mills, pp. 821–45. Amsterdam: North Holland.

———. 2000. "Urban Sprawl: Diagnosis and Remedies." *International Regional Science Review* 23 (2): 160–71.

———. 2001. "Urban Sprawl: Lessons from Urban Economics." *Brookings-Wharton Papers on Urban Affairs,* 65–97.

Brueckner, Jan K., and Hyun-A Kim 2003. "Urban Sprawl and the Property Tax." *International Tax and Public Finance* 10 (1): 5–23.

Brueckner, Jan K., Jacques-François Thisse, and Yves Zenou. 1999. "Why Is Central Paris Rich and Downtown Detroit Poor? An Amenity-Based Theory." *European Economic Review* 43 (1): 91–107.

Brueckner, Jan K., and Yves Zenou. 2003. "Space and Unemployment: The Labor-Market Effects of Spatial Mismatch." *Journal of Labor Economics* 21 (1): 242–66.

Bruegmann, Robert. 2005. *Sprawl: A Compact History.* University of Chicago Press.

Burchfield, Marcy, Henry G. Overman, Diego Puga, and Matthew A. Turner. 2006. "Causes of Sprawl: A Portrait from Space." *Quarterly Journal of Economics* 121 (2): 587–633.

Cheshire, Paul C., and Stefano Magrini. 2006. "Population Growth in European Cities: Weather Matters—but Only Nationally." *Regional Studies* 40 (1): 23–37.

Couch, Chris, Lila Leontidou, and Karl-Olov Arnstberg. 2007. "Introduction: Definitions, Theories and Methods of Comparative Analysis." In *Urban Sprawl in Europe: Landscapes, Land-Use Change and Policy*, edited by Couch, Leontidou, and Gerhard Petschel-Held, pp. 3–38. Oxford, U.K.: Blackwell Publishing.

Coulson, N. Edward, Derek Laing, and Ping Wang. 2001. "Spatial Mismatch in Search Equilibrium." *Journal of Labor Economics* 19 (4): 949–72.

Cullen, Julie B., and Steven D. Levitt. 1999. "Crime, Urban Flight, and the Consequences for Cities." *Review of Economics and Statistics* 81 (2): 159–69.

Freeman, Scott J., Jeffrey T. Grogger, and Jon Sonstelie. 1996. "The Spatial Concentration of Crime." *Journal of Urban Economics* 40 (2): 216–31.

Fujita, Masahisa. 1989. *Urban Economic Theory: Land Use and City Size.* Cambridge University Press.

Fujita, Masahisa, Jacques-François Thisse, and Yves Zenou. 1997. "On the Endogenous Formation of Secondary Employment Centers in a City." *Journal of Urban Economics* 41 (3): 337–57.

Galster, George, and others. 2001. "Wrestling Sprawl to the Ground: Defining and Measuring an Elusive Concept." *Housing Policy Debate* 12 (4): 681–717.

Glaeser, Edward L., and Matthew E. Kahn. 2001. "Decentralized Employment and the Transformation of the American City." *Brookings-Wharton Papers on Urban Affairs*, 1–64.

———. 2004. "Sprawl and Urban Growth." In *Handbook of Regional and Urban Economics,* vol. 4: *Cities and Geography*, edited by J. V. Henderson and J.-F. Thisse, pp. 2481–527. Amsterdam: North-Holland.

Glaeser, Edward L., and Jesse M. Shapiro. 2003. "Urban Growth in the 1990s: Is City Living Back?" *Journal of Regional Science* 43 (1): 139–65.

Henderson, Vernon J., and Arindam Mitra. 1999. "The New Urban Landscape: Developers and Edge Cities." *Regional Science and Urban Economics* 26 (6): 613–43.

Nechyba, Thomas J., and Randall P. Walsh. 2004. "Urban Sprawl." *Journal of Economic Perspectives* 18 (4): 177–200.

Ogawa, Hideaki, and Masahisa Fujita. 1982. "Multiple Equilibria and Structural Transition of Nonmonocentric Urban Configurations." *Regional Science and Urban Economics* 12 (2): 161–96.

Patacchini, Eleonora, and Yves Zenou. 2008. "Ethnicity and Crime in London." Unpublished manuscript. Stockholm University.

Rose-Ackerman, Susan. 1975. "Racism and Urban Structure." *Journal of Urban Economics* 2 (1): 85–103.

Selod, Harris, and Yves Zenou. 2006. "City Structure, Job Search, and Labor Discrimination: Theory and Policy Implications." *Economic Journal* 116 (514): 1057–087.

Smith, Tony E., and Yves Zenou. 1997. "Dual Labor Markets, Urban Unemployment, and Multicentric Cities." *Journal of Economic Theory* 76 (1): 185–214.

Song, Yan, and Yves Zenou. 2006. "Property Tax and Urban Sprawl: Theory and Implications for U.S. Cities." *Journal of Urban Economics* 60 (3): 519–34.

———. 2009 (forthcoming). "How Differences in Property Taxes within Cities Affect Urban Sprawl" *Journal of Regional Science*.

Verdier, Thierry, and Yves Zenou. 2004. "Racial Beliefs, Location and the Causes of Crime." *International Economic Review* 45 (3): 731–60.

Wheaton, William C. 1974. "A Comparative Static Analysis of Urban Spatial Structure." *Journal of Economic Theory* 9 (2): 223–37.

Yinger, John. 1976. "Racial Prejudice and Racial Residential Segregation in an Urban Model." *Journal of Urban Economics* 3 (4): 383–96.

Zenou, Yves. 2009. *Urban Labor Economics*. Cambridge University Press.

SOMIK V. LALL
World Bank

CHRISTOPHER TIMMINS
Duke University

SHOUYUE YU
Duke University

Connecting Lagging and Leading Regions: The Role of Labor Mobility

How can policies improve welfare of people in economically lagging regions of countries? The answer to this question is not straightforward, and policymakers in developed as well as developing countries struggle in making choices between the market solution of promoting out-migration and the intervention option of promoting economic growth in specific regions. In most countries, policy discussions of improving welfare in lagging regions often focus on targeted interventions or incentives for moving production to these places. While these efforts are likely to be politically attractive, there is considerable evidence highlighting the limited effectiveness of targeted incentives. And when incentives go against the grain of market forces, they can subtract from, rather than add to, national economic growth.

At the same time, policymakers have often viewed internal migration—or labor mobility—from lagging to leading regions, or rural to urban areas, as a consequence of failed place-based policies. And in many countries, policies raise barriers to the movement of labor. Consider the household registration system (the *hukou* system) in China, which has been a barrier to rural-urban migration. Not having a *hukou* in urban areas means that migrants do not qual-

The research for this paper has been co-funded by the World Development Report and the Spatial Team in the World Bank. The authors have benefited from discussions and comments from Alex Anas, Jan Brueckner, Gary Burtless, Paul Dorosh, Forhad Shilpi, Antonio Estache, Indermit Gill, Vernon Henderson, Marisela Montoliu, Janet Pack, Truman Packard, Harris Selod, Hyoung Gun Wang, and seminar participants at the World Bank and the BWPUA conference at Brookings.

This volume is a product of the staff of the International Bank for Reconstruction and Development at the World Bank. The findings, interpretations, and conclusions expressed in this paper do not necessarily reflect the views of the executive directors of the World Bank or the governments they represent. The World Bank does not guarantee the accuracy of the data included in this work. The boundaries, colors, denominations, and other information shown on any map in this work do not imply any judgment on the part of the World Bank concerning the legal status of any territory or the endorsement or acceptance of such boundaries.

151

ify for public education or health benefits. This can produce large interregional wage differences. Recent research indicates that removing such mobility restrictions would reallocate labor across areas, reduce wage differences, and lower income inequality (Whalley and Zhang 2007).

The World Bank's *World Development Report 2009* (*WDR 2009*) provides a new framework for territorial development, arguing that policies should focus on integrating lagging and leading regions—and not be exclusively concerned with stimulating growth in lagging regions. The *WDR 2009* highlights that enabling geographic mobility of labor and improving economic connectivity between lagging and leading regions are key ingredients for countries to gain from the geographic concentration of economic activities along with convergence in living standards. Which policies can help? Policies that are *spatially blind* in design can have the spatially sharpest effects. These include progressive income tax policies, the achievement of national minimum standards in basic health and education indicators, and removal of barriers to labor mobility. In addition, *spatially connective* policies such as transport and communication improvements physically link lagging and leading regions. *Spatially targeted* incentives should be policy instruments of last resort, only to be used when factor mobility is weak due to internal divisions from ethnic and linguistic fractionalization. In such cases, these type incentives may be considered but only after investing in information to identify sources of comparative advantage and to amplify the benefits from spatially blind and spatially connective policies.

In this paper, we focus on one aspect of the territorial integration challenge— the migration of labor from lagging to leading regions within countries. In particular, we are interested in understanding migration decisions in Brazil— a large developing country with no formal barriers to labor mobility. During years of high economic growth in the 1960s and 1970s, almost 40 million people left the countryside for cities—with a large share of those migrants moving from the lagging Northeast to the leading Southeast region (World Bank 2008). And even today, young workers migrate in large numbers.

Why people migrate depends on forces that "pull," as well as those that "push," them to leave. On the one hand, one big pull is economic density in leading regions of countries. Differences in economic opportunity between lagging and leading regions often provide the main motivation for internal migration. On the other hand, people are pushed off their land where agriculture is in severe decline, by the pressures of population growth, and where environmental change makes cultivation no longer viable. Historically, droughts have had sudden and prolonged impact on the distribution of the population, particularly in sub-Saharan Africa and South Asia.[1] Conflict has also pushed people to migrate across sub-Saharan Africa, and in many other developing regions.

But in many low- and middle-income countries, another important push propels internal migration—the lack of adequate public services in rural areas or in economically lagging regions. To a large extent, this topic has been overlooked in empirical analysis of migration decisions. However, in reality, the location of schools, health care centers, hospitals, and public and private amenities is correlated with the location of economic activity. In Africa, disparities in school enrollment and neonatal care between cities, towns, and villages are attributable to the near absence of schools and health facilities in outlying areas.[2] Evidence from Central Asia shows that in the isolated parts of Tajikistan, schools are inadequately heated, drinking water is scarce, and there are no arrangements to clear garbage and sewage.[3] So as market forces encourage the concentration of economic mass, public services are underprovided in smaller towns, villages, and lagging regions.[4] Although voluntary, migration in response to limited access to public services is more likely to add to congestion costs in cities than to contribute to agglomeration benefits.

In the empirical analysis, we examine the relative contribution of economic opportunities and amenities in leading areas ("pull") and the lack of access to basic public services in rural and lagging regions ("push") on internal migration decisions of Brazilians. We use household-level data that are representative samples down to the second level of subnational administration (for example, counties in the United States). These data record migration history over a short-term horizon (for example, 5 years) and relative to birth location.[5] Our empirical approach employs repeated cross-sectional data to control for time-invariant unobserved local attributes in a utility-based model of individual migration decisions. Even the best dataset will necessarily lack information about important amenities, local public goods, and geo-economic features that might motivate migration behavior. If these unobserved factors are correlated with migration determinants about which we do have information (for example, access to piped water, sewage, electricity, or health care), they can bias our conclusions

1. Iliffe (1995) on the historical impact of drought on population distribution in Africa; Bryceson (1999) on the Sahel and Sudan; and Hardoy and Satterthwaite (1989) on Mauritania. Wandschneider and Mishra (2003), cited in Deshingkar and Grimm (2004), on the drought-induced migration of 60,000 people out of Bolangir, in the Indian state of Orissa, in 2001.

2. Sahn and Stifel (2003).

3. Anderson and Pomfret (2005).

4. Venables and Kanbur (2005).

5. We focus on birth location, where missing observations are less of a concern.

about the role those observed determinants play in migration decisions. Following Bayer, Keohane and Timmins (2009), we incorporate repeat cross-sectional data on migration behavior into a two-stage discrete choice model that allows us to easily overcome many of these biases, with important implications for our conclusions regarding many of these factors.

Our analysis confirms the importance of public service differentials in influencing long-run migration decisions. In particular, we find that in addition to looking for better jobs, working-age men migrated from the lagging Northeast region to get better access to basic public services such as piped water, electricity, and health care. How much are migrants willing to pay for public services? A full-time minimum wage worker earning Rs$7 per hour (about US$2.30 in February 2008) was willing to pay Rs$390 per year in compensating wage differentials to have access to better health services, Rs$84 for better access to sewage services, and Rs$42 for better access to electricity.

What do these findings imply for urbanization and territorial development policies? First, rather than only focusing on providing spatially targeted incentives to stimulate economic growth in lagging regions, policies should focus on building human capital that enables people to become geographically mobile. Second, investing in basic public services and core infrastructure in lagging regions should be of high priority. Access to these services will directly improve welfare in lagging regions and will reduce the push factors that induce migration. By overlooking the provision of basic social services in economically lagging regions, policymakers can inadvertently influence the choice to migrate, motivating households to move for reasons other than to exploit economic opportunities. While the move improves the welfare of these individuals, the economy may end up worse off as they are more likely to add to congestion costs in cities rather than to contribute to agglomeration benefits.

The paper proceeds as follows. In the next section, we discuss the analytic model, which uses a simple model of location choice that depends upon earning opportunities and local public goods to illustrate that the latter matter in individual migration decisions. In the third section, we describe the results from estimating the model. In the last section, we offer our conclusions.

Modeling the Determinants of Migration

Theories of economic growth and convergence have motivated economic thinking on what causes people to move and what such movements mean. Whether couched in a classical framework or in the recent models of endogenous growth, when people are free to move, they will pursue private gain and compete away differences in wages between locations.[6] There is abundant empirical work identifying the determinants of migration decisions, whereby migrants respond to geographic differences in incomes or wages. In the 1960s and 1970s, aggregate data at the subnational level were used to estimate modified gravity models of migration inspired by Newton's law of gravitation. In these models, migration flows are directly related to population size at the origin and destination and inversely related to distance between locations. These gravity models considered the effects of the push and pull factors in both areas of origin and destination. Today, this approach—which can only broadly describe population movements—has been replaced by finer micro-econometric methods (Lall, Selod, and Shalizi 2006).[7]

The typical migration equation at the microlevel specifies a binary variable (moving versus staying) as function of a set of explanatory variables. This approach focuses on the decision of individuals originally located in a given area to migrate. The migration choice can be modeled with a linear probability, a probit, or a logit model. One of the main problems with this approach is that it groups all potential destinations into a single "rest of the world" destination. This is often due to the lack of available and measurable data and because multivariate analyses are often less tractable. However, this is an important problem as potential migrants face a set of multiple destinations with different local opportunities. Workers may not only decide whether to migrate but also decide where to migrate, and they may be making these choices simultaneously. Without modeling the choice of where to migrate, it is impossible to determine the relative roles of different determinants of migration behavior. An emerging body of empirical analysis addresses this issue by considering polychotomous choice models, usually multinomial logits.

This type of model is used by Falaris (1987) who estimates a nested logit of individual internal migration across twenty-three states in Venezuela grouped in seven regions. Distance between states is used as a proxy for moving costs. Consistent with what theory would predict, he finds that wage differentials do indeed affect migration decisions in Venezuela. Our model of migration choice builds on this approach.

---

6. For a discussion of the classical framework, see Solow (1956) and Swan (1956); for models of endogenous growth, see Romer (1986) and Lucas (1988).

7. A discussion on gravity models can be found in Greenwood (1997).

Model

We first present a simple model that is geared toward the recovery of the value placed on specific local public services and amenities by potential migrants. The model as presented explicitly controls for local public services and amenities but does so nonparametrically, making it difficult to learn about the value of any one service or amenity in particular (such as access to electricity).

We begin by defining the individual indirect utility function of a potential migrant. As is done in traditional migration models, we assume that individuals receive utility from wage compensation while trying to avoid higher migration costs (Falaris 1987). In addition, we assume that individuals enjoy local public goods and amenities such as access to piped water and electricity. Consider an individual i from origin location j. We can write this person's utility, should he or she choose to reside in location k, as the following:

$$(1) \qquad \tilde{U}_{i,j,k} = \tilde{\beta} w_{i,j,k} - \tilde{\delta} \ln(D_{j,k} + 0.01) + X'_k \tilde{\gamma} + \tilde{\xi}_k + \tilde{\eta}_{i,j,k},$$

where $w_{i,j,k}$ = log wage earned by individual i in location k, $D_{j,k}$ = migration distance (in kilometers from origin j to location k), X_k = observable (by the econometrician) attributes of location k, $\tilde{\xi}_k$ = unobservable (by the econometrician) attributes of location k, and $\tilde{\eta}_{i,j,k}$ = idiosyncratic unobservable (by the econometrician) determinants of individual i's utility in location k.

For the purpose of easy interpretation, we rescale equation 2 so that the marginal utility of the natural log of wage is normalized to be 1. We remove the "~" from each parameter to reflect this rescaling.

$$(2) \qquad U_{i,j,k} = w_{i,j,k} - \delta \ln(D_{j,k} + 0.01) + X'_k \gamma + \xi_k + \eta_{i,j,k}.$$

We can now interpret estimates of γ as the marginal willingness to pay (as a percentage of wage) for a one-unit increase in any of the attributes in X_k.

This model makes a few simplifying assumptions. First, the migration cost is simply related to the migration distance. This is typical of previous analyses, but the model could be extended to treat migration cost as a function of the difference between origin and destination attributes. Second, we do not model the individual's labor market participation decision (that is, the individual's choice of working hours). Moreover, we also ignore the possibility of involuntary unemployment but plan to account for this possibility in future work by including unemployment rates in X_k.[8] This is in line with the emphasis in the Harris-Todaro model on expected labor market returns.

8. One could also make the distinction between formal and informal employment.

Suppose there are K locations and that individual i can choose one of them as his or her destination. This individual will then choose the utility maximizing location. If we assume that $\tilde{\eta}_{i,j,k} \sim i.i.d.$ *Type 1 Extreme Value*, the probability that individual i chooses a particular location k as his or her destination can be written as follows:

$$(3) \quad P(U_{i,j,k} \geq U_{i,j,l} \ \forall \ l \neq k) = \frac{\exp(\mu(w_{i,j,k} - \delta \log(D_{j,k} + 0.01) + X'_k \gamma + \xi_k))}{\sum_{l=1}^{K} \exp(\mu(w_{i,j,l} - \delta \log(D_{j,l} + 0.01) + X'_l \gamma + \xi_l))}.$$

Since the marginal utility of log wage has been rescaled to be 1, the model dictates that we explicitly estimate the logit scale parameter μ. Let N denote the total population. We would like to maximize the probability associated with the chosen destination of each individual (k_i^*). This implies the following log-likelihood function, where $I(k = k_i^*)$ is an indicator function that takes the value 1 if individual i chooses location k_i^*, such that

$$(4) \qquad \ell = \sum_{i=1}^{N} \sum_{k=1}^{K} \ln[P(U_{i,j,k} \geq U_{i,j,l} \ \forall \ l \neq k)] * I(k = k_i^*).$$

Using equation 3, the model predicts that the population of location k would be

$$(5) \qquad \hat{pop}_k = \sum_{i-1}^{N} P(U_{i,j,k} \geq U_{i,j,l} \ \forall \ l \neq k),$$

which, in equilibrium, should be equal to the observed population of location k (pop_k). This applies to all K locations. That is, in equilibrium,

$$(6) \qquad \hat{pop}_k = pop_k, \forall k = 1, \cdots, K.$$

We use this information to employ the two-stage estimation procedure in Bayer and Timmins (2007). In the first stage, we define the mean utility (that is, separate from idiosyncratic components) enjoyed by all migrants who choose location k:

$$(7) \qquad \theta_k = X'_k \gamma + \xi_k$$

and obtain estimates of μ, δ, and $\{\theta_k\}_{k=1}^{K}$. Bayer and Timmins (2007) show how, on the basis of equation 6, the contraction mapping formulated in Berry, Levinsohn, and Pakes (1995) and Berry (1994) can be used to simply calculate the vector $\{\hat{\theta}_k\}_{k=1}^{K}$ for any guess at remaining utility parameters $[\mu, \delta]$ and an arbitrary normalization (for example, the average value of $\hat{\theta}_k$ is set equal to zero). We can then estimate our parameters $[\mu, \delta, \{\theta_k\}_{k=1}^K]$ with a maximum likelihood procedure using the log-likelihood function, equation 4.

In the second stage, we decompose the estimates $\{\theta_k\}_{k=1}^K$ from the first stage according to equation 7. This would yield a vector containing the individual's marginal willingness to pay (as a percentage of the wage) for each element of the vector $\mathbf{X}_k$. Since ξ_k and $\mathbf{X}_k$ are likely correlated with each other (for example, cities with desirable public goods may be high quality in other unobserved dimensions), the simple ordinary least square (OLS) estimator of γ will be biased. Ideally, one might use an instrument for each endogenous component of $\mathbf{X}_k$. Given the number of potentially endogenous local attributes that might be important to the individual's migration decision, however, this solution is not practical. Instead, we deal with this problem by assuming that any correlation between $\mathbf{X}_k$ and ξ_k is only with components of X that do not vary over time (that is, ξ_k).

$$\theta_{k,t} = \mathbf{X}'_{k,t}\gamma + \underbrace{\varsigma_k + \upsilon_{k,t}}_{\xi_{k,t}}.$$
(8)

Assuming $E[\Delta\mathbf{X}_k\Delta\upsilon_k] = 0$, differencing this expression over time will remove any source of bias. While it is unlikely that this assumption holds perfectly, in practice it is a far better option than simply ignoring the role of correlated unobserved local attributes, and it will likely eliminate much of any potential endogeneity bias.

Practically, we expand the first stage of the model to include data from two census years, restricting the parameters $[\mu, \delta]$ to remain fixed over that time period. We then solve for two vectors, $\{\hat{\theta}_{k,1}\}_{k=1}^K$ and $\{\hat{\theta}_{k,2}\}_{k=1}^K$, using an extension of the Berry, Levinsohn, and Pakes (1995) contraction procedure. Finally, the unbiased estimates of γ can be obtained by estimating

(9) $$\Delta\hat{\theta}_k = \Delta\mathbf{X}'_k\gamma + \Delta\upsilon_k,$$

where

(10)
$$\Delta\hat{\theta}_k = \hat{\theta}_{k,2} - \hat{\theta}_{k,1}$$
$$\Delta X_k = X_{k,2} - X_{k,1}$$
$$\Delta\upsilon_k = \upsilon_{k,2} - \upsilon_{k,1}.$$

Data

The 1991 and 2000 Brazil censuses provide information on current residence and birth state for most individuals. Therefore, we define migration by an individual's current location relative to his birth state. That is, we use a long-run measure of migration. One could also employ a short-run definition of migration—that is, relative to where the individual was living one, two, or five years before—if necessary data are available. We use 3,659 AMCs (minimally comparable areas) as destination locations and twenty-seven states as origin locations. AMCs are similar to counties but are aggregated in some cases to make them comparable over time.

For each census year, we focus our attention on household heads who were between the ages of twenty-five and thirty-five. In this way, it is less likely that the same household head will show up in both the 1991 and 2000 samples. Moreover, by using individuals from this cohort, we focus our attention on first migration decisions—those made after an individual initially finishes school or leaves his or her parents' home. This move may be accompanied by marriage or the birth of a child, for example. Our goal is to avoid mixing these individuals with older individuals who may be making location decisions according to retirement considerations or who may have made location decisions many years in the past. Finally, we also control for individual attributes, since amenities and employment opportunities are likely to have different effects on migration behavior for different types of individuals. Given that age has already been restricted, we further divide those household heads according to their education level. Household heads with postsecondary education are excluded from the analysis.

The Brazilian censuses also contain information on employment and income. Recall that our current model ignores the possibility that the individual would be unable to find work. We therefore keep only those household heads who were employed. In the 2000 census, over 90 percent of all Brazilians between the ages of twenty-five and thirty-five (with less than college education) reported that they were working. Thus, dropping unemployed household heads is not a major problem in this context. For each household head in our sample, we can observe the individual's wage in the destination location where he or she actually resides. However, to model the individual's destination location decision, we need to know what the individual would earn in every other location. Properly recovering these counterfactual wages can be quite difficult. In this part of the paper, we adopt the relatively simple approach of using the average wage

Table 1. Summary of Regression Procedures to Predict Counterfactual AMC Wages

	2000			1991		
Variable	Mean of parameter estimates	Mean of std. err.	Std. dev. parameter estimates	Mean of parameter estimates	Mean of std. err.	Std. dev. parameter estimates
Age	0.0155	0.0014	0.0356	0.0109	0.0009	0.0299
Primary education dummy	0.2131	0.1302	0.3643	0.1336	0.0679	0.2680
Secondary education dummy	0.6636	0.2198	0.5217	0.6039	0.1783	0.5507
Female dummy	−0.4100	0.1533	0.4272	−0.4374	0.1875	0.4923
Occupation dummies						
1	0.1784	0.2679	0.6140	0.4611	0.2874	0.6873
2	0.3918	0.4337	0.9072	0.2959	0.3367	0.6998
3	0.1860	0.3247	0.7365	−0.3494	0.2332	0.5950
4	0.1851	0.4341	0.8089	0.0191	0.1440	0.4605
5	0.0156	0.4112	0.7394	0.1038	0.2568	0.5923
6	−0.1675	0.4092	0.7996	0.2645	0.2987	0.6850
7	−0.4817	0.3900	0.7959	0.2328	0.2886	0.6349
8	−0.0893	0.4021	0.7887	−0.1614	0.3107	0.6246
9	−0.1742	0.4039	0.7467	0.1776	0.2549	0.5270
10	−0.0608	0.3799	0.7384			
Constant	−0.1780	1.8395	1.3723	5.1162	1.1139	1.1206

AMC = minimally comparable areas.

earned by conditionally similar individuals in those other locations. Practically, this means that we run a separate log wage regression for each AMC:

$$(11) \qquad w_{i,j,k} = \mathbf{Z}_i' \alpha_k + u_{i,j,k},$$

where $\mathbf{Z}_i$ is a vector of variables describing individual i, including age, sex, education level, and occupation dummy variables, and α_k is a set of wage parameters for location k. Table 1 reports summaries of regression procedures to predict counterfactual wages.

We model moving costs as a function of migration distance, which is calculated from the longitude and latitude of the center of the individual's birth state and destination AMC. Except for a log-linear function of migration distance, we may also specify moving costs using a set of distance dummies.

Our primary interest is in the role played by regional differences in local public services on migration decisions. We focus on variables describing local infrastructure (such as percentage of households with access to piped water, sewage, and electric lights), access to health care (such as number of hospitals), and network infrastructure (for example, transportation costs to the state

Table 2. Regional Differences in Access to Public Services

Region	Percent water		Percent light		Percent sewage		No. of hospitals (per AMC)	
	1991	2000	1991	2000	1991	2000	1992	2000
North	18.1	41.0	48.0	65.5	0.9	2.2	4.0	4.6
Northeast	26.2	52.2	57.3	80.5	1.7	12.9	2.2	2.4
Southeast	56.9	72.2	85.9	95.8	43.2	57.7	2.1	2.1
South	48.9	65.4	89.8	97.0	3.5	13.4	2.4	2.3
Midwest	40.1	66.5	76.3	92.6	4.1	7.8	3.7	3.9

AMC = minimally comparable areas.

capital and São Paulo). Any list of local attributes would, however, necessarily be incomplete. As described above, we use census data from two years to control nonparametrically for all local attributes that do not vary over time. Table 2 summarizes regional differences in access to public services. Differences in water and sanitation services are quite stark. Access to piped water is 52 percent in the Northeast compared with 72 percent in the Southeast. In terms of access to sewage facilities, connection rates in the Northeast were 13 percent in 2000, 58 percent in the Southeast.

Main Findings on Migration Choice

We find strong evidence that individuals' migration decisions depend upon more than just returns in the labor market. Ignoring these nonpecuniary determinants may cause us to overstate the role of wages in driving migration decisions. This can be seen in tables 3 and 4, which describe the results of the procedure described above for those with less (zero to six years) and more (seven to twelve years) education.

Columns 1 to 4 of the lower panel of each table describe the results of cross-sectional procedures applied to each census year individually, ignoring moving costs. The likely effects of omitted variable bias are evident in the estimates of the utility parameters on access to piped water and number of hospitals. It is likely that each of these variables (particularly the number of hospitals in an AMC) is correlated with other desirable urban amenities. This has the effect of biasing upward the coefficient on each of these variables for both education groups. Access to electricity has a counterintuitive sign or is insignificant. While access to sewage shows the expected sign for those in the lower education group, it exhibits the counterintuitive sign (although it is insignificant) for the higher education group in 1991. In all, these results appear to be unstable

Table 3. Migration Estimation Results
Education = [0,6] years

	No moving costs second-stage without differencing		No moving costs second-stage differencing		Moving costs second-stage differencing	
	Estimate	t statistic	Estimate	t statistic	Estimate	t statistic
Stage 1						
Scale parameter	0.479	13.20	0.479	13.20	0.397	10.94
Moving costs[a]					-1.757	-10.87
Log likelihood	28591.164		28591.164		21456.657	

	1991		2000		Δ(1991–2000)		Δ(1991–2000)	
	1	2	3	4	5	6	7	8
	Estimate	t statistic	Estimate	t statistic	Estimate	t statistic	Estimate	t statistic
Stage 2								
Percent electric light	-1.35E-03	-0.72	-1.47E-02	-5.46	1.12E-02	8.61	2.89E-03	1.52
Percent piped water	2.15E-02	11.69	1.01E-02	4.86	1.99E-03	1.21	2.48E-03	1.04
Percent sewage	1.64E-03	1.14	6.07E-03	4.97	1.38E-03	1.22	6.35E-03	3.86
No. of hospitals	1.75E-01	31.35	1.81E-01	33.93	4.73E-02	5.4	2.79E-02	2.19
Transportation cost (SP)	1.87E-04	4.1	1.17E-04	2.25	-7.10E-04	-7.63	1.15E-03	8.44
Transportation cost (SC)	-3.70E-04	-3.93	-6.00E-04	-6.35	6.83E-04	2.15	-9.60E-04	-2.06
Constant	-1.25E+00	-6.27	5.11E-01	1.87	-2.93E-01	-8.3	-4.53E-02	-0.88
R^2	0.3522		0.3215		0.0886		0.0418	

AMC = minimally comparable areas.
a. "Moving costs" are measured as the natural log of the number of kilometers (in 1,000s) from the AMC of residence to the center of the individual's birth state.

Table 4. Migration Estimation Results

Education = [7,12] years

	No moving costs second-stage without differencing		No moving costs second-stage differencing		Moving costs second-stage differencing	
	Estimate	t statistic	Estimate	t statistic	Estimate	t statistic
Stage 1						
Scale parameter	0.138	19.95	0.138	19.95	0.253	7.75
Moving costs[a]					-2.598	-7.69
Log likelihood	25098.315		25098.315		18231.261	

	1991		2000		Δ(1991–2000)		Δ(1991–2000)	
	1	*2*	*3*	*4*	*5*	*6*	*7*	*8*
	Estimate	t statistic	Estimate	t statistic	Estimate	t statistic	Estimate	t statistic
Stage 2								
Percent electric light	2.60E-03	0.34	-4.68E-02	-4.07	3.85E-04	0.08	1.15E-02	3.68
Percent piped water	2.02E-01	26.74	1.68E-01	18.92	8.73E-03	1.48	4.52E-03	1.15
Percent sewage	-6.27E-03	-1.06	2.22E-02	4.25	1.63E-03	0.4	-3.00E-04	-0.11
No. of hospitals	7.17E-01	31.17	7.41E-01	32.55	8.29E-02	2.64	4.17E-02	1.99
Transportation cost (SP)	1.80E-03	9.59	1.05E-03	4.73	-1.57E-03	-4.69	4.12E-04	1.84
Transportation cost (SC)	-2.16E-03	-5.59	-1.79E-03	-4.46	1.53E-03	1.35	-9.20E-05	-0.12
Constant	-1.35E+01	-16.47	-9.16E+00	-7.85	-3.66E-01	-2.89	-3.03E-01	-3.59
R^2	0.4209		0.4917		0.0153		0.0088	

AMC = minimally comparable areas.

a. "Moving costs" are measured as the natural log of the number of kilometers (in 1,000s) from the AMC of residence to the center of the individual's birth state.

over time and likely reflect omitted variable biases caused by unobserved urban amenities.

Columns 5 to 6 report the results of a differencing procedure that ignores the costs of migration. While controlling nonparametrically for time-invariant unobservable local attributes, this specification ignores the fact that it may be difficult, for example, for someone born in the Northeast to migrate to locations in the Southeast or South of Brazil. The signs of most of the coefficients correspond to expectations; very few of the parameter estimates are, however, statistically significant (only access to electricity and the number of hospitals for those in the lower education group and the number of hospitals for those in the higher education group are significant). For both groups, an increasing cost of transporting commodities to São Paulo (a measure of national market connectedness) enters negatively into utility, while the cost of transporting commodities to the nearest state capital (a measure of local market connectedness) enters positively. This latter result is counterintuitive.

Columns 7 to 8 report the results of our most complete model. Here, we differentiate over time and control for migration costs. Doing so, we find that percentage with sewage services (percent sewage), number of hospitals (no. of hospitals), and transportation cost to the nearest state capital (SC) all enter significantly and with the expected sign into the utility of those with less education, while percentage with electricity (percent electric light) and percentage with piped water (percent piped water) are only marginally insignificant. This reflects the fact that local public goods are indeed important in this group's migration decision process. For the more educated group, number of hospitals and percentage with electricity both enter significantly with the expected sign. For this group, however, transportation cost to the nearest state capital and percentage with sewage services do not seem to matter. It is likely that this group is not on the margin in terms of its access to sewage services (or piped water, for that matter), so a marginal improvement in access to either of these public goods is not likely to provide much inducement for choosing a particular destination. Increasing access to electricity and hospitals is more likely to be important for this group on the margin.

For both groups, increased transportation cost to São Paulo enters into utility positively and significantly in this specification. This result may initially seem counterintuitive. However, after controlling for access to health care and other forms of infrastructure (such as proximity to a state capital), this variable may simply be a proxy for a low cost of living (a desirable amenity).

We can interpret the coefficients on each variable as the percentage of the individual's wage that he is willing to pay for a one unit increase in each variable. For example, an individual from the higher (seven to twelve years) education group would be willing to pay 4.17 percent of wages in exchange for an additional hospital in the individual's AMC and 1.15 percent of wages in exchange for an additional percentage point of the population being covered by electric lights. An individual from the lower education group would be willing to pay only 0.3 percent of wages in exchange for another percentage point increase in the population covered by electric lights but would be willing to pay 0.6 percent in exchange for an additional percentage point increase in the population with access to sewage services. Since we use the log wage in the model, it reflects that people with higher education pay a smaller percentage of their wage for amenities. But their absolute payment for amenities is higher than that of people with lower education. And for some amenities, better-educated people are not marginal, and therefore they do not really benefit from an improvement at the margin (that is, connecting more people up to a sewer line likely does not help a rich person, since he or she was probably already hooked up to the sewer line, but the less-educated person is more likely to benefit from that improvement).

Conclusions

In this paper, we examine the determinants of internal migration, paying particular attention to the role of amenities such as access to health and education services and urban infrastructure in migration decisions of working-age individuals. We use Brazilian census data for the analysis and find that the poor from the country's lagging regions not only migrate in search of better economic outcomes but that they are often pushed from their hometowns where they are deprived of access to basic public services such as health care, water supply, and electricity.

These findings have important implications for territorial development and urbanization policies in Brazil. First, economic activities in industry and services are concentrated in the country's leading areas, benefiting from internal scale economies as well as positive externalities from agglomeration. In Brazil and elsewhere, fiscal incentives and infrastructure programs that have tried to develop industrial clusters in lagging regions have been largely unsuccessful (World Bank 2008, Lall, Selod, and Shalizi 2006, Carvalho, Lall, and Timmins 2006, World Bank 2005). However, our results show that people have been leaving lagging regions in search of better economic opportunities—particularly in the Southeast. Policies should encourage this mobility of labor, and the best way is to help in improving human capital accumulation in lagging regions. Considerable evidence shows that education is the best instrument for overcoming the barriers of distance. One of the biggest success stories comes from the United States, where a rise in the schooling of African Americans is believed to have been an important causal factor behind their "Great Migration" out of the South (Margo 1988).

The Northeast in Brazil has the worst education attainment in the country—the labor force has 4.6 years of schooling compared with the average of 6.4 years nationwide and 7.3 years in the Southeast. There are estimates suggesting that average incomes in the Northeast would increase by more than half if the local populace had the same education profile as people in the Southeast have (Mont'Alverne and others 2004). And neoclassical economic thinking suggests that mobility of labor will contribute to interregional convergence. Since higher wages at the destination reflect an initial shortage of workers relative to capital—or a large endowment of capital per worker—the arrival of new migrants will slow the accumulation of capital per worker and the growth of wages. In contrast, the accumulation of capital per worker in the places migrants leave will speed up as they go, accelerating wage growth for workers who stay behind. By this mechanism, incomes in different locations are predicted to eventually converge.

Second, improving access to public services in lagging regions should be a high priority. While the geographic concentration of economic activities generates increasing returns and helps accelerate economic growth, public policies can help convergence in access to social services. By overlooking the provision of basic social services in economically lagging regions—such as schools, primary health centers, and even basic public infrastructure—policymakers can inadvertently influence the choice to migrate, motivating households to move for reasons other than to exploit economic opportunities. While the move improves the welfare of these individuals, the economy may end up worse off as they are more likely to add to congestion costs in cities than to contribute to agglomeration benefits. Also, by improving the provision of these services, policymakers can directly improve welfare of the poor in lagging regions.

Comments

Alex Anas: This interesting article is about migration from economically lagging rural regions to economically leading urban regions in developing countries. The authors present an empirical study focusing on migration into Brazil's vibrant Southeast from the lagging areas of the country.

Of central interest in any empirical study should be the theoretical determinants that would be important in formulating a well-specified model for empirical analysis. My comments have two parts. In the first, I will examine the question: What does the theory in urban economics tells us about the determinants of rural-to-urban migration? In the second part I will comment on selected aspects of the empirical analysis provided by the authors.

The Determinants of Rural-to-Urban Migration: Lessons from Urban Economics

The open-city model of urban economics is particularly applicable to the situation of a developing country with a large rural population. In figure 1, I illustrate this model in full. The x-axis measures the population concentrated in a leading region or large urban area. The horizontal line is the utility that a citizen can obtain by living in a lagging or rural area. The figure assumes that regardless of how many people concentrate in the urban area, the level of utility in the rural area remains unchanged. The inverse U-shaped curve is the level of utility per person that can be obtained in the urban area as a function of the urban population.

Note that when the urban population is small, adding more people to the urban area increases utility because of agglomeration effects that build quickly, but as the urban area grows and density increases, externalities such as crowd-

Figure 1. Open-City Model of Urban Economics

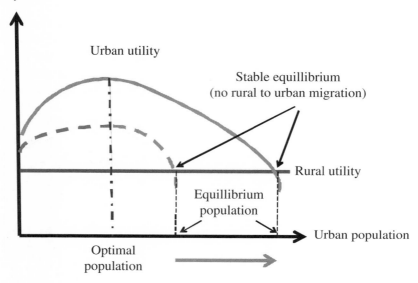

Utility level

ing, traffic congestion, poor sanitation, and so on also increase and the level of utility per person begins to fall (represented by the declining portion of the inverse U-shaped curve). As long as the urban utility level is above the rural one, rural to urban migration continues. This migration dynamic means that the stable equilibrium population of the urban area will be bigger than the optimal population. The former occurs where the declining portion of the inverse U-shaped urban utility curve intersects the rural utility level. The optimal population occurs where the urban utility curve peaks.

The open-city model implies an inefficient allocation of resources: urban populations are larger than optimal and cannot achieve a higher level of utility than rural populations can obtain. If this seems counterintuitive at first, recall the reasons for it. The higher concentration of population in the urban area has caused rents to go up and the unpriced pollution, sanitation, and congestion externalities to increase. Meanwhile the presence of human capital, agglomeration, and other positive externalities in urban areas means that urban producers can offer lower wages (than otherwise) to attract workers to the urban area. The final result is encapsulated by the well-known capitalization hypothesis. Attractive migration destinations are places where, ceteris paribus, land is expensive and labor compensation is relatively low. Unattractive migration destinations do not abound with positive externalities, but they are rich in the absence of at least some of the negative externalities. They are characterized by relatively higher wages and lower rents.

The authors mention the role of public services in migration. How do public service improvements affect the rural to urban migration equilibrium? The answer is in figure 1. Suppose that politicians invest in infrastructure improvements in the urban area. Ceteris paribus, the inverse U-shaped curve shifts up as these investments make the urban area more attractive for migrants. But after the additional rural-to-urban migration occurs, the new stable equilibrium urban population increases without any gain in urban utility. What has happened is that the benefit of better public services has become capitalized into rents as more people have flocked to the urban area to benefit from the improved services.

The above dismal prediction of the open-city model poses a public policy dilemma. It is obvious from figure 1 that permanent welfare improvements can come only by raising the rural utility level, not by raising the urban one. An increase in rural utility would decongest cities, reducing the urban population toward its optimum level. In reality, however, increasing the rural utility level is a virtually insurmountable challenge. The reason is that the lack of scale economies in the widely dispersed rural populations would require gargantuan and spatially ubiquitous spending by governments seeking to improve rural utility levels. By contrast, investing in flashy urban projects (for example, a new subway system in the large city) is both cheaper and much more appealing to voters who perceive these investments as beneficial even though all they do is to increase the urban size without creating real benefits after the additional migration that is induced.

I believe the open-city model to be important in understanding the welfare economics of rural-to-urban migration. The model is also useful in deflating potential myths that have emerged recently. One of these myths is mentioned by the authors. They note that the *hukou* system of urban population controls in China have not been beneficial. According to the open city model, however, this is far from clear. The answer is again in figure 1. Suppose that the government limits migration from rural to urban areas so that the urban population is near its optimal size. This is a nonequilibrium solution in which the urban area is put on a higher utility level than is the rural area, by shutting the door (or greatly raising the cost) on the rural population that would migrate there. But the result of this intrusive policy is that the average utility level in the country is higher than the rural utility level. More precisely, those who migrated to the cities despite the *hukou* restrictions clearly had a benefit, or otherwise they would not have done so. Those who stayed in the rural areas did not see their utility lowered, and those who were already in the urban area enjoy a higher level of utility because the *hukou* prevented the full incremental migration that would have further congested the urban area. Loss in agglomeration benefits are irrelevant as long as the *hukou* policy is active on the declining portion of the inverse U-shaped curve, where more population creates more costs than benefits.

There are other insights from urban economics that bear on the article's central theme. One of these has to do with the role of social networks in rural-to-urban migration. More precisely, consider the likely scenario that migrants move to the city because their friends or relatives have already moved there. Such social networks have ambiguous effects on economic opportunity. On the one hand, having a friend in the big city should make the migrant more willing to move there for a lower wage. On the other hand, the friends can help the migrant find cheaper housing, a better-paying job, or better access to public services. While I am inclined to believe that the latter effects dominate the former, I know of no formal research that either supports or contradicts my intuition.

Finally, there is the well-known model of Harris and Todaro that explained rural-to-urban migration in the face of high and persistent unemployment in the urban areas. As my colleague Edwin Mills pointed out during the conference, it may indeed be the case that the supposed involuntary unemployment of rural migrants in the large cities may be all smoke. It may indeed be the case that hard-to-observe informal and even illegal employment is keeping such migrants busy indeed. But, in the context of the authors' article, there is yet another reason to be cognizant of this model. The authors have stressed the importance of better urban public services as a cause of rural-to-urban migration. If these factors are really important, then it should be at least in part true that keeping the expected urban wage constant, higher unemployment or longer unemployment spells are tolerated by migrants to urban areas with better and more accessible urban services. Perhaps this is a hypothesis that the authors could test in the future.

A Few Thoughts on the Model Used by the Authors

An attractive aspect of the article is the use of a discrete choice model (logit) to explain the migration decision. The authors contribute meaningfully to that literature.

One of the less satisfying aspects of the empirical model is the specification of the utility function in which wages are entered specifically as explanatory variables but rents are ignored, which does not account well for the capitalization hypothesis. Again, wearing my urban economist hat, I have trouble with this. Apart from data limitations on rents, I can only anticipate a possible justification that I have heard before from others but never agreed with. One might be that rents at the migration destination k are indirectly captured by the X_k variables, so they are endogenous not exogenous. But so are wages. As well, rents paid by various types of migrants will vary in the same destination because of the immensely sophisticated differentiation that occurs in housing markets, just as wages will also vary (which the authors do take into account) because of the differentiation that occurs in the labor markets.

Finally, I would have liked to see the wage elasticities of labor supply calculated from the estimated logit. Since the model treats considerable variation among migrants and includes a variety of labor destinations, it would be of interest to learn how the elasticity of labor supply varies among larger and smaller urban destinations and for different types of migrants.

Jan K. Brueckner: Migration to cities from the rural or other disadvantaged areas of developing countries has been a long-time focus of development economists, who often rely on the conceptual framework of the Harris-Todaro model. That model attempted to explain the puzzle of continuing migration flows in the face of urban unemployment by identifying expected income, in a probabilistic sense, as the force luring migrants toward cities. The key insight is that, when urban wages are sufficiently high relative to rural wages, an appreciable likelihood of urban unemployment need not deter migrants since the city offers an attractive *expected* income despite the low chance of actually finding a high-wage urban job. In a Harris-Todaro equilibrium, rural-urban migration stops when the urban unemployment rate has risen to the point where rural incomes and expected urban incomes are equal.

In addition to this unemployment mechanism, additional forces may play a role in equilibrating rural-urban migration. Once such force, explored in a series of my own papers, is escalation in the urban cost of living in response to migration, particularly land and housing costs. As migrants crowd into cities, housing costs rise, and this escalation reduces the urban standard of living and limits the appeal of further migration. In this extended model, urban unemployment and rising housing prices jointly serve to equilibrate rural-urban migration flows.

172 Brookings-Wharton Papers on Urban Affairs: 2009

Such migration flows also depend on other elements of the economic environment in the origin and destination regions. While wages, unemployment rates, and housing costs are among these elements, the paper by Lall, Timmins, and Yu brings a welcome focus on another overlooked factor: public service levels. Superior access to public health facilities, schools, water, electricity, and sewage may motivate migration just as powerfully as the lure of better incomes. The chapter provides new and useful empirical estimates that document the strength of these attractive forces.

Even though this evidence shows that public services do indeed play a role in migration decisions, the equilibration forces described above do not operate so explicitly in this case. In particular, even though unemployment and housing costs rise as migrants pour into cities, an urban government may be committed to maintaining public service levels, which would then not deteriorate as the population swells. In this case, the labor and housing markets must do all the equilibrating work. However, if public service budgets are fixed or do not increase to match population growth, then public service levels will decline as the migrant population swells, and this force will operate in conjunction with rising unemployment and higher housing costs to limit the extent of migration. Thus, public service "congestion" could be added to the list of equilibrating forces in an expanded Harris-Todaro model.

Regardless of which view applies, Lall, Timmins, and Yu have identified an underappreciated policy lever that governments might use to exert control over migration flows. If a national government wishes to slow migration into a country's largest cities from rural areas or smaller hinterland cities, it could take steps to increase spending on public services in these origin regions. Given the findings of the authors, such spending would make migration less attractive, retarding the unwanted migration flows. In countries such as China, where migration flows are massive and tend to subvert the government's *hukou* system, improvement of rural public services would provide a means for limiting population pressure in the largest cities. A similar policy could be employed in Brazil, the focus of the authors' empirical work.

References

Anderson, K., and R. Pomfret. 2005. "Spatial Inequality and Development in Central Asia." In *Spatial Disparities in Human Development: Perspectives from Asia*, edited by Ravi Kanbur, Anthony J. Venables, and G. Wan. Tokyo: United Nations University Press.

Bayer, P., N. Keohane, and C. Timmins. 2009 (forthcoming). "Migration and Hedonic Valuation: The Case of Air Quality." *Journal of Environmental Economics and Management*.

Bayer, P., and C. Timmins. 2007. "Estimating Equilibrium Models of Sorting across Locations." *Economic Journal* 117 (518): 353–74.

Berry S. 1994. "Estimating Discrete Choice Models of Product Differentiation." *RAND Journal of Economics* 25: 242–62.

Berry, S., J. Levinsohn, and A. Pakes. 1995. "Automobile Prices in Market Equilibrium." *Econometrica* 63 (4): 841–90.

Bryceson, D. 1999. "Sub-Saharan Africa Betwixt and Between. Rural Livelihood Practices and Policies." Working Paper Series 43. Leiden, Netherlands: University of Leiden, African Studies Centre.

Carvalho, A. S., S. V. Lall, and C. Timmins. 2006. "Regional Subsidies and Industrial Prospects of Lagging Regions." Policy Research Working Paper Series 3843. Washington: World Bank.

Deshingkar, P., and S. Grimm. 2004. "Voluntary Internal Migration: An Update." Paper commissioned by the Urban and Rural Change Team and the Migration Team, Policy Division, Development for International Development (DFID) and the Overseas Development Institute (ODI) (London, September).

Falaris, E. 1987. "A Nested Logit Migration Model with Selectivity." *International Economic Review* 28: 429–43.

Greenwood, M. 1997. "Internal Migration in Developed Countries." In *Handbook of Population and Family Economics*, vol. 1B, edited by M. R. Rosenzweig and O. Stark, chapter 12, pp. 647–720. Amsterdam: North-Holland.

Hardoy, J. E., and D. Satterthwaite. 1989. *Squatter Citizen: Life in the Urban Third World*. London: Earthscan Publications.

Iliffe, J. 1995. *Africans: The History of a Continent*. Cambridge University Press.

Lall, S. V., H. Selod, and Z. Shalizi. 2006. "Rural-Urban Migration in Developing Countries: A Survey of Theoretical Predictions and Empirical Findings." Policy Research Working Paper Series 3915. Washington: World Bank.

Lucas Jr., R. E. 1988. "On the Mechanics of Economic Development." *Journal of Monetary Economics* 22 (1): 3–42.

Margo, R. A. 1988. "Schooling and the Great Migration." Working Paper 2697. Cambridge, Mass.: National Bureau of Economic Research.

Mont'Alverne, A. J., P. C. Ferreira, and M. A. Salvato. 2004. "Regional or Educational Disparities? A Counterfactual Exercise." Working Paper 532. Brazil: Fundação Getulio Vargas (FGV), Graduate School of Economics.

Romer, P. M. 1986. "Increasing Returns on Long-Run Growth." *Journal of Political Economy* 94 (5): 1002–037.

Sahn, D. E., and D. C. Stifel. 2003. "Urban-Rural Inequality in Living Standards in Africa." *Journal of African Economies* 12 (4): 564–97.

Solow, R. 1956. "A Contribution to the Theory of Economic Growth." *Quarterly Journal of Economics* 70 (1): 65–94.

Swan, T. 1956. "Economic Growth and Capital Accumulation." *Economic Record* 32: 334–61.

Venables, A. J., and R. Kanbur. 2005. *Spatial Inequality and Development, Overview of the UNU-WIDER Project*. Oxford University Press.

Wandschneider, T., and P. Mishra. 2003. *Rural Non-Farm Economy and Livelihood Enhancement*. Washington: National Resources Institute.

Whalley, John, and Shunming Zhang. 2007. "A Numerical Simulation Analysis of (Hukou) Labour Mobility Restrictions in China." *Journal of Development Economics* 83 (2) (July): 392–410.

World Bank. 2005. "Brazil: Regional Economic Development: (Some) Lessons from Experience." Washington: World Bank.

———. 2008. *World Development Report 2009: Reshaping Economic Geography*. Oxford University Press.

TOMOYA MORI
Kyoto University

TONY E. SMITH
University of Pennsylvania

A Reconsideration of the NAS Rule from an Industrial Agglomeration Perspective

Japan experienced rapid urbanization after the World War II as indicated, for example, by the fact that the population share of Densely Inhabited Districts (DID), nearly doubled between 1950 and 2000, from 34.9 percent to 65.2 percent, while accounting for only 3.3 percent of the national land.[1] Moreover, this rapid urbanization does not appear to be a simple proportional increase of economic activities in all urban areas. Rather, the spatial distributions of industries and population within the 258 metro areas (cities) of Japan are quite skewed. The population of the largest city, Tokyo, exceeded 30 million in 2000 and accounted for more than a quarter of the national population. The ten largest cities together accounted for more than a half of the national population. Moreover, if the *industrial diversity* of a given city is defined in terms of the number of industries exhibiting significant agglomeration within that city (see the section on cluster-based choice cities and industries below), then the population sizes of cities also appear to be highly correlated with their industrial diversities (see the section on the hierarchy principle).

We especially thank Gary Burtless, Gilles Duranton, Vernon Henderson, Wen-Tai Hsu, Yannis Ioannides, Edwin Mills, Art O'Sullivan, Janet Pack, John Quigley, and Ping Wang for stimulating discussions. This research has been partially supported by The Murata Science Foundation, The Grant in Aid for Research (Nos. 17330052, 18203016, 19330049) of the Ministry of Education, Culture, Sports, Science and Technology of Japan.

1. *Densely Inhabited Districts* are defined in the Population Census of Japan (Japan Statistics Bureau 1980, 2000) as a geographic areas having a residential population of at least 5,000 with a population density greater than $4,000/km^2$. These DIDs are also used in the World Urbanization Prospects (United Nations 2007) definition of "urban shares" of population.

A similarly drastic urbanization has been observed, for example, in South Korea where the "urban share of population" nearly quadrupled from 21.4 percent in 1950 to 79.6 percent in 2000. The corresponding percentages for the United States, western Europe, and western Asia are from 64.2 percent to 79.1 percent, 63.8 percent to 75.3 percent, and 16.5 percent to 40.4 percent, respectively.

175

Against this background, our main interest is to ask whether these skewed spatial distributions of industries and population exhibit any clear relationship, or whether they might simply have happened by chance. In Mori, Nishikimi, and Smith (2008), a strong empirical regularity was identified between the size and industrial composition of cities in Japan. This regularity, designated as the Number-Average Size (NAS) Rule, asserts a negative log-linear relation between the number and average population size of those cities where a given industry is present, that is, of the *choice cities* for that industry. More recently, this same regularity (with comparable definitions of industries and cities) has been reported for the United States by Hsu (2008).

But despite the strong empirical regularity of the NAS Rule, there still remains the statistical question of whether such location patterns could simply have occurred by chance. Of particular importance here is the focus of this rule on the presence or absence of industries in each city, rather than on the percentage distribution of industries across cities. Indeed, chance occurrences of certain choice cities may be quite likely if, for example, one includes cities where only a single industrial establishment happens to appear. Hence there is a need to clarify exactly what constitutes a *substantial industrial presence* in a given city. Although it is possible to characterize *substantial* in terms of some threshold number or share of industrial establishments or employment, such conventions are necessarily ad hoc. Hence an alternative approach is proposed in a companion paper, Mori and Smith (2009b), which characterizes *substantial* in terms of significant industrial agglomeration. More specifically, this approach utilizes the statistical procedure developed in Mori and Smith (2009a) to identify spatially explicit patterns of significant clustering (agglomeration) for each industry. In this context, the desired choice cities for each industry are taken to be those (economic) cities that share at least a part of a significant spatial cluster for the industry and therefore are designated as *cluster-based choice cities*.

With this new definition, it is shown in Mori and Smith (2009b) that the NAS Rule not only continues to hold for Japan but in some ways is even stronger. In particular, the few industrial outliers identified for the NAS Rule in the original analysis of Mori, Nishikimi, and Smith (2008) are shown here to be *without exception* industries for which no significant spatial agglomerations can be identified. Hence these results serve to suggest that the NAS Rule may in fact be an observable consequence of underlying coordination between spatial agglomerations of industry and population.

But unlike the original analysis in Mori, Nishikimi, and Smith (2008), the NAS Rule in Mori and Smith (2009b) is examined only for 2001. To that end, there remains the question of whether this rule continues to exhibit the same persistence over time that was seen in the original analysis. The results for 1981 have now been completed, and indeed they confirm persistence of the NAS Rule over this twenty-year period.[2] Thus the main objective of the present paper is to develop these new results and to compare them with the original analysis in Mori, Nishikimi, and Smith (2008).

This persistence is particularly remarkable given that it does not arise from simple proportional growth, such as a proportional increase in the number of cluster-based choice cities across industries or a proportional increase in the average sizes of these cities. On the contrary, there has been a substantial churning of these choice cities across industries (as developed later in the section on churning of cluster-based choice cities and industries).

It was also shown in Mori, Nishikimi, and Smith (2008) that there is an intimate theoretical connection between the NAS Rule and both the classical Rank Size Rule for cities and Christaller's (1966) Hierarchy Principle for industrial location behavior. Thus a final objective of the present paper is to analyze the persistence of these two additional regularities with respect to cluster-based industry-choice cities over the given twenty-year period.

To develop these results, we begin in the next section with an overview of both the city and industry data employed in this analysis. The third section, after the data section, then focuses on cluster-based choice cities (and cluster-based choice industries), as constructed in Mori and Smith (2009b). These cities are analyzed with respect to their relative employment concentrations and their key churning properties with respect to industry mix. This is followed in the subsequent section with a review of the NAS Rule itself and a presentation of the new findings of persistence. In the same section, this pattern of persistence is extended to the Hierarchy Principle and Rank Size Rule. Finally, the paper concludes with a brief discussion of ongoing work and directions for further research.

Data

The data used in the present analysis is very similar to that used in the original two-period analysis of Mori, Nishikimi, and Smith (2008). In the discussion below,

---

2. This involved restricting the admissible set of industries to those that are comparable between the two time periods. It should also be mentioned here that several months of computer time were required to generate sufficient random cluster patterns for testing the significance of agglomerations in each of these observed industrial location patterns.

Figure 1. Municipality Boundaries, 2001

Source: National Statistics Center of Japan (2009).

we focus on the differences between the two. We begin with city data and then consider industrial data.

Cities

The basic regional units in the present study that are used to identify economic cities and industrial agglomerations are municipalities. The 3,230 municipalities used in Mori, Nishikimi, and Smith (2008) were based on data in 2000. In the present paper, the municipality boundaries in 2000 are converted to the latest definition used in 2001, which creates certain minor differences. More important, the 13 major municipalities (such as Tokyo, Osaka, Nagoya, and Kyoto) have been divided into their individual *wards*, which are comparable in size to most other municipalities. This increases the total to 3,363 as of October 1, 2001. Finally, since industrial agglomerations are identified in terms of road-network distances (see the industry clusters section), we focus on the 3,207 municipalities that are geographically connected to the major islands of Japan (that is, Honshu, Hokkaido, Kyushu, and Shikoku) via a road network (refer to figure 1). The excluded municipalities account for only 1.6 percent of the total population in both 1980 and 2000 and should not have a significant effect on the analysis.

In terms of these basic regional units, an (*economic*) *city* is formally defined to be an Urban Employment Area (UEA), as proposed originally by Kanemoto and Tokuoka (2002). Each UEA is designed to be an urban area of Japan that is comparable to the metropolitan areas (MAs) of a Core Based Statistical Area (CBSA) in the United States.[3] Hence each UEA consists of a core set of municipalities designated as its business district (BD) together with a set of suburban municipalities from which workers commute toward the BD. Following Kanemoto and Tokuoka (2002), UEAs are constructed as aggregations of municipalities by a recursive procedure that is detailed in Mori, Nishikimi, and Smith (2008). Basically this construction starts with a large "seed" municipality, designated as the central municipality of the UEA. This in turn is extended to a BD and an approropriate set of suburban municipalities. However, the analysis in Mori, Nishikimi, and Smith (2008) used only Metropolitan Employment Areas (MEAs), that is, UEAs with central municpality populations of at least 50,000. In the present analysis, we include all UEAs as defined by Kanemoto and Tokuoka (2002) that have central municipality populations of at least 10,000. Those with central munipality populations below 50,000 are designated as Micropolitan Employment Areas. This broader definition yields 309 cities (UEAs) in 1980 and 258 cities in 2000 (compared with the respectively smaller sets of 105 and 113 MEAs used in Mori, Nishikimi, and Smith 2008).

Industries

As in Mori, Nishikimi, and Smith (2008), the industrial employment data used for the analyses in this paper are classified according to the three-digit Japanese Standard Industry Classification (JSIC) taken from the Establishment and Enterprise Census of Japan in 1981 and 2001 (Japan Statistics Bureau 1981, 2001) and are applied to the respective population data in 1980 and 2000. But unlike in Mori, Nishikimi, and Smith (2008), the present analysis focuses on manufacturing. For while services and wholesale-retail industries tend to be found almost everywhere, that is, they are ubiquitous, manufacturing industries exhibit a much larger diversity of location patterns at the three-digit level. Therefore, as observed in Mori, Nishikimi, and Smith (2008), the NAS Rule itself is far more interesting for manufacturing industries.[4]

3. For the definition of a CBSA, see U.S. Office of Management and Budget (2000).
4. This can be seen quite dramatically in figure B1 of appendix B in Mori, Nishikimi, and Smith (2008), where the 125 manufacturing industries shown (see footnote 14) are a subset of those used here.

There were 152 and 164 manufacturing industries at the three-digit level in 1981 and 2001, respectively. Hence, to achieve comparability between industrial location patterns in these two years, industries in each year have been aggregated in a manner that yields the largest number of common classifications with a positive number of establishments for both years. This aggregation resulted in 147 common manufacturing industrial classifications for both years.[5] This number is further reduced to 139 industries that exhibit at least some degree of significant agglomeration (as discussed in industry clusters below).

Cluster-Based Choice Cities and Industries

As stated in the introduction, the central objective of this paper is to reexamine the NAS Rule with respect to cluster-based choice (cb-choice) cities for each industry. Since the identification of cb-choice cities for industries is developed fully in Mori and Smith (2009a, 2009b), we only sketch the main ideas below. Given the definition of cities above, the focus here will be on the identification of significant industrial clusters. These clusters are used to define cb-choice cities for each industry when we discuss the definitions of cluster-based choice cities and industries. From the city perspective, there is a completely parallel concept of cb-choice industries for each city. This is followed with a brief consideration of the relative industrial employment concentration in cb-choice cities relative to all other cities. Finally, the churning of industrial locations is considered from both industry and city viewpoints in the last subsection.

Industrial Clusters

Our approach to the identification of significant clusters of regions (municipalities) for a given industry is closely related to the statistical clustering procedures proposed by Besag and Newell (1991), Kulldorff and Nagarwalla (1995), and Kulldorff (1997). To test for the presence of clusters, these procedures start by postulating an appropriate null hypothesis of no clustering. In the present case, this hypothesis is characterized by a uniform distribution of industrial locations across regions.[6] Such clustering procedures then seek to determine the single most significant cluster of regions with respect to this hypothesis. Candidate clusters are typically defined to be approximately cir-

5. See appendix A for the details of this industrial aggregation.
6. Here *uniformity* is defined with respect to an areal measure of the economic area of each region (municipality). Details of this measurement procedure are given in Mori and Smith (2009a).

cular areas containing all regions having centroids within some specified distance of a given reference point (such as the centroid of a central region). The approach developed in Mori and Smith (2009a) extends these procedures in two ways. First, the notion of a circular cluster of regions is extended to the more general (metric-space) concept of a *convex solid*, as defined with respect to the shortest travel-distance metric on the given set of regions.[7] Next, individual (convex solid) clusters, C, are extended to the more global concept of cluster schemes. If the set of relevant regions (municipalities), r, is denoted by R, then each cluster scheme, $\mathbf{C} = (R_0, C_1, \ldots C_{k_C})$, is taken to be a partition of R into one or more disjoint clusters, $C_1, \ldots C_{k_C}$, together with the residual set, R_0, of all noncluster regions. Each cluster scheme then induces a family of possible location probability models, called cluster probability models, $p_C = [p_C(j) : j = 1, \ldots, k_C]$, in which it is implicitly hypothesized that industrial establishments are more likely to be located in one of the cluster regions than in a noncluster region (and where $p_C(R_0) = 1 - \Sigma_j p_C(j)$). Each cluster probability model, p_C, thus amounts formally to multinomial sampling models on its underlying cluster schemes, $\mathbf{C}$.[8]

In this context, the local problem of finding a single, most likely cluster is replaced by the global problem of finding a cluster probability model that best fits the full set of industry locations. In turn, this is seen to be an instance of the general statistical goodness-of-fit problem, that is, the problem of selecting a best-fit model from among a family of candidate probability models for a given set of sample data. While many model-selection criteria have been proposed for doing so, the criterion chosen here is the Bayesian Information Criterion (BIC) first proposed by Schwarz (1978).[9] Essentially this criterion involves a trade-off between the likelihood of the given sample data under each candidate model and the number of parameters (cluster probabilities) used in the model.[10]

To find a best cluster model with respect to this criterion, it would of course be ideal to compare all possible cluster schemes that can be constructed from the given system of regions. But even for modest numbers of regions, this is a

7. Here *shortest travel distance* is defined with respect to *road-network distance*, as detailed in Mori and Smith (2009a).

8. Other models of this type include the model-based clustering approach of Dasgupta and Raftery (1998), and the Bayesian approach of Gangnon and Clayton (2000, 2004). See Mori and Smith (2009a, footnote 7) for further discussion.

9. Among the many other model-selection criteria that are applicable here, the most prominent are Akaike's (1973) Information Criterion (AIC) and the Normalized Maximum Likelihood (NML) Criterion by Kontkanen and Myllymäki (2005). A comparison of these criteria in the present context will be presented in Smith and Mori (2009).

10. Further details are given in Mori and Smith (2009a, 2009b).

practical impossibility. Hence the approach taken in Mori and Smith (2009a) is to develop a heurisitic algorithm that searches among the set of candidate models for the best model with respect to the BIC criterion. To do so, one starts by finding the best cluster probability model with an underlying cluster scheme consisting of exactly one single-region cluster (municipality). More elaborate cluster schemes are then grown by adding new disjoint clusters or by either expanding or combining existing clusters until no further improvement in the BIC model-selection criterion is possible. The final result is thus guaranteed to yield at least a locally best cluster scheme with respect to this criterion.[11] If the set of manufacturing industries is denoted by I, then let the best cluster scheme found for industry, $i \in I$, be denoted by $\mathbf{C}_i = (R_{i0}, C_{i1}, ..., C_{ik_i})$.

Cluster schemes for each of the 147 manufacturing industries were constructed for 1981 and 2001. Since the construction procedure and analysis of these cluster schemes is identical for both years, we drop time distinctions and simply take $\mathbf{C}_i$ to be a generic representation of both cluster schemes for each industry i. In addition it should be noted that both cluster schemes for each of these 147 industries contain at least one cluster, and hence are nondegenerate.

But even when cluster schemes are nondegenerate, there remains the statistical question of whether such clustering could simply have occurred by chance. Indeed, even completely random location patterns will tend to exhibit some degree of clustering.[12] Therefore, for each industry i, one can ask how the optimal criterion value, BIC_i, obtained for $\mathbf{C}_i$ compares with typical values obtained by applying the same cluster detection procedure to randomly generated spatial data. This testing procedure can be formalized in terms of the null hypothesis of complete spatial randomness, which asserts that individual establishment locations are independently and uniformly distributed over the economic areas of regions. Under this hypothesis, therefore, the probability, $P(r)$, that any given establishment will locate in region (municipality), $r \in R$, is taken to be proportional to the size of economic area of region r. Monte Carlo simulation can then be employed to estimate the sampling distribution of BIC_i under this hypothesis, and a one-sided test can be performed to determine whether the observed value of BIC_i is significantly large relative to this distribution. Those industries with clustering that is not significant at the 5 percent level are said to exhibit spurious clustering.[13]

---

11. See Mori and Smith (2009a) for further details.
12. In fact, the complete absence of clustering is statistically consistent with a significantly dispersed (ubiquitous) pattern of industrial locations, which is the complete opposite of clustering (agglomeration).
13. See Mori and Smith (2009a).

Among the 147 industries for which clusters were identified, all were extremely significant (with p values close to zero) except for 8 industries where complete spatial randomness could not be rejected at the 5 percent level. These include six arms-related industries (JSIC381, 383–387), together with tobacco (JSIC194), and coke manufacturing (JSIC273). Besides the small numbers of establishments in these industries, they also are rather special in other ways.[14] Tobacco manufacturing and arms-related industries are highly regulated industries, so that their location patterns are not determined by market forces. Finally, coke production is a typical declining industry in Japan (steel industries have gradually replaced coke production with less expensive powder coal after the 1970s).

Thus our present analysis is based on the remaining 139 industries that exhibit some degree of significant clustering. For these industries, the percentages of establishments included in clusters range from 39.1 percent to 100 percent (with an average of 94.1 percent) in 2001, while the corresponding percentages in 1981 range from 51.8 percent to 100 percent (with an average of 95.7 percent).[15]

Definition of Cluster-Based Choice Cities and Cluster-Based Choice Industries

For each industry with significant clustering, we can now define its set of corresponding cluster-based choice cities as follows. First, if the set of all cities (UEAs) in a given year is indexed by U, and if the subset of cities with positive employment in industry i is indexed by $U_i^+ \subseteq U$ (where again we drop time distinctions), then a city, $k \in U_i^+$, is designated as a cluster-based choice city for industry i, if and only if there is some cluster, $C_i \in \mathbf{C}_i$, such that

$$(1) \qquad\qquad\qquad UEA_k \cap C_i \neq \varnothing.$$

In other words, UEA_k is a cb-choice city for i, if and only if (iff) it shares at least one positive i-employment municipality with some cluster in $\mathbf{C}_i$.[16] Let the set of cb-choice cities for i be indexed simply by U_i. To distinguish this notion from the original set of choice cities, U_i^+, proposed in Mori, Nishikimi, and Smith

---

14. All have less than 40 establishments, with an average of 7.89 establishments (compared with the average of 6,183 establishments for the other industries in 2001). Establishment location data are not available for tobacco manufacturing (JSIC194) in 1981 since it was operated by the national government.

15. For further discussion, see Mori and Smith (2009b).

16. Here it should be noted that the "convexity" requirement on clusters in $\mathbf{C}_i$ implies that a cluster may contain some municipalities with no i employment. Hence as a minimum condition, cb-choice cities for i are required to share cluster municipalities in $\mathbf{C}_i$ with *positive* i employment.

(2008), it is convenient to designate all cities in U_i^+ as presence-based (pb) choice cities for industry i.

Note that the intersection in equation 1 can be interpreted in terms of individual cities as well as industries. In particular, one may designate industry i as a cb-choice industry for city k iff $k \in U_i^+$ and equation 1 holds for some cluster, $C_i \in \mathbf{C}_i$. As a parallel to U_i, one may then index the set of cb-choice industries, $i \in I$, for city k by I_k. Hence, in the same way that the number ($\#U_i$) of cb-choice cities for a given industry reflects its location diversity, the number ($\#I_k$) of cb-choice industries for a given city reflects its industrial diversity. These diversity measures exhibit great variation across industries and cities alike. With respect to the 139 industries studied, $\#U_i$ ranges from 14 to 275 (with an average of 116.3) cities in 1981, and ranges from 12 to 227 (with an average of 101.7) cities in 2001. Similarly, for the 309 cities identified in 1980, $\#I_k$ ranges from 2 to 139 (with an average of 52.3) industries in 1981, and for the 258 cities identified in 2000, $\#I_k$ covers the full range from 1 to 139 (with an average of 54.8) industries. We shall examine some additional empirical properties of these dual relations in the last subsection below.

Industrial Concentration in Cluster-Based Choice Cities

Next, recall that the primary motivation for the present definition of cb-choice cities was to characterize substantial industry presence in terms of agglomeration behavior. Hence we next consider how this endogenous approach relates to more exogenous threshold approaches in terms of industrial concentration. Such concentration can be measured in terms of either employment or numbers of establishments in cities. The key finding here is that with respect to both these measures, cb-choice cities for industries do indeed exhibit larger concentrations than do other cities in which the industry is present.

To state this more precisely, let E_{ik} and N_{ik} denote respectively the employment size and number of establishments of industry i in city k. Then, the employment-concentration ratio, R_i^{emp}, of average i-employment in cb-choice cities, U_i, to that in all other cities with positive i-employment, $U_i^+ - U_i$, is given by:

(2)
$$R_i^{emp} \equiv \frac{\dfrac{1}{\#U_i}\sum_{k \in U_i} E_{ik}}{\dfrac{1}{\#U_i^+ - \#U_i}\sum_{k \in U_i^+ - U_i} E_{ik}}.$$

Similarly, the establishment-concentration ratio, R_i^{est}, of the average number of *i*-establishments in cb-choice cities, U_i, to that in all other cities with positive *i*-employment, $U_i^+ - U_i$, is given by:

$$(3) \qquad R_i^{est} \equiv \frac{\dfrac{1}{\#U_i}\sum_{k \in U_i} N_{ik}}{\dfrac{1}{\#U_i^+ - \#U_i}\sum_{k \in U_i^+ - U_i} N_{ik}}.$$

The frequency distributions of concentration ratios, R_i^{emp} and R_i^{est}, over all 139 industries, *i*, with significant clustering in 2001 are shown in figures 2 and 3, respectively. Here R_i^{emp} ranges from 1.17 to 121.00 (with an average value of 15.19), and R_i^{est} ranges from 1.47 to 71.74 (with an average value of 15.05). Notice in particular that *all* ratios are greater than one. Hence it is clear that cb-choice cities for each industry *i* do indeed exhibit relatively large concentrations without imposing ad hoc threshold sizes on such concentrations.

Churning of Cluster-Based Choice Cities and Cluster-Based Choice Industries

Recall from the section above that for each time period there is a wide range in the locational diversities of industries and the industrial diversities of cities. But even more important is the fact that there has been a considerable amount of churning of industries across cities and vice versa. One way to examine these effects is to consider changes in the number of cb-choice cities for each industry *i* between 1981 and 2001, as shown in figure 4. Here figure 4(a) shows these changes as calculated using the respective city boundaries identified for each year. Figure 4(b) shows these changes using the 2000 city boundaries for both years (so that only changes in industrial agglomeration patterns are reflected). In both figures, industries are ordered by their locational diversity (that is, by the number of cb-choice cities) in 1981. The vertical bar shown for each industry is divided into two segments. The length of the upper segment corresponds to the number of new cb-choice cities for this industry in 2001 that were not cb-choice cities in 1981, and the length of the lower segment is the number of old cb-choice cities in 1981 that ceased to be cb-choice cities by 2001. These two diagrams suggest that regardless of changes in city boundaries, there are significant numbers of both exiting and entering cb-choice cities for most industries.

An alternative way to examine these churning effects is to measure changes in the set of cb-choice cities for each industry between these two years. If the

Figure 2. Average Employment Size of Cluster-Based Choice Cities Relative to That of Presence-based Ones

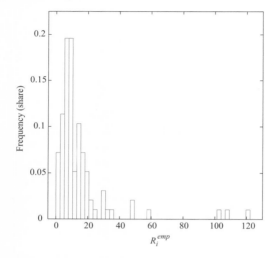

Source: Japan Statistics Bureau (2001) and authors' calculations.

Figure 3. Average Establishment Count of Cluster-Based Choice Cities Relative to That of Presence-based Ones

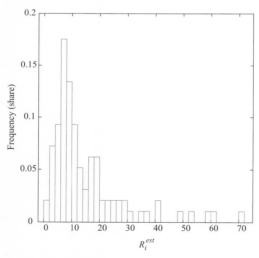

Source: Japan Statistics Bureau (2001) and authors' calculations.

Figure 4. Change in the Number of Choice Cities

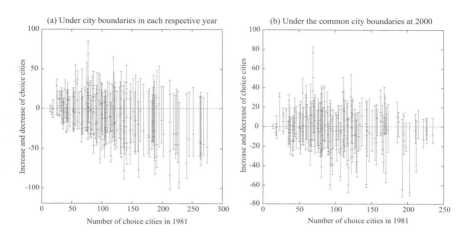

Source: Japan Statistics Bureau (1980, 1981, 2000, 2001) and authors' calculations.

sets of cb-choice cities for each industry $i \in I$ in 1981 and 2001 (with respect to 2000 city boundaries) are denoted respectively by U_i^{1981} and U_i^{2001}, then the churning of cb-choice cities for i can be measured as follows:

$$(4) \qquad CHURN_i^{cities} = 1 - \frac{\#(U_i^{1981} \cap U_i^{2001})}{\#(U_i^{1981} \cup U_i^{2001})}.$$

Hence complete churning corresponds to $CHURN_i^{cities} = 1$, where all cb-choice cities for industry i have changed from 1981 to 2001. Similarly, $CHURN_i^{cities} = 0$ implies no churning. The frequency distribution of these churning values across all 139 industries with significant clustering is shown in figure 5. The values of $CHURN_i^{cities}$ range from 0.06 to 0.78 with an average of 0.41. Here more than half of the cb-choice cities for thirty-nine (28.1 percent) of these industries were replaced during this twenty-year period (and more than a quarter were replaced for at least 80 percent of the industries). In short, these industries have exhibited dramatic churning of their locations during this period. Similar rapid adjustments of industrial locations have been documented for France and the United States by Duranton (2007).[17]

---

17. The employment share–based measure of churning of industrial locations adopted by Duranton (2007) is somewhat problematic when relatively disaggregated industries are considered (as in the present study) since employment shares may often be zero.

Figure 5. Churning of Choice Cities

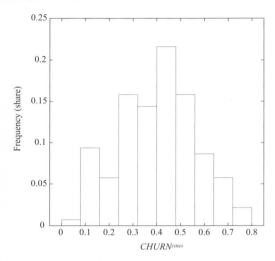

Source: Japan Statistics Bureau (1980, 1981, 2000, 2001) and authors' calculations.

Such churning can also be measured from the city perspective. Here we focus on the 258 cities identified in 2000 and use their 2000 boundaries for analysis. As a parallel to the industries analysis above, we first consider changes in the number of cb-choice industries for each city, k, during this twenty-year period, as shown in figure 6. Here cities are ordered on the x-axis in terms of their industrial diversity (that is, number of cb-choice industries) in 1981. The length of the upper segment of the vertical bar for each city k now corresponds to the number of new cb-choice industries for k in 2001 that were not cb-choice industries for k in 1981, and the length of the bottom segment corresponds to the number of cb-choice industries for k in 1981 that had ceased to be cb-choice industries for k by 2001.

It is clear from the figure that the change in industrial composition is smallest for the most diversified and the least diversified cities. This is partly due to the fact the industry classification is fixed, so that the number of choice industries has little room for increase in the most diversified cities. Similarly, there is little room for decrease in the least diversified cities. But, as figure 6 shows, there is also little decrease for the most diversified cities, and little increase for the least diversified cities. So the industrial diversification of cities at both ends of the spectrum appears to be relatively stable during this twenty-year period.

Figure 6. Change in the Number of Choice Industries of Cities

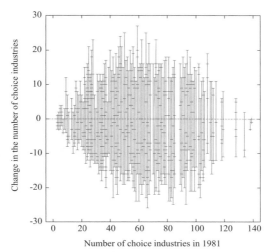

Source: Japan Statistics Bureau (1980, 1981, 2000, 2001) and authors' calculations.

Thus, churning of cb-choice industries occurs mostly in cities with intermediate levels of industrial diversity.

As with industries, these churning effects can also be examined by measuring changes in the sets of cb-choice industries for cities. To do so, let the sets of cb-choice industries for each city k in 1981 and 2001 (with respect to 2001 city boundaries) be denoted by I_k^{1981} and I_k^{2001}. Then the churning of cb-choice industries for k can be measured as follows:

$$(5) \qquad CHURN_k^{indus} = 1 - \frac{\#(I_k^{1981} \cap I_k^{2001})}{\#(I_k^{1981} \cup I_k^{2001})},$$

where complete churning of industries for k again corresponds to $CHURN_k^{indus}$ = 1, and where $CHURN_k^{indus} = 0$ again implies no churning. The frequency distribution of $CHURN_k^{indus}$ across all cities, k, is shown in figure 7. Here the values of $CHURN_k^{indus}$ take on the full range from 0.0 to 1.0, with an average of 0.58. As with cb-choice cities above, there is substantial churning of cb-choice industries. Here more than half of the cb-choice industries for 77 (30.0 percent) of these 258 cities are replaced (and more than a quarter were replaced for 216, or 83.7 percent, of these cities).

Figure 7. Churning of Choice Industries between 1981 and 2001

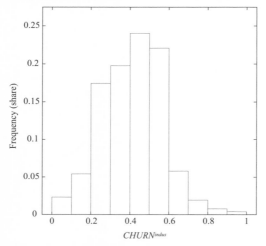

Source: Japan Statistics Bureau (1980, 1981, 2000, 2001) and authors' calculations.

The NAS Rule and its Associated Empirical Regularities

Given the definitions and preliminary findings above, we turn now to the major results of this paper. Here we begin with the NAS Rule itself below and consider its persistence properties for the case of Japan under our new definition of cluster-based choice cities. These persistence properties are then extended to the associated Hierarchy Principle and Rank Size Rule in the next two sections, respectively.

The NAS Rule

In the present setting, the Number-Average Size (NAS) Rule first formulated in Mori, Nisikimi, and Smith (2008) (in terms of pb-choice cities) now asserts that there is a log-linear relationship between the number and average size of cb-choice cities for industries. With respect to this new definition of choice cities, the main result of the present paper is shown in figure 8.

In figure 8, the logs of both the number of cb-choice cities ($\#CITY$) and average size of cb-choice cities ($\overline{SIZE}$) are plotted for the relevant 147 manufacturing industries in 1981 and 2001.[18] The specific points corresponding to the eight

---

18. In terms of the notation in the section on definitions of cb-choice cities and industries above, for each industry i, $\#CITY_i = \#U_i$ and $\overline{SIZE}_i$ is the average size of all cities in U_i.

Figure 8. Average Size versus the Number of Choice Cities of Industries

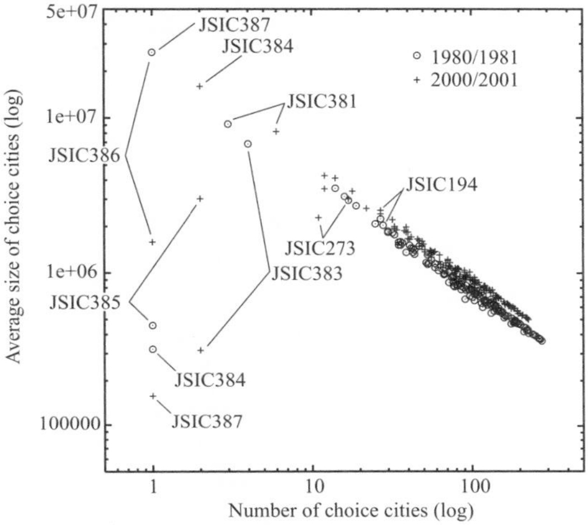

Source: Japan Statistics Bureau (1980, 1981, 2000, 2001) and authors' calculations.

industries with spurious clustering are indicated in figure 8, and they show that *all outliers* are in this group. Hence for those 139 industries with significant clustering, the relations shown for each year are almost exactly log linear. This can be verified by a simple OLS regression, which yields the following results for each year:[19]

$$(6) \quad 1980 - 1981 : \log(\overline{SIZE}) = 16.92 - 0.734 \log(\#CITY), R^2 = 0.996,$$
$$\underset{(0.0309)}{} \quad \underset{(0.00668)}{}$$

$$(7) \quad 2000 - 2001 : \log(\overline{SIZE}) = 17.01 - 0.716 \log(\#CITY), R^2 = 0.996,$$
$$\underset{(0.0286)}{} \quad \underset{(0.00635)}{}$$

where the values in parentheses are standard errors. It should be noted that since the dependent variables are neither normally distributed nor independent by construction, the linear estimates in equations 6 and 7 are best regarded as "curve fitting" rather than genuine statistical models (as pointed out by Eaton and Eckstein (1997, p. 452, footnote 19).[20] However, it should also be emphasized that

19. Because our city data are for 1980 and 2000 while our industry data are for 1981 and 2001, we shall sometimes denote these two periods by 1980/1981 and 2000/2001, respectively.

20. It should also be noted that if city sizes are distributed according to a power law (as implied by the Rank Size Rule below), then as pointed out by Gabaix and Ioannides (2004, section 2.2.1), the standard errors in these regressions may be grossly underestimated. But in the present case, with R^2 values almost 1, it should be clear that such standard errors add little in the way of new information.

these strong log-linear relations are not simply the result of some underlying tautology. In particular, the drastic outliers in figure 8 suggest that for industries without strong agglomeration tendencies, this NAS Rule may not be relevant at all. Hence it can be conjectured that insofar as agglomeration behavior is a reflection of economic factors, the NAS Rule is most relevant for industries where location decisions are largely governed by economic considerations.

Aside from the obvious strength of this log-linear relation, it should also be emphasized that the slopes of these two regression lines are almost the same. This can again be tested by pooling the data for both time periods, introducing a time dummy and applying standard F tests to evaluate coefficient shifts. While the statistical validity of such a test is again questionable in terms of normality and independence, the results clearly support invariance of the slope coefficient. However, the intercept does exhibit a significant shift, as can easily be seen from figure 8. So while both the numbers and average sizes of cb-choice cities for individual industries have changed, they have done so in a manner that leaves their elasticity of substitution invariant. More specifically, a 1 percent increase in the number of cb-choice cities for an industry from 1981 to 2001 corresponds roughly to a 0.7 percent decrease in the average size of these cities during the same twenty-year period.

The stability of this relation is even more remarkable in view of the dramatic churning of industries across cities during this period (as discussed in the section on churning above). In addition, there has also been a substantial reordering of city sizes themselves (as discussed below). The invariance of the NAS Rule adds further support to the conjecture that this implicit coordination between industrial and population locations is driven by the same underlying economic forces over time. Although the exact nature of these forces remains an open question, the recent model proposed by Hsu (2008) suggests that scale economies of production may constitute one important contributing factor.

The results in Hsu (2008) together with the original analysis in Mori, Nishikimi, and Smith (2008) show that this NAS Rule is intimately connected with two other well-known classical regularities of city systems, namely, Christaller's (1966) Hierarchy Principle and the Rank Size Rule of city size distributions. Hence the invariance of the NAS Rule above suggests that these two regularities may also exhibit invariance properties. We now consider each of these regularities in the context of our present manufacturing data.

The Hierarchy Principle

The Hierarchy Principle originally proposed by Christaller (1966) asserts that industries found in cities of a given size will also be found in all cities of larger sizes. The approach of Mori, Nishikimi, and Smith (2008) was to redefine this principle in terms of industrial diversity (that is, the number of choice industries for a city) rather than by population size. Hence our present version of the Hierarchy Principle asserts that industries in cities with a given level of industrial diversity (that is, a given number of cb-choice industries) will also be found in all cities with larger industrial diversities. This version is formally somewhat weaker than the original population version of Christaller and hence constitutes a necessary condition for the classical Hierarchy Principle.[21] The main advantage of this reformulation is that it allows the Hierarchy Principle to be tested without altering the industrial diversity structure of the city system. Moreover, this weaker version is in reality very closely related to the classical version. In the present case, Spearman's rank correlation between the industrial diversity levels and populations of cities is around 0.75 for both 1980/1981 and 2000/2001.

Before testing this principle in the present setting, it is useful to consider the city-industry relationships depicted graphically in figure 9, using 2001 data. Here, cities, k, are ordered by their industrial diversities (number of cb-choice industries) on the horizontal axis, and industries, i, are ordered by their locational diversities (number of cb-choice cities) on the vertical axis. A plus symbol (+) in position (k, i) indicates that k is a cb-choice city for industry i (and equivalently, that i is a cb-choice industry for city k). If we distinguish such positions as positive, then the Hierarchy Principle asserts that for each positive position (k, i), then there must also be a + in every column position $(\cdot, i)$ to the right of (k, i), indicating that all cities with industrial diversities greater than or equal to city k are also cb-choice cities for industry i. Hence it is clear from the figure that while the Hierarchy Principle does not hold perfectly, the row density of + values increases from left to right in virtually every row. Hence there is clearly a strong level of agreement with the Hierarchy Principle that could not have occurred by chance.[22]

A formal statistical test of this assertion was developed in Mori, Nishikimi, and Smith (2008). To apply this test in the present context, it suffices to outline the basic elements of the test in terms of figure 9 (see Mori, Nishikimi, and Smith 2008, section 4 for a detailed development). To do so, observe first

21. See footnote 40 in Mori, Nishikimi, and Smith (2008).

22. Note that this figure bears a strong resemblance to figure 7 in Mori, Nishikimi, and Smith (2008). The key difference for our present purposes is the new cluster-based definition of choice cites for industries. However, it should be noted that the inclusion of Micropolitan Employment Areas in the present analysis greatly expands the range of cities with small industrial diversities (at the left end of the city scale). It should also be noted that the SIC classification system for industries is by no means exact; some level of disagreement in such hierarchical relations is unavoidable.

Figure 9. Industry-Location Events

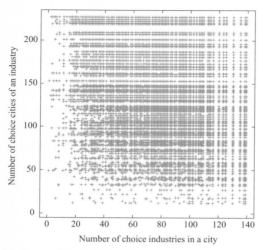

Source: Japan Statistics Bureau (2000, 2001) and authors' calculations.

that each occurrence of a full row of + values to the right of a positive position (k, i) can be regarded as a "full hierarchy event" at (k, i) in the sense that it is fully consistent with the Hierarchy Principle. However, in cases where only small fraction of + values are missing, it is natural to regard this as being closer to a full hierarchy event than if all + values were missing. To distinguish between such cases, it is appropriate to designate the fraction of positive positions to the right of each positive (k, i) as the fractional hierarchy event, H_{ki}, at (k, i). Thus $0 \leq H_{ki} \leq 1$, with $H_{ki} = 1$ denoting a full hierarchy event at (k, i). Note also that since by definition each positive position (k, i) generates a unique fractional hierarchy event (of which it is the left end point), the number, h, of fractional hierarchy events is precisely the number of positive positions (+ values) in the figure. Hence, as a measure of overall consistency with the Hierarchy Principle, we designate the average of these fractional hierarchy events as the (observed) hierarchy share,

$$(8) \qquad\qquad p_0 = \frac{1}{h} \sum_{ki} H_{ki},$$

for the given system of cities and industries. By definition, $0 \leq p_0 \leq 1$, with $p_0 = 1$ now denoting exact agreement with the Hierarchy Principle, that is, all fractional hierarchy events are full.

In this context, one possible null hypothesis for testing the Hierarchy Principle would be that this figure is the realization of a stochastic process in which *h* of these + values are assigned randomly to (k, i) pairs (without replacement). However, it can be argued that this null hypothesis is too strong in the sense that it not only ignores industrial hierarchies but also ignores the basic urban structure of the city system itself. For example, major cities such as Tokyo and Osaka are implicitly treated as indistinguishable from even the smallest micropolitan cities in Japan. To preserve actual urban structure to some degree, we thus choose to hold the industrial diversity of each city fixed.[23] To test this Hierarchy Principle, the null hypothesis, H_0, adopted here is that the observed distribution of + values in figure 9 is the realization of a stochastic process that assigns random + values in a manner that preserves the industrial diversity of each city, that is, preserves the number of + values in each column of the figure. Since the industrial diversity of city k is given by the number of its cb-choice industries, $\#I_k$, it follows that this process is easily realized by randomly selecting $\#I_k$ cb-choice industries from I for each city k. By constructing a large number of such realizations, say 1,000, and calculating the hierarchy share, p_m, for each realization, $m = 1, \ldots, 1000$, one can then test the Hierarchy Principle by simply checking whether the observed hierarchy share, p_0, is unusually large relative to this sample of typical share values under H_0.

The results of this (one-sided) test in the present case provide a strong rejection of H_0 in favor of significantly large hierarchy shares. In particular, for the 2001 data in figure 9, the observed hierarchy share is $p_0 = 0.775$, while the simulated hierarchy shares under H_0 ranged from 0.622 to 0.631.[24] Thus, even when the industrial diversity structure of this city system is held fixed, the statistical evidence in favor of the Hierarchy Principle is overwhelming. A parallel application of this test to the 1981 data produced essentially the same findings, with an observed hierarchy share of $p_0 = 0.772$ and a simulated range of hierarchy shares from 0.612 to 0.618 under H_0. The similarity of these values shows that in spite of the dramatic churning of both industries and city sizes during this twenty-year period, the overall hierarchical structure of industrial locations has remained remarkably stable.

Finally, it is of interest to consider the implications of these results for the NAS Rule itself. The relation between this rule and the Hierarchy Principle is seen most easily in terms of the broader definitions of these concepts in Mori, Nishikimi, and Smith (2008), in which the classical Hierarchy Principle (in terms of city size) was used and choice cities for each industry i were taken to

23. Recall that since industrial diversity is highly rank correlated with city size, this convention tends to preserve the ordering city sizes as well.

24. The observed value of p_0 is so far above this range that larger simulation sizes would surely yield similar results.

include the larger set, U_i^+, of all cities where i is found. If this classical Hierarchy Principle were to hold exactly, and if we denote the smallest choice city for i by $\tilde{k}_i \in U_i^+$, then U_i^+ would consist precisely of all cities with populations at least as large as $\tilde{k}_i$. Moreover, $\#U_i^+$ would then be the number of cities at least as large as $\tilde{k}_i$, which is by definition the (population) rank of city $\tilde{k}_i$. Under these conditions, the NAS Rule is equivalent to a negative log-linear relation between the rank of city $\tilde{k}_i$ and the average of all city sizes at least as large as $\tilde{k}_i$, designated in Mori, Nishikimi, and Smith (2008) as the upper-average city size for $\tilde{k}_i$. If the rank and upper-average city size of each city, k, are denoted respectively by $RANK_k$ and $\widehat{SIZE}_k$ then the plot of $\log\widehat{SIZE}$ against $\log(RANK)$ for all cities in plot b of figure 10 in Mori, Nishikimi, and Smith (2008) showed a remarkably close relation to a plot of the actual values of $\log(\overline{SIZE})$ and $\log(\#CITY)$ in plot a of figure 10.[25]

In the present context, both the definitions of choice cities (as cb-choice cities) and the Hierarchy Principle (in terms of industrial diversity) have changed. However, as noted at the beginning of this section, the rank correlation between city size and industrial diversity continues to be high. This, together with the test results above (as well as the direct evidence in figure 9), suggests that the average size of cb-choice cities in $U_i(\subset U_i^+)$ should still agree reasonably well with the upper-average city size for the smallest cb-choice city, $k_i \in U_i$. This relation is demonstrated in figure 10 below, which bears a striking resemblance to figure 10 in Mori, Nishikimi, and Smith (2008). Here, using data for 2001, $\log\widehat{SIZE}$ is again plotted against $\log(RANK)$ for all cities in plot b of figure 10. Similarly, for the present definition cb-choice cities, $\log(\overline{SIZE})$ is plotted against $\log(\#CITY)$ in plot a of figure 10.[26] It is clear, therefore, that the present restriction to cb-choice cities (as well as the inclusion of Micropolitan Employment Areas) has made little difference. These relations are both very close, where the slightly flatter slope of the NAS Rule again reflects imperfections in the Hierarchy Principle.

Note also that if $\underline{SIZE}_k$ denotes the average of all city sizes smaller than city k, then in the same way that $\widehat{SIZE}_k$ represents the natural upper bound on $\overline{SIZE}_k$, the value $\underline{SIZE}_k$ represents a natural lower bound. In these terms, the plot of $\log(\underline{SIZE})$ against $\log(\#CITY)$ in plot c of figure 10 shows that within its feasible range of values, $\log(\overline{SIZE})$ is almost identical with its upper bound. As

---

25. As in footnote 18 above, for each industry i, $\#CITY_i$ here represents $\#U_i^+$, and $\overline{SIZE}_i$ is the average size of all cities in U_i^+.

26. Plot a is identical with the plot of 2001 data in figure 8, in which all industries with spurious clustering have now been removed.

Figure 10. City Size Distribution and the NAS Rule

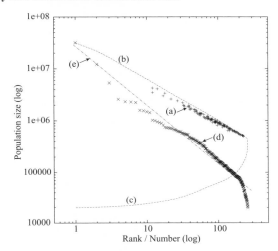

Source: Japan Statistics Bureau (2000, 2001) and authors' calculations.

observed in Mori, Nishikimi, and Smith (2008), this serves to further under-score the extremely nonrandom nature of plot a.

Finally, in view of the closeness of plot a to this upper bound in plot b, it is of interest to ask whether the stability of the NAS Rule in equations 6 and 7 above is also reflected in this upper-bound relation between $\log \widehat{SIZE}$ and $\log(RANK)$. The corresponding regression results for 1980/1981 and 2000/2001 are shown below:

$$(9) \quad 1980 - 1981 : \log(\widehat{SIZE}) = \underset{(0.00692)}{17.37} - \underset{(0.00143)}{0.806} \log(\# RANK), R^2 = 0.999,$$

$$(10) \quad 2000 - 2001 : \log(\widehat{SIZE}) = \underset{(0.00718)}{17.52} - \underset{(0.00154)}{0.805} \log(\# RANK), R^2 = 0.999.$$

As with the NAS regressions in equations 6 and 7 above, an F test using equations 9 and 10 confirms that only the intercept has shifted in any significant way. In fact, the slope of this Hierarchy relation appears to be even more stable than the NAS Rule over this twenty-year period.

The Rank Size Rule

Finally we turn to the Rank Size Rule for systems of cities, which asserts that if all cities are ranked by population size, then the $RANK_k$ and $SIZE_k$ of cities, k, are (approximately) negatively log-linearly related, that is, that for all cities,

(11) $\log(SIZE) \approx \sigma + \theta \log(RANK)$.

The classical version of this rule also asserts that $\theta \approx -1.0$. For the present case, a plot of $\log(SIZE_k)$ against $\log(RANK_k)$ for all cities, $k \in U$, is shown in plot d of figure 10. Here again, this plot is qualitatively similar to plot c of figure 10 in Mori, Nishikimi, and Smith (2008), showing that the restriction to cb-choice cities (and inclusion of Micropolitan Employment Areas) has made little difference. Log linearity is again most evident in the central range of the plot, while the relative slopes at each end are much steeper.[27] At each extreme it appears that other socioeconomic mechanisms may be at work (as discussed further in Mori, Nishikimi, and Smith (2008)).

But our present interest focuses mainly on the relation between the Rank Size Rule in equation 11 and the NAS Rule. In Mori, Nishikimi, and Smith (2008), it was shown that in the presence of the classical Hierarchy Principle, the NAS Rule (with respect to the larger sets of choice cities U_i^+ for industries i) is asymptotically equivalent to this Rank Size Rule, that is, they satisfy the same asymptotic power law (see Mori, Nishikimi, and Smith 2008, corollary 1). Hence the above stability results for the NAS Rule in equations 6 and 7, and for the Hierarchy Principle in equations 9 and 10, suggest that stability over this twenty-year period may also be exhibited by the Rank Size Rule. Regressions of $\log(SIZE)$ on $\log(RANK)$ in periods 1980/1981 and 2000/2001 produced the following results:

(12) $1980 - 1981 : \log(SIZE) = \underset{(0.0582)}{16.85} - \underset{(0.0120)}{1.094} \log(\# RANK), R^2 = 0.964,$

(13) $2000 - 2001 : \log(SIZE) = \underset{(0.0786)}{17.11} - \underset{(0.0168)}{1.130} \log(\# RANK), R^2 = 0.946.$

Here again an F test shows that only the intercept has shifted significantly and hence that the slope of this overall relation has remained fairly stable. The regression line for 2000/2001 in equation 13 is shown in plot e of figure 10.[28]

As with the NAS Rule discussed above, this stability of the Rank Size Rule is even more remarkable in view of the substantial shuffling of population ranks

27. Here, there is a slight kink at cities with populations of about 300,000 and a much sharper dip at cities below 70,000.

28. Since the data for the Rank Size relation in 1980/1981 strongly overlap the data for 2000/2001, it is difficult to show both on the same figure. Thus we choose to display only the latter.

Figure 11. Change in the Ranking of Cities Existing in Both Years

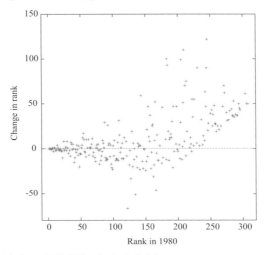

Rank in 1980

Sources: Japan Statistics Bureau (1980, 2000) and authors' calculations.

among cities. For the 246 cities that existed in both 1980 and 2000 (by our definition of cities), the changes in population ranks of these cities in 2000 are plotted against their corresponding 1980 ranks in figure 11. As is clear from the figure, while the largest cities remained relatively stable, most cities actually moved up in the rankings, with an average jump in rank of 10.25.[29] But there is also a great deal of variation in movement. For example, there are cities like Uozu with large upward jumps—from 245th (49,512) in 1980 to 123th (134,411) in 2000—and other cities like Okaya with large downward jumps—from 122th (371,850) in 1980 to 189th (435,367) in 2000.[30] In addition to this movement, there were

29. This same phenomenon (largest cities remaining stable) is observed in other countries as well. For the United States in particular, see, for example, Black and Henderson (2003).

30. The numbers in parentheses are the population levels of the city for 1980 and 2000, respectively. The most significant growths and declines of cities in the studied period seemed to be triggered by the expansion of Shinkansen (bullet train) lines. For instance, the extension of the Shinkansen line from Tokyo to Fukuoka in 1975 leads to the population growth of Fukuoka as a new center of Kyushu region from 1,762,794 to 2,323,604 (31.8 percent) and from sixth to fifth in the population rankings, while it also caused the population decline by 6.64 percent and from eighth to eleventh in the population rankings of Kitakyushu, the traditional regional center of Kyushu, located 50 km east of Fukuoka. Okayama experienced even more drastic population growth from 744,735 to 1,484,742 (99.4 percent) and moved up from fourteenth to tenth in the size ranking. There are two major reasons for this disproportionate growth. One is that Okayama became a transshipment point of the extended Shinkansen line between Tokyo and Fukuoka mentioned above. The other is the completion of the Seto-oh-hashi in 1988, the bridge connecting the main island to Shikoku island via Okayama.

Figure 12. Change in the Ranking of Cities with Boundaries Fixed at 2000

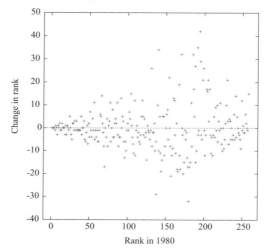

Source: Japan Statistics Bureau (1980, 2000) and authors' calculations.

also changes in the sets of cities themselves (again with respect to our definition of cities). Most of the reduction in cities from 309 in 1980 to 258 in 2000 was due to the absorption of one city by another. In fact, most cities that exhibited large upward jumps in the rankings grew by absorption of nearby cities.[31]

One problem with these observations is that changes in the number of cities between 1980 and 2000 make it somewhat difficult to interpret the changes in rankings above. Thus even though these absolute rankings are the ones used in the regressions of equations 12 and 13, it is useful for our present purposes to consider changes in the relative rankings of the 246 cities existing in both years. This can be done by simply ranking these cities from 1 to 246 in 1980 and recording the changes of these ranks in 2000. But even here it can be argued that such changes might be due largely to the changes in city boundaries between 1980 and 2000 (resulting from our city definitions above). Hence it is useful to consider changes in these relative rankings using the city boundaries in 2000 for both years.[32] These changes in relative rankings are shown in figure 12. By construction, the average change in rankings of cities is now zero. But the range of such changes from –32 to 42 again shows wide variation (with

31. For instance, Uozu, with a population of 49,512, moved up 122 ranks by absorbing Kurobe with a population of 72,259. Similarly, Kitagami with a population of 76,633 moved up 100 ranks by absorbing Hanamaki with a population of 97,389.

32. See Overman and Ioannides (2001) for a discussion of the choice of geographical areas for cities when making intertemporal comparisons of city sizes.

Figure 13. Change in the Sizes of Cities Existing in Both Years

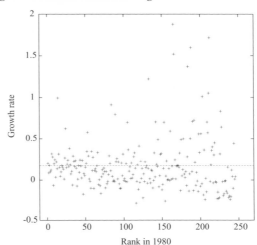

Source: Japan Statistics Bureau (1980, 2000) and authors' calculations.

a standard deviation of 10.1). Thus even in terms of relative rankings with fixed boundaries, the changes in rankings over this twenty-year period have been dramatic.

In addition to changes in rankings, there has also been very uneven growth among cities. In figure 13, the population growth rates of these 246 cities are plotted against their absolute rankings in 1980. The sizes of these cities increased by 17.5 percent on average, with a standard deviation of 32.4 percent. Note also from the figure that variation in growth rates appears to be higher for smaller cities.

In figure 14 below, growth rates are plotted using fixed city boundaries from 2000. Here the average growth rate, 1.81 percent, is now much smaller since the (usually larger) city boundaries in 2000 are used. But even here it is remarkable that the growth rates of cities range from –36.2 percent to 44.3 percent, with a standard deviation of 13.1 percent.

Finally, returning to the Rank Size Rule itself, it is of interest to compare the regression results in equations 12 and 13 with both the classical Rank Size Rule and the NAS Rule. Notice first that the overall slope of each regression is close to –1.0, and hence appears to be in rough agreement with the classical Rank Size Rule. But it is clear for the regression line shown in plot e of figure 10 for 2000–01 data that this slope is in fact a compromise between the slopes for each of the three data segments in plot d decribed above.[33] In particular, the

33. This same type of compromise is also exhibited by the regression line for 1980/1981 (not shown).

Figure 14. Change in the Sizes of Cities with Boundaries Fixed at 2000

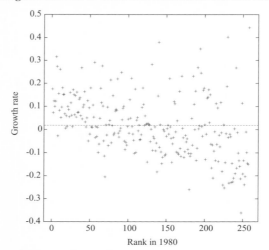

Sources: Japan Statistics Bureau (1980, 2000) and authors' calculations.

slope of the middle range in plot d, for which log linearity is most evident, is seen to be much flatter and is indeed much closer to that of the NAS regression in equation 7 above than it is to -1.0.[34] Moreover, it can be argued that this central range is dominant in the sense that the slope of the upper average relation in plot b essentially mirrors that of this range. In fact, Mori, Nishikimi, and Smith (2008, Theorem 2) have shown that the log linearity of the rank-size distribution and that of the upper-average distribution are asymptotically equivalent with the same log slope. So, while no definitive conclusions can be drawn from such limited observations, they do suggest that the theoretical relations between the NAS Rule and both the Rank Size Rule and Hierarchy Principle developed in Mori, Nishikimi, and Smith (2008) are empirically most evident for cities in this dominant central range.

Concluding Remarks

The main purpose of this paper has been to examine the temporal stability properties of the NAS Rule under the sharper definition of cluster-based choice cities for industries proposed by Mori and Smith (2009b). In particular, it was shown above that for Japanese manufacturing industries between 1981 and

---

34. A regression using only this middle segment yields a slope of -0.767.

2001, the stability of this rule under presence-based choice cities continues to hold for cb-choice cities as well. In addition, it was shown that, as in Mori and Smith (2009b), similar stability properties are exhibited by the two other regularities closely related to the NAS Rule, namely the Hierarchy Principle for industries and the Rank Size Rule for cities.

These stability results are even more remarkable given the substantial shuffling of both industries and city sizes between these two years. For the NAS Rule in particular, the results in equations 6 and 7 show that in spite of dramatic changes in both the cb-choice cities for specific industries and even the sizes of these cities themselves, the elasticity of substitution between the number and average size of these cb-choice cities across industries has remained essentially constant. While the corresponding log-linear relationship for the Rank Size Rule in equation 11 is not as sharp, the overall elasticity of substitution between city sizes and ranks in equations 12 and 13 has also remained essentially constant (and slightly larger in magnitude than for the classical model). Thus, while the underlying adjustment processes that preserve these relations remain to be established, it would appear that such processes must be relatively fast in comparison to this twenty-year span.

In addition, the joint stability of these three relations serves to reinforce the close relationships between them. With respect to the Rank Size Rule in particular, these relations suggest that rather than considering simple independent growth models of cities, such as Gibrat's Law and its extensions (see Gabaix and Ioannides 2004), better explanations of the skewed distribution of city sizes might be given in terms of the colocation behavior of populations and industries over time.

It should also be noted that while the present results for the NAS Rule involve only two points in time for a single country (Japan), this regularity appears to be far more robust. As mentioned at the beginning, the results of Hsu (2008) suggest that this same regularity can be seen in the United States as well. More generally, it appears that the NAS Rule is also evident in relatively self-contained subregions of nations. In particular, if one takes patterns of interregional travel behavior to define relatively self-sustained subsystems within nations (in the same way that commuting patterns have been used to define cities), then for Japan there is a natural nesting of four monopolar regional systems identified by their central cities as "Tokyo" ⊃ "Osaka" ⊃ "Nagoya," and "Tokyo" ⊃ "Sapporo".[35] Our preliminary investigations show that the NAS Rule holds with roughly the same slope coefficient for the "Tokyo," "Osaka,"

---

35. Data on interprefectural passenger trips using mass transport modes were obtained from the Ministry of Land, Infrastructure, Transport and Tourism of Japan (2000).

"Nagoya," and "Sapporo" regions. These initial findings suggest that international comparisons of such regularities would perhaps be most meaningful by identifying self-contained economically comparable subregions for testing purposes. Such questions will be pursued further in subsequent research.

Finally, it should be emphasized that while the NAS Rule implies a regularity between the number and average size of cb-choice cities for each industry, it says little about the actual distribution of industries across cities. Hence from a regional policy perspective, neither the existence nor the stability of NAS by itself allows specific conclusions to be drawn about this distribution. However, when taken together with the closely related Hierarchy Principle, there are some policy implications that can be drawn. Indeed, if the Hierarchy Principle were to hold exactly, then the set of cb-choice cities for each industry i would be completely determined by the number of such cities, that is, would consist of the $\#U_i$ cities with largest industrial diversities. In such a case, cities k could only hope to attract new industries i for which k would then qualify as a cb-choice city for i and all cities with larger industrial diversity were already cb-choice cities. While such rigid rules are of course unrealistic, they nonetheless suggest that in regional systems where these regularities are sufficiently strong, cities are more likely to attract industries for which this addition would either create or enhance a meaningful local clustering of that industry and would be consistent with the current locational hierarchy for that industry. In particular, this suggests that smaller cities may be more likely to grow by attracting lower-order industries that would not be too isolated in that city. Such policy implications will be considered more fully in subsequent work.

Appendix

Industry Aggregation

There are 152 and 164 classifications in the three-digit manufacturing industries in 1981 and 2001 defined in the Establishments and Enterprise Census of Japan (1981, 2001). Industrial classifications have been basically disaggregated over the twenty-year period. Thus, in the present paper, the classifications in 2001 have been basically aggregated to those in 1981. Besides the conversions of the classifications between the two periods specified in the census, however, the following conventions have been adopted to make classifications at these two time points comparable.

1. Since "forged and cast steel manufacturing" (JSIC316) and "cast iron product manufacturing" (JSIC317) in 1981 have been aggregated to "ferrous metal machine parts and tooling products" (JSIC266) in 2001, we redefined JSIC316 to represent a union of JSIC316 and JSIC317 in 1981 and JSIC266 in 2001.

2. Since the union of "headgear manufacturing" (JSIC213) and "other apparel and textile accessory manufacturing" (JSIC215) in 1981 is equivalent to the union of "Japanese style apparel and socks ('tabi')" (JSIC155) and "other textile apparel and accessories" (JSIC156) in 2001, these are labeled JSIC215.

3. Since "wooden footwear manufacturing" (JSIC224) and "other wooden product manufacturing" (JSIC229) in 1981 have been aggregated to "miscellaneous manufacture of wood products, including bamboo and rattan" (JSIC169) in 2001, we let JSIC229 represent this aggregated classification.

Comments

Yannis M. Ioannides: This paper reconsiders the so-called Number-Average Size (NAS) Rule by investigating the rule by means of new definitions for cities and the presence of industries in cities. It is built around an empirical finding with data from Japan that shows that a regression of the average population size of cities, where an industry is present, against the number of such cities yields a very precisely estimated log-linear relationship. This paper differs from previous work by Mori, Nishikimi, and Smith (2008), which relies on a traditional definition of a city and of the presence of an industry.

To appreciate this difference, consider that urbanization and industrial concentration are often dramatized by means of pictures of countries (or land masses) from space. Clustering of lights and their brightness is very suggestive of clustering of economic activity. What conclusions can one draw about firms' location decisions from such pictures, or from the underlying geocoded data, when industrial concentration may not observe jurisdictional boundaries?

In the remainder of this comment I first outline the paper and discuss its key findings, then seek to put them in the perspective of the industrial agglomeration literature. I conclude with a critique of the findings and suggestions for future research.

Mori and Smith's paper in this volume reaffirms the validity of the NAS Rule, which they report first in Mori, Nishikimi, and Smith (2008). Mori and Smith use "clustered-based" choice cities of industries for two cross sections, 1980/1981 and 2000/2001, of Japanese data. Mori, Nishikimi, and Smith look only at choice-based cities of each industry, which are those hosting "significant" agglomeration of an industry. Mori and Smith use a different definition of Urban Employment Areas (UEAs) that expands the data to include smaller urban concentrations. That is, unlike Mori, Nishikimi, and Smith who use only Metropolitan Employment Areas (MEAs), which are UEAs with central municipality populations of at least 50,000, Mori and Smith include those with central municipality populations of at least 10,000. This broader definition yields 309 cities (UEAs) in 1980 and 258 cities in 2000 (compared with the smaller sets of 105 and 113 MEAs, respectively, used by Mori, Nishikimi, and Smith). Mori and Smith determine agglomerations of each industry that are significant by means of a statistical clustering technique, which they develop in two other papers (Mori and Smith 2009a, 2009b).

Specifically, the measures that are typically used for studies of industrial agglomeration are based on data collected according to jurisdictional boundaries. For the United States, these include states or local jurisdictions. The U.S. Bureau of the Census provides data at different spatial scales, such as U.S. metropolitan areas, U.S. census regions, and so on. Similar procedures are used elsewhere, which in the European Union involve NUTS (Nomenclature of Territorial Units for Statistics) and are designed to handle various spatial scales.

Mori and Smith use cluster analysis to detect whether the observed spatial distribution of establishments is not random and may be explained best by using statistical model selection criteria for finding the "best cluster scheme." For each of a number of statistical techniques, such as likelihood-ratio tests, Akaike's information criterion, and Schwartz's Bayesian Information Criterion, the authors compute the difference between the particular measure when it is based on the observed distribution and when it is based on complete spatial randomness. The best cluster scheme is the one that maximizes this difference.

This sounds straightforward, but there is a difficulty: the method requires defining spatial partitions, but the number of possible partitions of the space can be enormous. For this reason, these authors propose a cluster detection procedure that detects, in general, one cluster per industry. This designates a partition of the national economic space where an industry's concentration is significantly most pronounced.

I wish to explain this process a bit further. I adopt the authors' notation, according to which an economy's continuous (location) space Ω, is subdivided into disjoint municipalities, $\Omega_r, \Omega_{r'} \subseteq \Omega$ with municipalities indexed by the set $R = \{1, ..., k_R\}$. The municipalities partition the economy's space: $\cup_{r=1}^{k_R} \Omega_r = \Omega$. Suppose that establishment locations over space Ω may be described in terms of an industry-specific probability distribution function. Location decisions of different establishments in an industry may be treated as independent random samples from this unknown distribution. The class of all possible location models corresponds to the set of probability measures on Ω.

Suppose next that we identify groups of municipalities within which an industry's locational activity is more intense, that is possibly disjoint *clusters* of municipalities, defined by subsets of the index set R: $C_j \subset R, j \in C = \{1,...,$

k_c}. All clusters make up a cluster scheme, **C**, which is a partition of the index set of municipalities, $\mathbf{C} = (R_0, C_{1,...}, C_{k_c})$.

For example, let the jurisdictions be U.S. states. In that case, a cluster could be the group of the New England states {Massachusetts, Connecticut, Rhode Island, New Hampshire, Vermont, Maine}. The areal extent of cluster Cj is the union of the areas of all of its constituent jurisdictions, $VCj = \cup_{r \in C}^{k_R}$, the entire land area of New England. The probability that an establishment locates in New England is $p_C(j) = P_C(\Omega_{C_j}), j \in C$.

Mori and Smith define choice cities of industries and choice industries of cities as follows. In the institutional context of Japan, consider Urban Economic Areas, $UEA_k \subseteq U$ and cluster schemes for different industries. Let UEA_k overlap territorially with cluster C_j in cluster scheme **C**, $UEA_k \cap C_j \neq \varnothing$. Then, city UEA_k is said to be a choice city of industry j, that is, industry j establishments may be found in city k. Let U_j be the set of choice cities of industry j. Conversely, industry j is a choice industry of city k. Let the set of choice industries of city k be I_k. The more spatially diverse an industry is, the larger the number of its choice cities U_j (the location diversity of industry j), and the less localized it is.

The authors construct cluster schemes for each of the 147 manufacturing industries for 1981 and 2001. Of these, for eight industries, complete spatial randomness could not be rejected. Of the remaining 139 industries, the percentages of establishments included in clusters range from 39.1 percent to 100 percent (with an average of 94.1 percent) in 2001, while the corresponding percentages in 1981 range from 51.8 percent to 100 percent (with an average of 95.7 percent).

Consider the ratio, for each industry, of the mean of employment among all cluster-based cities (the cities that are included in the industry's cluster, that is, the choice cities of that industry) to the mean of employment among those that are not in its cluster (the nonchoice cities of that industry, where the industry might be merely present) but do contain positive employment by plants of that industry. A similar measure can be defined in terms of establishment counts, instead of employment. Both these measures, when plotted are remarkably regular; see figures 2 and 3 in Mori and Smith. Both figures suggest that these magnitudes are skewed to the right. This regularity is tantalizing. It would behoove the authors to see whether these frequency distributions could be predicted on the basis of the sampling process that generates the respective measures.

Mori and Smith also show that, over a twenty-year period, industrial location decisions are subject to a lot of churning. This is illustrated by figures 4 to 7 in the paper. That is, during 1980/1981–2000/2001, smaller and less diversified cities tend to stay smaller and less diversified, and larger and more diversified cities also tend to stay larger and more diversified cities. At the same time, the locations at which agglomeration of industries take place vary quite a lot. Remarkably then, Mori and Smith find a statistical regularity—that is, a linear regression, across the three-digit manufacturing industries in their data set, of the log of the average size of industry choice cities against the log of their number gives a nearly perfect fit. This is the NAS Rule, pictured in figure 9, along with the outliers. They also find it to be remarkably stable over time. This stunning fit, which as the authors state should best be regarded as "curve fitting," rather than a genuine statistical model, is indistinguishable from perfect linearity. Furthermore, Holmes and Hsu (2009) report estimates of the coefficient of the average size using U.S. data (3-digit NAICS identifier for MSA and CMSAs in 2000) and the overall fit, at 0.7477 (standard deviation = 0.00255) and $R^2 = 0.9991$, respectively, that are remarkably close to those of Mori and Smith.[1]

The authors also report regressions along the lines of the Rank Size Rule. Figure 10 plots the logarithm of population size against the logarithm of the rank, for the same definition of choice-based cities that was used in their NAS Rule, along with the corresponding linear regression lines. The resulting fits for the Rank Size Rule are very different, in my opinion, from those of the NAS Rule. As the authors state, the overall slope of each regression is close to –1.0, but they are significantly different, as I see it, from the classical Rank Size Rule. As they put it, "but it is clear for the regression line shown in plot e of figure 10 for 2000/2001 data that this slope is in fact a compromise between the slopes" for the middle range and the two extreme ones. The regression line cuts through what is roughly a concave plot.

Here we have a genuine instance of "glass half full" versus "glass half empty." The authors state that "while no definitive conclusions can be drawn from such limited observations," they do suggest that the theoretical relations between the NAS Rule and both the Rank Size Rule and Hierarchy Principle developed in Mori, Nishikimi, and Smith (2008) are empirically most evident for cities in this dominant central range." In comparison, Duranton (2007) and Rossi-Hansberg and Wright (2007) propose good theoretical explanations for the concavity of the city size distribution.

Specifically, Mori, Nishikimi, and Smith offer an elegant result on equivalence between NAS and Rank Size Rules (see Mori, Nishikimi, and Smith 2008, Theorem 1). A critical step that allows them to prove their Theorem 1 is that

1. NAICS = North American Industry Classification System; MSA= metropolitan statistical area; CMSAs = consolidated metropolitan statistical areas; S.D. = standard deviation.

when cities are indexed, the indexes of cities where an industry is present (its choice cities) form an interval. Specifically, let industry types be defined by index $i \in \mathbf{I}$, with industry i occupying a measurable subset $\mathbf{R}_i \subset \mathbf{R}$ of the cities in $\mathbf{R}$. Let $\mathbf{R}_i$ be an interval, $\mathbf{R}_i = [0, r_i]$, where r_i denotes the rank of the smallest population units occupied by industry i. This assumption encompasses a strict version of the Hierarchy Principle. In general, this principle holds that if an industry is present in a city, it would also be present in all cities that are larger than itself. Intuitively, there are cities with gas stations only, but a larger city with an opera will have gas stations, as well.

Let n_i denote the number of cities where industry i is present, and the number of choice cities of industry i as

$$n_i = \int_{R_i} dr.$$

The average size of choice cities of industry i is

$$\bar{R}_i = (1 / n_i) \int_{R_i} \rho(x)\, dx.$$

Cities are ranked by their sizes: rank$(r) = \rho(r)$. The empirical NAS Rule is expressed as

$$\text{If } \bar{R}_i = \alpha n_i^{-\beta}, \text{ then } \rho(r) = \alpha r^{-\beta} \Leftrightarrow \bar{R}_i = \alpha(1-\beta)^{-1} n_i^{-\beta}.$$

Taking logs of both sides in the last equation above gives the log of $\bar{R}_i$ as a linear function of the log of n_i. Theorem 1 states that for any economy for which Christaller's Hierarchy Principle holds, the Rank Size Rule and the NAS Rule are equivalent.

In contrast, Rossi-Hansberg and Wright (2007) use a complete theory of urban structure and growth to argue that larger cities likely operate in industries that experienced a history of above-average productivity shocks, and thus they can be expected to grow slower than average in the future, while the opposite is true of smaller cities. Furthermore, urban growth rates exhibit reversion to the mean, which implies "that the log rank-log size relationship will in general (apart from particular realizations of the shocks) be concave or, in other words, that the invariant distribution for city sizes has thinner tails than a Pareto distribution with coefficient 1."[2]

The authors' linking the NAS Rule with the Rank Size Rule does not strengthen their finding, in my opinion, for two reasons. One is that the Rank

2. Rossi-Hansberg and Wright (2007, p. 612).

Size Rule might be in the eye of the beholder. A second is that the Rank Size Rule is not an immutable fact. Ioannides and others (2008) use international city size data to show that adoption of information and communication technologies causes, ceteris paribus, an increased concentration of the city size distribution and thus a decreased Zipf's coefficient. Still, this misgiving of mine should not be held against the significance of the authors' contribution that is reported in the paper.

Still, the conceptual interrelationships between the NAS and Rank Size Rules, on the one hand, and the Hierarchy Principle, on the other, are very interesting and too tantalizing to ignore. To model them, one could start from a model of plant location, perhaps along the lines of Ellison and Glaeser (1997). Such a model assigns probabilities to location decisions of different firms, from which probabilities can be computed for different realizations of strings of zeroes and ones. Such strings feature prominently in the authors' graphical representations of the Hierarchy Principle. Location choices that depend on industry presence and city size could provide a link from the Hierarchy Principle, a qualitative relationship, to the NAS and Rank Size Rules. In this connection, theoretical results by Hsu (2008), however special, are very promising in that they can provide an overarching theme linking qualitative and quantitative aspects of location.

I conclude that I am most amazed by and respectful of the authors' NAS Rule, both as reported here as well as in Mori, Nishikimi, and Smith (2008). Furthermore, the consistency of the findings across different definitions of urban areas, not to mention the care with which the search of cluster schemes is implemented, is also impressive. I am all the more anxious and hopeful to see that a full theory underlying these findings would be developed. The potential for informing the design for urban and regional development policies is also considerable. Policies must respect the fact that industries tend to cluster and in ways that are related to the size of the urban areas hosting them.

John M. Quigley: The careful and well-documented paper by Tomoya Mori and Tony Smith makes four distinct and interesting contributions. First, it presents and explicates a new measure of the regularity of city types within a country, the so-called Number-Average-Size Rule. Second, it shows how this new measure is related to a group of standard and well-known economic and geographic measures of empirical regularity across cities. Third, the paper demonstrates that the Number-Average-Size measure is generated by agglomerative factors in the economic geography of regions, not simply by chance.

More specifically, it shows that the empirical regularities observed in Japan at a couple of points in time do not arise from some competing "dartboard model" or some random set of fluctuations. Fourth, it presents a comprehensive description of the computation of these measures, and the hierarchical significance of these measures, for all the 3,200 municipalities in Japan.

What is the new measure of the distribution of city sizes, the Number-Average-Size Rule? The rule asserts that the logarithm of city size (that is, population) is a linear function of the logarithm of the number of industries that are represented in that city. The threshold for representation is pretty clear, and the statistical model employed by the authors fits the data remarkably well, at least for Japanese cities. Essentially all the variation in Japanese city sizes is explained by the heterogeneity of the industrial composition of those cities. This is true for two cross sections of municipalities measured two decades apart, in 1980 and in 2001. Moreover, the estimated slopes of the regression relationships are virtually identical in these cross sections measured twenty years apart.

How is this new measure related to standard measures of the urban hierarchy? Seventy-five years ago, Walter Christaller developed a simple principle of urban hierarchies that was based upon introspection and his close observation of villages, towns, and cities in Germany. In villages, the grain grown in the surrounding farms was auctioned in local markets. In the next tier of places, towns, the grain was milled into flour and shipped onto larger towns. But some was baked into bread and sold in those small towns and also in the villages that supplied the grain in the first place. From these observations came the specific hunch that all economic activities in a city will also be found in cities of larger sizes.

And from this, Christaller's famous Rank Size Rule follows. The Rank Size Rule holds that the logarithm of city size is linearly related to the logarithm of the rank of that city in the hierarchy of cities. Christaller formulated this law on the basis of introspection and the observations of rural life. From purely an empirical viewpoint, the Rank Size Rule has also been remarkably durable. It has been applied to the urban hierarchy of many countries in many time periods (see Berliant 2008 for a review). And there has been great attention paid to theoretical constructs that would justify the remarkable regularities observed. (See Simon 1955; Gabaix 1999; Gabaix and Ioannides 2004.)

Specifically, Mori and Smith demonstrate in their paper that a specific weak formulation of Christaller's hunch unifies the Number-Average Size Rule and the Rank Size Rule. Specifically, assume that those industries in cities of a given industrial diversity will also be found in cities of higher industrial diversity.

Under this assumption, the authors show that Christaller's Rank Size Rule is isomorphic to their Number-Average Size Rule.

More important, the assumption that a large city like Tokyo has A slots for different industries while a smaller city like Osaka has B slots for different industries ($A > B$) facilitates a direct test of the extent to which the joint frequency distribution of population in cities and the number of industries in those cities could arise by chance.

The authors take great care to standardize the linkage between population and industries for Japanese cities—standardization is by characteristics of transport systems and demographics. The empirical analysis demonstrates rather convincingly that the Number-Average Size Rule does not arise from the random or quasi-random location of industries or from quirks in geography or the transport system.

The authors demonstrate that there have been enormous changes in the hierarchy of Japanese cities. Below the thirty largest cities, there has been a great deal of movement—with some cities going up the hierarchy and some moving downward over relatively short periods of time. Despite this vast churning of cities in the hierarchy, the Number-Average Size Rule operates in any cross section. This is the most compelling finding in the paper.

My principal criticism of the analysis so far is that it is essentially mechanical. So far, the authors have not been able to dig into the economic or social behavior of households and firms that might give rise to these spatial regularities.

If it is true that city size is associated with a more heterogeneous industrial structure, is economic output similarly associated? Is output per worker, that is, productivity, associated as well? Can better city organization be inferred from a city's deviation from its predicted placement according to the Number-Average Size Rule? There is a hint of an argument about this in the paper, but it is not taken very far.

But we could well imagine taking the Number-Average Size Rule seriously in economic research, not just in spatial or geographical descriptions. Recall, there are a number of studies that have explored the variations in the Rank Size Rule across countries—to what extent does the exponential decay parameter vary across the hierarchy in different countries? With policies? With the political economy? With favoritism accorded to the capital city?

One could imagine that the parameter of the Number-Average Size Rule, the exponential decay, varies across countries—with the level of development or the extent of active regional policies to attract (or direct) types of industries to different places. To what extent is this measure of industrial structure consistent with agglomerative urbanization economies? In Japan or in comparison with other places?

At this point, the challenge to the authors is to test whether the careful spatial measurement in this paper is useful in understanding the behavior of the economic and social agents in the urban hierarchy.

References

Akaike, H. 1973. "Information Theory as an Extension of the Maximum Likelihood Principle." In *Second International Symposium on Information Theory*, edited by B. N. Petrov and F. Csaki, pp. 267–81. Budapest: Akademiai Kiado.

Berliant, Marcus. 2008. "Central Place Theory." In *The New Palgrave Dictionary of Economics*, 2nd ed. New York: Palgrave Macmillan.

Besag, J., and J. Newell. 1991. "The Detection of Clusters in Rare Diseases." *Journal of the Royal Statistical Society, Series A* 154: 143–55.

Black, D., and V. Henderson. 2003. "Urban Evolution in the USA." *Journal of Economic Geography* 3: 343–72.

Christaller, W. 1966. *Central Places in Southern Germany*, translated by C. W. Baskin. Upper Saddle River, N.J.: Prentice Hall. Originally published as *Die zentralen Orte in Süddeutschland* (Gustav Fischer, 1933).

Dasgupta, A., and A. E. Raftery. 1998. "Detecting Features in Spatial Point Processes with Clutter via Model-Based Clustering." *Journal of the American Statistical Association* 93: 294–302.

Duranton, G. 2007. "Urban Evolutions: The Fast, the Slow, and the Still." *American Economic Review* 97 (1): 197–221.

Eaton, J., and Z. Eckstein. 1997. "Cities and Growth: Theory and Evidence from France and Japan." *Regional Science and Urban Economics* 27: 443–74.

Ellison, Glenn, and Edward L. Glaeser. 1997. "Geographic Concentration in U.S. Manufacturing Industries: A Dartboard Approach." *Journal of Political Economy* 105 (5): 889–927.

Gabaix, X. 1999. "Zipf's Law for Cities: An Explanation." *Quarterly Journal of Economics* 114: 737–67.

Gabaix, X., and Y. M. Ioannides. 2004. "The Evolution of City Size Distributions." In *Handbook of Regional and Urban Economics*, vol. 4, *Cities and Geography*, edited by J. V. Henderson and J.-F. Thisse, pp. 2341–378. Amsterdam: North-Holland.

Gangnon, R. E. and M. K. Clayton. 2000. "Bayesian Detections and Modeling of Spatial Disease Clustering." *Biometrics* 56: 922–35.

———. 2004. "Likelihood-Based Tests for Localized Spatial Clustering of Disease." *Environmetrics* 15: 797–810.

Holmes, Thomas J., and Wen-Tai Hsu. 2009. "Optimal City Hierarchy: A Dynamic Programming Approach to Central Place Theory." Working Paper. Chinese University of Hong Kong, Department of Economics (January).

Hsu, Wen-Tai. 2008. "Central Place Theory and Zipf's Law." Working Paper. Chinese University of Hong Kong (December).

Ioannides, Yannis M., Henry G. Overman, Esteban Rossi-Hansberg, and Kurt Schmidheiny. 2008. "The Effect of Information and Communication Technologies on Urban Structure." *Economic Policy* 54: 203–42.

Japan Statistics Bureau. 1980. *Population Census*.

———. 1981. *Establishments and Enterprise Census of Japan*.

————. 2000. *Population Census.*

————. 2001. *Establishments and Enterprise Census of Japan.*

Kanemoto, Y., and K. Tokuoka. 2002. "The Proposal for the Standard Definition of the Metropolitan Area in Japan." [In Japanese.] *Journal of Applied Regional Science* 7: 1–15.

Kontkanen, P., and P. Myllymäki. 2005. "Analyzing the Stochastic Complexity via Tree Polynomials." Technical Report 2005-4. Helsinki Institute for Information Technology.

Kulldorff, M. 1997. "A Spatial Scan Statistic." *Communications in Statistics: Theory and Methods* 26: 1481–496.

Kulldorff, M., and N. Nagarwalla. 1995. "Spatial Disease Clusters: Detection and Inference." *Statistics in Medicine* 14: 799–810.

Ministry of Land, Infrastructure, Transport and Tourism of Japan. 2000. *Inquiry for Passenger Trip Flow among Prefectures.*

Mori, Tomoya, Koji Nishikimi, and Tony E. Smith. 2008. "The Number-Average Size Rule: A New Empirical Relationship between Industrial Location and City Size." *Journal of Regional Science* 48 (1): 165–211.

Mori, Tomoya, and Tony E. Smith. 2009a. "A Probabilistic Modeling Approach to the Detection of Industrial Agglomerations." Working Paper.

————. 2009b. "Spatial Coordination of Population and Industrial Agglomerations: The Central Place Theory and the City Size Regularities Revisited." Working Paper.

National Statistics Center of Japan. 2009. "Portal Site of Official Statistics of Japan." Statistics Bureau, Ministry of Internal Affairs and Communication (www.e-stat.go.jp/SG1/estat/eStatTopPortalE.do).

Overman, H., and Y. M. Ioannides. 2001. "Cross-Sectional Evolution of the US City Size Distribution." *Journal of Urban Economics* 49: 543–66.

Rossi-Hansberg, Esteban, and Mark L. J. Wright. 2007. "Urban Structure and Growth." *Review of Economic Studies* 74: 597–624.

Schwarz, G. 1978. "Estimating the Dimension of a Model." *Annals of Statistics* 6: 461–64.

Simon, Herbert. 1955. "On a Class of Skew Distribution Functions." *Biometrika* 44: 425–40.

Smith, T. E., and T. Mori. 2009. "On the Model-Based Clustering for the Detection of Industrial Agglomerations." Working Paper.

United Nations. 2007. *World Urbanization Prospects.*

U.S. Office of Management and Budget. 2000. "Standards for Defining Metropolitan and Micropolitan Statistical Areas." *Federal Register* 65 (249) (December 27).